T0295959

EXTRACTION POLITICS

RSA·STR

THE RSA SERIES IN TRANSDISCIPLINARY RHETORIC

The RSA Series in Transdisciplinary Rhetoric is a collaboration with the Rhetoric Society of America to publish innovative and rigorously argued scholarship on the tremendous disciplinary breadth of rhetoric. Books in the series take a variety of approaches, including theoretical, historical, interpretive, critical, or ethnographic, and examine rhetorical action in a way that appeals, first, to scholars in communication studies and English or writing, and, second, to at least one other discipline or subject area.

Nicholas S. Paliewicz

EXTRACTION POLITICS

Rio Tinto and the Corporate Persona

THE PENNSYLVANIA STATE UNIVERSITY PRESS
UNIVERSITY PARK, PENNSYLVANIA

Library of Congress Cataloging-in-Publication Data

Names: Paliewicz, Nicholas S., author.
Title: Extraction politics : Rio Tinto and the corporate
    persona / Nicholas S. Paliewicz.
Other titles: RSA series in transdisciplinary rhetoric.
Description: University Park, Pennsylvania : The Pennsylvania
    State University Press, [2024] | Series: The RSA series in
    transdisciplinary rhetoric | Includes bibliographical
    references and index.
Summary: "Investigates how the mineral mining company
    Rio Tinto constructs rhetorical personae in the places it
    operates and transforms environments, communities, and
    entire landscapes"—Provided by publisher.
Identifiers: LCCN 2023052079 | ISBN 9780271097060
    (hardback)
Subjects: LCSH: Rio Tinto (Group) | Mineral industries—
    Political aspects. | Mineral industries—Environmental
    aspects. | Mineral industries—Southwest, New. | Corporate
    image. | Rhetoric.
Classification: LCC HD9506.G74 P355 2024 | DDC
    338.8/8722—dc23/eng/20231207
LC record available at https://lccn.loc.gov/2023052079

The Pennsylvania State University Press is a member of the
Association of University Presses.

It is the policy of The Pennsylvania State University Press to
use acid-free paper. Publications on uncoated stock satisfy the
minimum requirements of American National Standard for
Information Sciences—Permanence of Paper for Printed
Library Material, ANSI z39.48-1992.

In loving memory of Iaithrang Nongbri

Contents

Illustrations

Acknowledgments

This project would not be possible without the direct and indirect support from countless individuals, communities, and organizations. For me to try to take credit for all the content in these pages would be an inaccuracy. This book is just as much an accomplishment on the part of the persons and groups named here—and so many more—as it is my own. While identifying all of those that contributed to the evolution of this book is a near impossible task (or at least a book in itself), I must at least make an attempt to acknowledge, albeit partially, a few of those who cannot be separated from my complicated signature.

The seeds for this project were sowed during my doctoral education at the University of Utah, which is when I first encountered the Bingham Canyon Mine (BCM) as a horrifying site that was no doubt what Jennifer Peeples has called the "toxic sublime" in her award-winning essay in *Environmental Communication*. It was during this time (2011) that I began researching some of the environmental politics surrounding this mine with friend and colleague Katie Hunt, who was equally intrigued by this massive hole. Neither of us could understand how or why anyone would possibly write about anything else, so we began working on a class project about local public hearings concerning Rio Tinto Kennecott's plans to extend the life of the mine through what was called the Cornerstone Expansion Project. Our focus was on the indecorous voices that both of us witnessed while attending these hearings, and we virtually presented our findings about this rhetorical phenomenon at the biannual Conference on Communication and the Environment in Uppsala, Sweden. Years later, we published a related book chapter with Danielle Endres on "The Radical Potential of Public Participation Processes." Readers will note a continued discussion about indecorous voices in chapter 5. All of this is to say special thanks goes to Katie, as well as Danielle, for contributing to the intellectual development of this project at an early stage.

In fascinating ways, the BCM, over time, became less of a sublime force and more mundane and commonplace (even, in a way, invisible). I became intrigued by this phenomenon and took it up in one of my dissertation chapters on the topic of corporate personhood. I recall many discussions with friends and colleagues such as Megan O'Byrne, Guy McHendry, Maria Blevins, Shireen Ghorbani, Antonio De La Garza, Matthew Richards, Betsy Brunner, and Joshua Trey Barnett that helped inform my thinking about the meaning of this mine, not to mention the nurturing from mentors Kevin DeLuca, Danielle Endres, Michael Middleton, Marouf Hasian Jr., and Brett Clark. Special thanks to my friend, colleague, and (at the time) roommate Brian Cozen for his encouragement and willingness to entertain different ways of seeing the mine. Thanks also to friends William Saunders and Reena Antonishak for letting me stay on their couch multiple times for research trips and conferences that took me through Los Angeles. I am also grateful for all the productive feedback on Rio Tinto–related papers from Emma Bloomfield.

Research on Rio Tinto really began when I was hired at the University of Louisville (2015). Thanks to all of the staff persons and colleagues in the Department of Communication, especially Al Futrell, Kandi Walker, and John Ferré, for supporting this work on the departmental and human levels. Thanks also to the Commonwealth Center for the Humanities and Society (CCHS) for its fellowship, which supported this project with a stipend and course release in 2020–21. I am grateful to all the other fellows—Paul Griner, Kristi Maxwell, Rachel Singel, Angela Storey, Jennifer Westerfeld—in addition to the director John Gibson for contributing to such a rich intellectual climate on the topic "Anthropocene, Environment, and Modernity." These virtual meetings no doubt widened my thinking about resource colonialism, Rio Tinto, and the Anthropocene from new and exciting interdisciplinary perspectives. Special thanks to Pete Bsumek for his willingness to join this group of fellows as an expert guest speaker and discussant. Thanks also to the CCHS (program coordinator Janna Tajibaeva) in addition to the Office of the Dean in the College of Arts and Sciences and the Office of Research and Innovation at the University of Louisville for contributing to subvention funds for the index.

I am also tremendously grateful for the support of this project from the editorial office at Penn State University Press. Thanks to former acquisition editor Ryan Peterson for originally taking an interest in this project, to Josie DiNovo for carefully handling this monograph as it went to production, and to Archna Patel for prudently managing the review process during a time of transition, in addition to her helpful feedback during the final stages of editing. Thanks also to freelance copyeditor Dana Henricks for taking great care of this monograph during the copyediting stage of production. Special thanks also to the thoughtful and meticulous feedback from Timothy Johnson and Leah Ceccarelli, who provided the best possible kind of feedback that no doubt improved the quality of this monograph.

Parts of this monograph also appeared in various journal articles published by Taylor & Francis and Michigan State University Press. Content derived from Taylor & Francis journals includes the following four articles: "The Country, the City, and the Corporation: Rio Tinto Kennecott and the Materiality of Corporate Rhetoric," *Environmental Communication* 12, no. 6 (2018): 744–62 (https://doi.org/10.1080/17524032.2017.1416421); "Decolonizing Oak Flat: Apache Stronghold's Place-Based, Temporal, and Mnemonic Dissensus at Public Hearings," *Environmental Communication* 16, no. 5 (2022): 664–79 (https://doi.org/10.1080/17524032.2022.2036216); "Industrial Pioneerism in the Beehive State: Rio Tinto and the Corporate Persona," *Western Journal of Communication* 86, no. 1 (2022): 60–82 (https://doi.org/10.1080/10570314.2021.2016939), copyright © 2022 Western States Communication Association, reprinted by permission of Taylor & Francis Ltd, www.tandfonline.com, on behalf of 2022 Western States Communication Association; and "Thinking Like a Copper Mine: An Ecological Approach to Corporate Ethos and Prosōpon," *Rhetoric Society Quarterly* (2023): 1–16 (https://doi.org/10.1080/02773945.2022.2129757) copyright © 2023 The Rhetoric Society of America, reprinted by permission of Taylor & Francis Ltd, www.tandfonline.com, on behalf of 2023 The Rhetoric Society of America. Thanks to Taylor & Francis Ltd, www.tandfonline.com, for its permission to reprint parts of these works for chapters 1 and 3, specifically. Additionally, a version of chapter 4, as well as parts of chapter 5, originally appeared as "De/Linking Copper: Masking and Unmasking Extractive Coloniality at Chi'chil Biłdagoteel (Oak Flat)," *Rhetoric, Politics and Culture* 1, no. 2 (2021): 97–127 (https://doi.org/10.1353/rhp.2021.0016), published by Michigan State University Press.

As a result of all of this support from friends, colleagues, mentors, community members, reviewers, journals, and editors, this monograph is a sort of assemblage that speaks with not just one voice but many. The most important of these voices, however, are those from family members. Thanks to parents and in-laws for their enduring love and support. Special thanks to Cory, Ryan, John, Thomas, and Drew for all the mental and emotional support while camping, hiking, canoeing, and fishing in the upper Midwest and West. Thanks also for your geological expertise, Cory, especially as it pertains to borates (chapter 2). Most of all, thanks to my wife, Rida Wahlang, for supporting this project in the most important of ways and for tolerating all this talk about Rio Tinto, personae, and Reagan over the years (even in my sleep, apparently). And to both Amora and baby Ivy, my favorite humans. I love you all, more.

Introduction | The Corporation That Therefore I Am

President Ronald Reagan was not quite himself when he delivered the annual Churchill lecture at London's famous Guildhall in the summer of 1989. If he had Alzheimer's disease at that time, it did not show. Reagan was absent in other ways. Mainly, for the purposes of this monograph, he spoke, and not for the first time, as a corporate persona.[1] In the past Reagan played various roles in vintage ads for General Electric, Union Pacific, Chesterfield Cigarettes, and Royal Crown Cola, but this time he sponsored a more discreet but no less ubiquitous company in his promotion of the democratic possibilities of the microchip: an international mining company called Rio Tinto.

Advancing Rio Tinto's extractivist interests throughout the world, and especially in the American Southwest, Reagan strategically used mineral-bearing technologies as seemingly neutral realpolitik "matters of fact" to bridge troubled waters between the East and West. Technology was dubbed the "oxygen of the modern age," and communication technology was Reagan's weapon for transcending the United States's entrenched divisions with the Soviet Union and the People's Republic of China. "The Goliath of totalitarian control will rapidly be brought down by the David of the microchip," he said before an audience of about one thousand, hosted by the English-Speaking Union.[2]

Reagan may not have mentioned Rio Tinto by name, but this *Geist*-like corporation was, intentionally or not, one of the main benefactors of his speech, and it could not have missed the relevance of this speech to its global operations. Rio Tinto was present subjectively *through* Reagan as an implied corporate network that would carry out Reagan's implicit calls for heightened extractivism to create the technology needed for global peace and prosperity. After all, Rio Tinto's global headquarters were located just down the street from Guildhall in London's mining financial district.

Communication technology does not come from thin air.[3] Nor do the mineral metals that sustain it (e.g., copper, lithium, palladium, cadmium, gold, and silver). As this book shows, these taken-for-granted commodities in the age of information and networks create very material "metabolic rifts" for ecological systems and greatly affect persons, cultures, and place-based identities for those that live near these mines.[4] Rio Tinto is therefore presented with difficult exigencies across its many different vistas of terranean and subterranean rhetoric.

What is Rio Tinto? That is one of the main questions of this book. Rio Tinto is one of the largest and most essential companies most people have never heard of and yet are quite possibly connected to at this very moment. Founded in the nineteenth century, Rio Tinto has become an international mining conglomerate with at least sixty projects and operations in thirty-five countries.[5] With 46,500 employees, Rio Tinto reported $44.6 billion in gross revenue in 2020, making it one of the top three largest metals and mining companies in the world (behind only Glencore and BHP).[6] From gold to aluminum, copper to uranium, coal to borax, Rio Tinto is the juggernaut behind modern, taken-for-granted commodities such as cell phones, automobiles, computers, and even renewable energy technologies (e.g., solar panels, geothermal systems, electric vehicles). Demands for Rio Tinto's minerals and metals have risen dramatically in pandemic times, not to mention in response to the climate change crisis. From these increased demands for resources and the technologies they build, Rio Tinto has built a twenty-first-century empire that "envelops the entire space of . . . civilization."[7]

The Rio Tintos of the world remind us that communication technologies, like the energies that flow through them, are far from neutral and atomistic. They rely on natural resources extracted from the earth, and they have material effects on ecosystems, economies, and cultures that must be accounted for as we plunge deeper into the Anthropocene—a geological epoch defined by humanity's irrevocable impact on the planet. With increased dependencies and shortages of the metals that make up electric vehicles, smartphones, gaming consoles, computers, televisions, and their semiconductors in pandemic times, natural resources and their extractive companies are increasingly becoming what Bruno Latour has called "dingpolitik" (politics of things) "matters of concern" and less realpolitik "matters of fact."[8] This is especially true considering the historic transition we have experienced from the "public sphere" to the "public screen."[9]

Rio Tinto is an elusive global traveler cloaked beneath layers of black-boxed technologies, extractive processes, and political allies (e.g., Reagan). The company would not even come to the surface if not for the sublime presences of its open-pit mines. Whereas average consumers unknowingly rely on its resources on a day-to-day basis, those that live within the vicinities of these mines have very different sets of relations that provide researchers with a unique window to study how Rio Tinto builds potentially passable rhetorical identities in the places it dwells.

This book is all about Rio Tinto and its vast extractive economies, flows of resources, and networks of subjectivity and agency. Although research in environmental communication has studied different rhetorical strategies of coal, chemical, and energy companies, and also their counterpublic movements, research is limited when it comes to the rhetorical practices of hard-rock mining companies. Through Rio Tinto, I hope to show how extractive companies *alchemically* create rhetorical presences in the places and spaces they extract. In an era of dwindling natural resources yet surging demand, Rio Tinto can teach publics and critics what the future of extractivism may look like as we head deeper into the twenty-first century. While extractivism, or *extractivismo*, is a concept derived from the Global South, namely Latin American political climates, this book shows that North America is also the site for present and future extraction politics. Recognizing this creates new opportunities for cross-continental alliances through elevated consciousnesses about how extractivism works.[10] It may also expand our understanding of how extractive coloniality works as an agentic global force.

From the outset it should be known that this project approaches Rio Tinto as a rhetorical actor that shapes meanings and orientations toward the environment. In the following pages, I narrow in on rhetoric's abilities to alchemically transform objects, environments, and even persons into something deemed more valuable. What Ronald Walter Greene calls "money/speech" is an important component of understanding Rio Tinto's rhetoric. To Greene "money/speech" defines the ways the Supreme Court of the United States has interpreted corporate financial contributions to political campaigns and advocacies as constitutionally protected "speech." Money/speech accounts for the ways capitalism "incorporates rhetorical communication into its regime of accumulation and its modes of regulation" in ways that have created an "overdetermined articulation of money and advocacy that can appear in different rhetorical forms."[11] For instance, Emma Bloomfield has argued neoliberalism—what many have argued is our current regime of economic governance—has created a system where the markets themselves are agentic actors both "alive" and "hungry" with "economic autonomy that should not be violated" (e.g., "neoliberal piety").[12] As an agentic actor, Rio Tinto uses money/speech, among other *things*, to build localized place- and space-based identities. In doing so, Rio Tinto rhetorically mediates its complicated identity politic.

One of the main arguments this book will make is that Rio Tinto is a networked rhetorical subject, which allows the company to extract without experiencing any of the ecological costs associated with extraction. The term "subject" here is not used casually as it speaks to a historical tension within philosophy that since Descartes has assumed subjectivity, or the ability to exist as a knowing subject, is defined by a human's unique capacity to think, reason, and speak. Rio Tinto of course does none of these as an abstract corporate actor with no mind, body, soul, or flesh; yet it nevertheless exists as an actor "subjectivized," or articulated as a subject, through legal discourses that recognize corporations as constitutionally protected subjects (e.g., "money/speech"), cultural apparatuses that hail them as desirable (e.g., wealthy patrons of sports arenas such as "Ford Field"), and political decision-making processes where they participate in important debates that affect the "public sphere" (e.g., global warming, gun rights, tobacco consumption). As developed in the following chapter, Rio Tinto exists as a unique kind of "poststructural" actor defined by different assemblages, absences, and traces as opposed to a fully-present singular subject (e.g., the Cartesian kind).

A 2018 visit to Rio Tinto's headquarters, a short "tube" ride away from Guildhall, made these absences clear. Here, in London's St. James's Square, Rio Tinto—the singular, human actor—is nowhere to be found. Sure, one can find employees at the front desk, and others coming in and out of the building, but none of them are Rio Tinto, the essential subject. The building itself is mundane with a façade that blends in with surrounding architecture. Far from the alcazar I had in mind, Rio Tinto looks innocuous and mundane (see fig. 1).

The employees were also friendly, even funny. While they would not allow me to go beyond a gated entrance, I was permitted to casually browse the foyer, which was full of comfortable furniture, reading material, and a map of global operations. How can this place be the essence of one of the largest mining companies in the world that somehow simultaneously exists in thirty-five countries? Is this the same company that Reagan discursively implied when he was hailing the future of

Fig. 1 | Rio Tinto's London headquarters. Photo taken by the author.

technology just a few blocks away? If this building and all of its spaces are not the agentic Rio Tinto, who speaks for Rio Tinto? Where and how does it exist?

To locate Rio Tinto we must look beyond its metropole (London) to its mines, where it exists at the most basic level as an extractive agent of immense ecological, social, and cultural change. By the time this book is complete, I will make the argument that Rio Tinto is a colonial assemblage that, like the colonial "overseer" in the sugar plantations in the Caribbean (viz., Hispaniola [Haiti and Dominican Republic]), extracts from afar as a knowing, seeing, ordering subject. Is Rio Tinto all that different than the former British Empire? While both are/were global actors that form a colonial/modern regime of governance based in London, Rio Tinto is also unique in that it is subjectivized as a singular actor that transcends nations and states in free market economies, which raises important questions about the nature of Rio Tinto's being. As such we must begin this interrogation with an ontological probing of Rio Tinto to determine the nature of its rhetorical existence at its different mines.

By visiting three different submerged places in the American Southwest— Boron, California; Salt Lake City (SLC), Utah; and Oak Flat, Arizona—I will show that Rio Tinto crafts different rhetorical personae to mediate its extractive ontologies through discursive and material "masks." I call these different masked identities *corporate personae*, which function very differently than traditional personae because not only are they from an authorless agent, but they are, though not exclusively, place-based and affective (see chapter 1). In this way, Rio Tinto is a global traveler that extracts a wide range of resources cross-continentally as a modern-day resource colonialist, or colonial assemblage.

Before we can draw this conclusion about Rio Tinto's being, however, we must foremost determine Rio Tinto's ontological nature without any preconceived assumptions about how it exists (chapter 1). This is important because it allows us to determine the nature of Rio Tinto's being—a worthwhile pursuit in and of itself given Rio Tinto's corporate existence in a post–*Citizens United* world. Throughout the course of this book, we will travel to different mines in the American Southwest to see how Rio Tinto rhetorically exists in personified form. We will see how, for instance, Rio Tinto invokes metaphors of pioneerism, progress, and frontierism as vehicles for extractivism at its mines.

What some have called the "extractivist frontier" is very much alive as a dominant narrative frame.[13] From Columbus to Buffalo Bill, the frontier myth has defined American national identities and shaped rhetorical agencies. "Since the beginning," observes Janice Hocker Rushing, the pioneer spirit has shaped the American dream and infused its rhetoric."[14] For instance, In *The Frontier of Science*, Leah Ceccarelli convincingly argues that the frontier myth, and its different clusters of metaphors, has shaped the evolution of scientific exploration. Since the twentieth century, scientists have burnished their ethos with frontier imageries before lay audiences that may otherwise reject their work.[15] In similar ways, Rio Tinto draws from this myth to deflect environmental criticism about its extractive practices. Drawing from this frontier myth, Rio Tinto posits itself as a sort of masculine, risk-taking individual fulfilling its manifest destiny to extract, exploit, and strike it rich in the American West. While this rhetoricity may not be apparent to most transglobal natural resource consumers, those who visit these sites encounter the full range of *rhetorical resources* that Rio Tinto uses to stabilize not just its own presence but also the visual presences (and absences) of their mines.

Reagan is an example of a corporate person that advanced Rio Tinto's rhetorical motives, even if he did not know it. He never stopped being an actor, which is why, among other reasons, he lives on as a rugged frontiersman at Rio Tinto's Visitor's Center at the Borax Mine in Boron, California—the first stop on our ontological journey (chapter 2). Sitting atop the "biggest and richest deposits of borax on the planet," in Boron, California, the Borax Mine Visitor's Center allows visitors to encounter a wealth of cultural artifacts that commemorate Reagan, and the Hollywood persona he carried with him, in the annals of Rio Tinto's corporate history. Visitors who travel to this place of corporate rhetoric will find that Rio Tinto uses Reagan's celebrated "pioneer" persona to infuse the Borax Mine, and its otherwise invisible minerals and metals, with rhetorical life. This agentic corporate personality is especially poignant given that Reagan was featured in more than a few commercials for "20 Mule Team Borax"—a brand of borax cleaner that came from the Borax Mine—which was once featured on the hit radio and TV series, *Death Valley Days*. Images of Reagan and the twenty-mule team are ubiquitous throughout this "corporate town" of Boron, not least of which includes the Twenty Mule Team Museum. In more ways than some, Boron is a place-based version of a *chemical* utopia that, among other things, contributed to the invention of "nature" at Death Valley National Park (DVNP).[16] Reagan is therefore more than some simulacra that keeps shadowed the true face of Rio Tinto; he is an example of how Rio Tinto creatively uses persons—and also objects, places, and spaces—as media for translating its identity or personality.

Rio Tinto also has a much larger networked identity that adapts its different parts to meet certain place-based exigencies. In chapter 3, for instance, I show how Rio Tinto is capable of drawing from very different rhetorical resources to craft another iteration of this frontier identity in Salt Lake City, Utah, which is home to Rio Tinto Kennecott's Bingham Canyon Mine (BCM). At this colossal mine, oftentimes celebrated as "the largest" and "richest hole on Earth," Rio Tinto uses its main resource, copper, as a *rhetorical resource* for crafting a pioneer persona uniquely adapted to the cultural significations of pioneerism among Mormon populations throughout the Salt Lake Valley. Even though more than a few environmental activists charge Rio Tinto for disproportionately contributing to the Salt Lake Valley's atrocious air pollution problem, Rio Tinto rebuts these challenges affectively. Through different material rhetorics at places of corporate community, Rio Tinto transforms the mine into a felt iconic object that is necessary for sustainable futures in "the Beehive State."

Rio Tinto's presences are not always so seemingly innocuous, as its extractivist practices are also illustrative of how resource coloniality simply works in the Anthropocene. In chapter 4, I engage Rio Tinto's involvement in plans to create the largest underground copper mine in North America at Superior and Oak Flat, Arizona. As with many other extractive operations, though, the proposed Resolution Mine is a textbook example of how extractivism racializes land in ways that disproportionately target Indigenous communities and persons of color.[17] The massive deposits of copper exist beneath ground sacred to the San Carlos Apache, and the project would devastate cultural attachments to this holy site. Rio Tinto has responded to heightened criticism by extending its pioneer persona in ways that paternalistically appropriate folksy, yet securitized, affects to stabilize its mercurial identity. Under the joint corporate name Resolution, Rio Tinto and BHP Billiton attach their corporate identities to the extant architecture of mining (e.g., mining shafts, smelters, mining towns) in this region of Arizona known colonially as the "Copper Triangle" or the "Pioneer District." This material rhetoric grafts Rio Tinto onto a legacy of mining that has "racialized the land," rendering it and the Indigenous persons that live there "terra nullius," while also constituting an extractive version of "the people" in Superior.[18]

These are some of the many different faces, or "masks," that Rio Tinto wears in its efforts to "pass" among different audiences as a necessitous corporate actor without having to settle in those ecological communities and bear the costs of extraction. As I argue in the concluding chapters, Rio Tinto is an extractive colonialist that mediates its networked identity through myriad object-oriented colonialities, or rhetorical colonialisms, that produce different, and not altogether coherent, dimensions of its corporate persona. While Rio Tinto emphasizes its rugged frontierism in Boron, its community partnerships in Salt Lake City, and its paternalistic qualities in Superior, these personalities and traits are extensions of a dominant pioneer persona that has for centuries defined dominant agencies of Western actors. Whether or not Rio Tinto can be essentialized as such is a question I address in the conclusion.

As I argue in chapter 1, these personae are much more than mere masks that hide or mislead publics about truer environmental realities. Corporate personae are ontological strategies that alchemically *create* corporate beings through the material and discursive flows of their natural resources. In this way, Rio Tinto is the Archimedes of the Anthropocene that not only transforms mountains into purified rare earth metals for communication technologies such "public screens," but it also invents its own corporate genesis in the places it dwells. How this happens is part of the basis of this book as I consider corporate rhetoric and their places and spaces of extraction.

Before we can arrive to these specific arguments about Rio Tinto's material, yet fragile, identity politics, we must first situate this work within relevant literature and unpack some of its theoretical and methodological underpinnings. The remainder of this chapter thus walks readers through some of the main concepts of this book. I begin with a discussion about the similarities and differences between coal and copper companies' neoliberal rhetorics in environmental communication. I then introduce the concept of alchemical rhetoric as one way to interpret Rio Tinto's materialistic rhetorical strategies and then discuss my methodological approach for investigation and preview the remaining six chapters.

Rio Tinto, the Peabody of Copper

In a way, this book is just as much about Reagan and his corporate networks as it is about Rio Tinto. Although networks that hold together Reagan and Rio Tinto are not always made apparent, Reagan remains at the core of contemporary industrial rhetorics and their rootedness in neoliberalism. He also played an important role in Rio Tinto's rhetorical history. Throughout his career, Reagan frequently played the part of a corporate subject with a persona that boosted corporate ethos with his Western pioneer persona.[19] This kind of rhetorical performance is exemplary of what Jen Schneider et al., authors of *Under Pressure: Coal Industry Rhetoric and Neoliberalism*, call corporate ventriloquism, which usefully describes how corporations, especially mining corporations, use different front groups, faces, or personas to "transmit messages" that advance deregulatory motivations rooted in neoliberal ideologies.[20]

For instance, the authors observe how Reagan was featured in General Electric's (GE) "Live Better Electrically" campaign where at least in one commercial with his wife Nancy, he showcases their "all-electric" home full of different electrical appliances in a post–World War II era. "When you live better electrically," Reagan concludes, "you lead a richer, fuller, more satisfying life. And it's something all of us in this modern age can have."[21] To Schneider et al., Reagan's role in this particular ad is illustrative of "energy utopia," a corporate rhetorical strategy that suggests "a particular energy source [is] key to providing a 'good life' that transcends the conflicts of environment, justice and politics."[22] As I have suggested, Reagan was also the dummy for corporate ventriloquists GE and Rio Tinto. With Reagan, after all, are the "roots of neoliberalism, American style, with a cultural politics featuring an idealized version of private life made possible by an abundance of electricity."[23] Reagan was no less rhetorical at Guildhall as he appeared to draw from those same rhetorical energies afforded by both coal and copper to end the Cold War.

Corporate ventriloquism and energy utopia are two of five strategies Schneider et al. name in their study of how coal companies strategically deflect criticism. Other strategies include what they name the industrial apocalyptic, technological shell game, and the hypocrite's trap, which illustrate the rhetorical wiliness of coal companies against heightened environmental pressures to clean up their environmental messes.[24] For coal companies, these rhetorical ploys thrive off of and reinforce dominant neoliberal ideologies that emphasize deregulatory, market-based approaches to environmental problems. Conceptually, neoliberalism refers to the ways industries invoke rhetorics for deregulatory, privatized, and anti-taxation practices that have their roots in Milton Friedman's work at the University of Chicago in the 1970s. Neoliberalism was also politically enacted in the United States by none other than Reagan himself, and also British prime minister Margaret Thatcher, in the 1980s. As a hegemonic ideology that "disseminates the model of the market to all domains and activities," neoliberalism to Wendy Brown reduces subjectivity and agency to *homo oeconomicus*, or the idea that humans themselves are configured "exhaustively as market actors" in a "market regime of governance."[25]

Neoliberalism has granted corporations of all stripes, especially natural resource companies, wide agencies to rhetorically engage publics with privileged status. A corpus of work in environmental communication has studied how corporate rhetorical strategies shape discourses and practices about the environment and mislead publics and consumers about their environmental practices.[26] Through what Schneider et al. call "the paradox of voice," neoliberal rhetorical strategies may appear to broaden the pluralities of voice but actually stymie the very voices they seem to promote by narrowing discourses to market-based rationalities from neoliberal ideological positions.

Unlike coal, which tends to be more visually and discursively apparent in American culture, most of Rio Tinto's metallic minerals remain hidden beneath layers of black-boxed technologies in the nation's unconscious. Reflective of the invisible, yet necessitous "underlands" that support rapid flows of commodities, capital, and energy on the terranean world, Rio Tinto's mines are demonstrative of the continuous ruptures of place in an epoch defined by humanity's irreparable impacts on the planet.[27] These "sunken networks of extraction, exploitation, and disposal support the surface world," and, notes Robert Macfarlane, are metonymic of an "ongoing occurrence experienced most severely by the most vulnerable."[28] While Rio Tinto may keep subterranean matters submerged beneath dominant consciousness, Rio Tinto's extractive politics also have a way of rising to the surface.

For instance, if readers are not aware of the 1969–88 Bougainville ecological crisis, which led to a deadly civil war (and genocide) over Rio Tinto's Panguna Mine in Papua New Guinea, readers may be familiar with Rio Tinto's desecration of the Juukan Gorge caves in Western Australia during the summer of 2020.[29] In its search for iron ore, Rio Tinto "blasted" several sites sacred to the Puutu Kunti Kurrama and Pinikura (PKKP) people in the western Pilbara region, destroying more than a few burial sites and sacred objects—including a four-thousand-year-old "plaited" strand of hair from several different people related to PKKP persons. The site had served as a "resting place" for Aboriginal ancestors since the last Ice Age.[30] "It was the sort of site you do not get very often, you could have worked there for years," said archaeologist Michael Slack. He asked, "How significant does something have to be, to be valued by wider society?"[31] This blunder caused many, including investors, to question the politics of Rio Tinto's mineral-infused technologies, which is why it did not take long for Rio Tinto to publicly apologize and accept the resignation of executive officer Jean-Sébastien Jacques. While Rio Tinto has attempted to rebuild its image as a company sensitive to Indigenous cultures and lands, the Oak Flat controversy at the proposed Resolution Mine indicates otherwise (chapter 4). These high-profile cases bring Rio Tinto's environmentally unjust practices to the international spotlight, but what about Rio Tinto's other extractive operations that remain beneath the surface?[32]

While most of Rio Tinto's extractive networks for resources such as iron ore, copper, and borax might be more submerged than the previous examples suggest, they are no less commonplace and impactful and merit equal scholarly attention. Although research in environmental communication and rhetoric have studied different rhetorical strategies of coal, tar sands, chemical, and energy companies—all of which greatly inform this book's reading of Rio Tinto's environmental rhetorics—research remains limited when it comes to the rhetorical practices of other minerals and metals under less environmental pressures or even new demands as global societies wean off coal. This is especially true in Reagan's information age, where hidden minerals such as borax and palladium quite literally hold screens together. These *elemental rhetorics* cannot necessarily be separated from the practices of fossil fuel companies given their numerous cross-dependencies and political intersections, but there are also different local and national challenges tied to mines where these resources are primarily extracted. Below I consider one of Rio Tinto's most predominant resources, copper. While Rio Tinto mines many different resources, including coal, it tends to focus on copper above all other resources. Copper is such an important part of Rio Tinto's operations that it in a way can be considered the Peabody of copper.[33]

The "Pressures" and Affordances of Copper

While there are many parallels between industrial rhetorics of coal and copper, there are also more than a few key differences, not least of which is somewhat competing rhetorical situations. Whereas coal is "under pressure," as Schneider et al. observe, from different environmental advocates and policymakers to cease and desist or diversify for more environmentally sustainable futures, copper is becoming increasingly called upon for many technological "solutions" to global climate change. Since copper is such an efficient conduit of energy, it is an indispensable element for virtually all technologies that require some form of electrical current. This includes renewable energy technologies such as solar panels, electric vehicles, geothermal systems, and "paperless" campaigns. In and by themselves renewable energy technologies are pushing demands for copper upward by at least 2.5 percent per year, with those trends rising into the future. Electric vehicles alone are expected to increase demands for copper by as much as 10 percent by 2030 (currently 1 percent). While global demands decreased by 2 percent in 2020 (20 million tons fewer than in 2019 because of COVID lock-downs and layoffs),[34] production and demand are projected to increase expo-nentially in the future as more companies invest in "green" technologies that rely on the red metal.[35] The COVID-19 pandemic is even more demonstrative of the staying power of the "age of copper" with millions working, and communicating, from home on screens.[36]

While the technologies that copper supports may be considered renewable, copper itself is not. There is a limited supply of it in the world, and as global dependencies for the element continue to surge it will only continue to be a hotly contested dingpolitik resource. Currently, total reserves of copper are nearly 830 million tons and annual demands are approximately 28 million tons. This means that, like coal, we have more than enough of the precious metal to meet global needs for the coming years, even with anticipated growth rates over the following decades.[37] Nevertheless copper companies keep on ramping up supply to maximize profits.

Copper also enables "public screens" and their "image events," which more than a few have used to conceptually read possibilities of radical environmental protest.[38] Where there are public screens and microchips there are possible traces of Rio Tinto and its minerals and hard-rock metals (e.g., gold, silver, copper, borates) from places such as the Bingham Canyon Mine and the Borax Mine. Consider how each iPhone requires at least forty-six different elements—most of which are mined by Rio Tinto on some part of the planet and come with extraordinary environmental effects.[39] Again, the global reliance on digital technologies during pandemic and postpandemic times even further supports this point. As I write, actual microchips, and their semiconductors, are in such demand for global economies that their shortages have reached "a crisis point" of epic proportions.[40]

While not all public screens or renewable energy technologies necessarily have resources mined by Rio Tinto—as if one could tell—they are both linked in some way to hard-rock mineral mining exemplified by Rio Tinto, which is one of the top three largest of its kind in the world. When it can, Rio Tinto operates off a politics of invisibility. As Jared Diamond notes in *Collapse*, the processes and presences of copper in everyday commodities, let alone the companies that do the extracting, are nearly entirely clandestine to the individual consumer.[41] Unlike coal and gas, two resources that consumers may have more attachments with—either through their national significations, their uses, and their brands—consumers "are eight steps removed" from the processes of extracting hard-rock mineral metals. Among other effects, this makes protesting or boycotting "a dirty mining company virtually impossible" even though the environmental effects of postmining "forever chemicals" are just as, if not more, damning than, say, a highly visible oil spill.[42] Boycotting copper-infused technologies would be even more profoundly untenable since consumers have no idea which products have tiny bits of copper in them or where they may have come from.[43] All of this also assumes that copper comes from just one company and not a merged company such as Resolution Copper (which is owned by both Rio Tinto and BHP Billiton) or many more.

Consumers do not shop for palladium, aluminum, or copper. Instead, they tend to seek out the most inexpensive car, computer, or smartphone where these invisible resources are instead bundled into countless commodities that are passed on from producer to manufacturer and salesperson. Nonelectric vehicle drivers may not know where their oil comes from when they fill up their tanks of gas, but they at least know the reputation of the refining company that has marketed its brand. At the very least, brand recognition allows consumers to boycott certain companies for certain environmental practices such as BP in the wake of the 2010 Deepwater Horizon crisis. One cannot do the same with copper, even though the metal is one of the most important resources for "sustainable" technologies in our age of anthropogenic global climate change.

When it comes to copper, there are very different rhetorical situations that grant extractive companies certain leverages and affordances not available to coal companies. While coal may be tied to nationalistic symbologies within the United States, copper tends to be more global in its reach while also necessary for possible futures and plainly invisible. To Tim Heffernan, "Worries about oil and gas hog all the airwaves," he says, "but copper is also essential to keep the world running: It threads through your house, your computer, your eco-correct hybrid car. And it's getting just as difficult, expensive, and environmentally menacing as oil to extract. We have entered the era of tough ore."[44]

Given this unique rhetorical exigency where copper is becoming increasingly hailed for sustainable futures, and its presences are less apparent than coal, how does Rio Tinto manage its rhetorical presences and absences? Below I introduce the concept alchemical rhetoric as one way of reading Rio Tinto's copper rhetorics at its mines and beyond.

Alchemical Rhetoric

Copper does not speak for itself. For it to be made present for publics and consumers, its bits of red metal require corporate agencies. As discussed further in the following chapter, Rio Tinto's process of calling forth resources such as copper and circulating them for consumption is not just materially extractive but rhetorically as well, for Rio Tinto's rhetorical presences depend on a constant process of reduction, colonization, and reappropriation for particular rhetorical motivations. Rio Tinto agentically uses its natural resources as *resources for rhetorical invention*. For instance, at places such as Salt Lake City, Rio Tinto appropriates its dominant resources, namely, copper, to highlight its mundane importance to modern life. Considering natural resources as rhetorical resources for invention is suggestive of Rio Tinto's alchemy, which is a form of magic that turns mines into monuments and copper into public screens.

As Kenneth Burke has observed, magic is one of three orders of rationalization, in addition to science and religion, for understanding humans' role in the universe. As the "schema which stressed mainly the control of natural forces" as opposed to human (religion) and technological (science), magic for Burke is a "primitive rhetoric" that fills gaps between poetics and science.[45] Burke's notion of magic is rooted in the idea that rhetoric itself is not just symbolic action but what he labels "hortatory" action that exhorts through "suasion with a potential for inducing action in human beings."[46] In *Rhetoric of Motives* Burke notes, "Whereas poetic language is a kind of symbolic action, for itself and in itself, and whereas scientific action is a preparation for action, rhetorical language is *inducement* to action (or attitude, attitude being an incipient act)."[47]

Magic is thus a form of "coercive command" that creates and re-creates reality. This is why to William A. Covino, to "do magic" is to "do rhetoric." Likewise, doing rhetoric is doing magic.[48] For Kevin Johnson, who reads the artist Eminem as the "magical product" of *The Eminem Show*, Burke's magic is also located within "a hegemonic scene, where magic as agency exists for the purpose of either challenging or perpetuating the scene."[49] In other words rhetoric is a "symbolic inducement" that shuffles and reshuffles symbolisms to achieve particular goals.[50]

As a sort of magic, Rio Tinto alchemically mediates its sites of extraction to stabilize its corporate presences. Alchemical rhetoric, as understood here, is a form of what Robin Jensen has called "chemical rhetoric" that shows how minerals and metals with chemical properties become vernacularly imbued in public places and spaces.[51] As Jensen observes, studying the vernacularism of chemical rhetoric, and from a critical rhetorical standpoint, it is one of several "lens[es]" for viewing chemical rhetoric as a "nonexpert communication" that has functioned "as a powerful public vocabulary featuring chemical terms, tropes, figures, appeals and/or narratives."[52] While chemistry as a technical field may have emerged from alchemy, alchemical rhetoric—which exists within Burke's order of magic—highlights the rhetorical performances of natural resource companies that go beyond technical language within the order of science to convince publics about the necessities, and continued valuations, of resources such as gold, silver, and copper as we move closer to what Burke satirically calls "Helhaven."[53] Alchemical rhetoric, as I show in the following chapter, is how corporations use natural resources for rhetorical invention, even corporate genesis.

While several scholars have discussed alchemy as a rhetorical genre, a political tactic, and a psychoanalytic form of Enlightenment, I take up alchemical rhetoric as a metaphor for the very real practices of Rio Tinto that create new realities by mixing different elements in places and spaces to create new rhetorical presences through countless technologies, objects, and even people that spread its hybridized identity across vast terrains.[54] Importantly, alchemy is not a faux truth in the classic sense. While Joshua Gunn and Thomas Frentz point out in their reading of the *Da Vinci Code* that the alchemical genre is a fake truth advanced in ways that expose the absurdities of realities in plain sight, alchemical rhetoric for our purposes emphasizes how different resources (e.g., base metals) can be used as a sort of rhetorical elixir for the creation of desired wealth. In a way, Rio Tinto achieves what many alchemists have attempted in the past by metaphorically turning base metals, especially copper, into gold. Copper is just one example of how Rio Tinto uses its resources to create new presences in the architecture of place, space, and community.[55]

Alchemical rhetoric is principally an agentic force that hybridizes places, spaces, objects, and persons to normalize certain distributions of sense and their affective economies and narratives, that solidify Rio Tinto's presences. For instance, as I show in chapter 2 (and as previously noted), Rio Tinto's alchemy works by creating a corporate town entirely centered around the Borax Mine and attaching itself to the social construction of "nature" at Death Valley National Park. While many can read this as a fake corporate town, or what Baudrillard may call a hyperreal simulation,[56] it is no less real than the mine itself. This is how places, objects, and even people become part of Rio Tinto's vast network. Recall how Reagan became an extension of Rio Tinto's network through his inducements to action at Guildhall. Through Reagan, Rio Tinto was able to transmit its messages to wide audiences about the necessity of technologies in the Information Age. Since Reagan's speech (1989), Rio Tinto has become part of new technologies—including renewable ones—that increase global dependencies on copper.

Rio Tinto is thus both chemist and magician. Using extracted resources such as copper rhetorically, Rio Tinto shapes and reshapes realities to induce action that valorizes its presences. For instance, consider the Spanish river called the *Río Tinto* (tainted river), from which Rio Tinto bears its name (see fig. 2). At the same time Reagan promoted the democratic possibilities of technology at Guildhall, the *Río Tinto* ran red in Spain's Huelva Province, and not for the first time. For thousands of years the *Río Tinto* has bled as a result of mining precious metals such as pyrites, copper, silver, and gold. While some contend that the water's bloody discoloration is mostly the result of a natural process of acid mine drainage, there is no doubt that the abandoned *Minas de Riotinto* (Rio Tinto Mines) played no small part in the river's unnatural transformation as one of the most toxic rivers on the planet. "In more than a thousand years," writes Richard West in *River of Tears*, "the countryside round the Rio Tinto did not recover from the effect of the fumes from the ancient smelters. No vegetation grew and no birds sang among the abandoned pit shafts."[57] Even the poet Lord Byron spoke of this area after visiting the mines at this time: "The dust we tread upon was once alive."[58]

Rio Tinto purchased the *Minas de Riotinto* from the Spanish government in 1873, forming Rio Tinto Zinc. Since the nineteenth century, Rio Tinto has acquired tremendous extractive agencies from this barren "moonscape" that have alchemically transformed this river, its resources, and its meaning before public audiences. Even mining waste is apparently valuable for Rio Tinto's alchemical process. As an alchemist of many different types, Rio Tinto has transformed the term "Rio Tinto" into an international corporation with great wealth from a dead, highly polluted river.

Fig. 2 | Río Tinto. Photo taken by Carlos Cantero.

Place itself has been alchemically transformed into a meaningful site of memory.[59] *Minas de Riotinto* is publicly remembered today not as a sacrifice zone but as a historical site that stirs memories of romance.[60] While mining operations have been deceased for hundreds of years, the *Minas de Riotinto*, located just outside Seville, Spain, continues to live large in the imaginations of many as an amusement park called *Parque Minero Riotinto* that, through Rio Tinto, celebrates its mining pasts. The mining park includes a museum, historic train rides through the mines, and tours in old mining shafts. Visitors can survey archaic mining tools, mineral assays, and pottery; journey through the mines as "a trip back in time through landscapes of another planet" (including a night train through ancient mines); and walk in the shoes of Roman miners in underground collieries. This shows how mining companies and their alliances rhetorically control "natural forces" by altering the scene through symbolic and extrasymbolic inducements. By effect *Minas de Riotinto* is alchemically made a place of celebration rather than an environmental sacrifice zone.

Another example I discuss further in chapter 3 is Rio Tinto's sponsorship of the Natural History Museum of Utah (aka the Rio Tinto Center), which has a 42,000-square-foot copper façade unearthed from the nearby Bingham Canyon

Mine. To Aaron Phillips the façade "elides extractivism at the BCM," but I wish to suggest it also makes the mine visible as a necessary storehouse for cultural education.[61] The way Rio Tinto mediates its rhetorical identity from mine to museum for its corporate benefit is an alchemical process that greatly informs rhetorical critics about rhetorical agency, resources, and invention in the Anthropocene.

These examples show how Rio Tinto draws from actual natural resources (e.g., copper) to create altogether new golden realities (and truths) that rhetorically commemorate places that are otherwise horrifying environmental sacrifice zones. As such they reveal how Rio Tinto acquires rhetorical agency through inducements to action predicated on the "control of natural forces" (i.e., natural resources).[62]

Importantly, this conception of alchemy is more than just an object-oriented approach to rhetoric, as it accounts for the way rhetoric, like Rio Tinto, is a force that has everything to do with transformative change. This occurs through different affective economies attached to rhetorical creations. As Sara Ahmed puts it, "emotions *do things*" in affective economies, "and they align individuals with communities—or bodily space with social space—through the very intensity of their attachments."[63] While *affect* for our purposes is more usefully understood as a presubjective sense that induces "the body's capacity to affect and be affected, to act and to perceive, unleashed," rather than emotions, Ahmed nevertheless helps understand how Rio Tinto's alchemical reactions at museums, stadiums, and public screens create public affective attachments that alter actions and attitudes toward those objects.[64]

Rhetoric in this way is a transformative yet irreducible force that still shapes attitudes and induces actions, but it is also located at the nexus of different material, affective, and symbolic milieus. Rio Tinto, in other words, is a rhetorical agent that exceeds the objects of its assemblage and thus points to some limits in what is referred to in philosophy and sociology as object-oriented ontology, actor-network theory, or material-semiotics that assume objects are defined only by their relations.[65] Rio Tinto exists through countless objects and relations, but it also exists as a corporate subject. The legal idea of corporate personhood, for instance, brings to life corporations as fictitious persons with legal prerogatives even though corporations exist as non- or more-than-human actors comprising many different objects and relations.[66] Corporate personhood is thus a premier example of alchemical rhetoric that has brought corporations to life as legal and market-based persons.

Alchemical rhetoric can be understood as a material form of greenwashing. To Phaedra Pezzullo, greenwashing involves not just the "'greening'" of "the appearances of products and commodity consumption" but also "the deliberate disavowal of environmental effects."[67] Rather than duping publics into believing something that is untrue, however, alchemical rhetoric creates altogether new more valued realities through a series of chemical reactions.[68] For instance, when copper is coupled with borax and palladium as one of forty-six elements that go into iPhone assemblages it becomes much more than the sum of its parts as new technological assemblage that is then branded as a fetishized object with a new value entirely unto itself.[69] Copper, as a base element, could be separated from the phone, but such disassembly would not inform us about the full rhetorical effect of copper that, mixed with other elements, creates the iPhone. Copper, by itself, may be rhetorical as "vibrant matter" but only when it is mixed, matched, and blended with other materialities does it becomes a potent resource for rhetorical invention.[70] Post-extraction copper becomes tied to countless new materialities with utterly different relations, yet these relations, and their alchemical creations, are no less real than copper's geological realties pre-extraction.[71] They are just different.

Rio Tinto works the same way as a corporate rhetorical actor imbued within its elements' alchemical creations. At its mines in the American Southwest, Rio Tinto becomes part of the very architecture of alchemical creations within certain cultures and communities. Rio Tinto's carefully created presences may distract from other, possibly more sustainable realities, but such worlds are far from faux and immaterial. They are real and concrete. As I am suggesting, the world consists of actors and networks, or assemblages, that constantly create or become. As Edward Abbey has said repeatedly on his trip "Down the River with Henry David Thoreau," which may as well have been the *Río Tinto*, "appearance is reality."[72]

A related example is that of the Ford Motor Company. In *Rhetoric Inc.: Ford's Filmmaking and the Rise of Corporatism*, Timothy Johnson argues that Ford used films produced from its Motion Picture Laboratory to weave its industrial culture into the fabric of American life in the early twentieth century. Through a blending of film theory, economic history, and rhetorical theory, Johnson studies Ford's film as a rhetorical force that contributed to the ascendence of American corporate culture through motion pictures that taught audiences how to live and work within the Fordist rhetorical economy. Johnson calls this rhetorical practice "incorporational rhetoric," which he defines as "the work of a massive, distributed system of actors and producers" that "is often executed simultaneously across a number of coordinated media" and "can sustain a consistent and cumulative presence for decades."[73] Johnson notes that the effectiveness of incorporational rhetoric is defined by "a new perceived 'reality' composed of a new kind of reason, new identities, and new spaces." This novel and transformative capacity of incorporational rhetoric is an important part of the process of alchemical rhetoric, and it aids understanding of how industrial corporations hegemonically shape public life through "systems of economic reason and action that appear natural and are ubiquitous."[74]

Alchemical and incorporational rhetoric both show how industrial corporations imbue their identities in everyday life as mundane, and oftentimes instructional, rhetorical actors. Per Ronald Walter Greene, this can be seen as a sort of "governing apparatus" and "technology of deliberation," wherein power is not hidden but in plain sight.[75] Alchemical rhetoric for our purposes specifically emphasizes the material dimensions of rhetoric that creates and transforms something new with greater social, cultural, or economic value. In a way, alchemical rhetoric is all about social change and creates spaces thinking and acting about how processes of alchemical transformation can be jammed, rerouted, or détournés (i.e., "monkey wrenched").[76] As I show in chapter 5, one way of doing this is through disrupting Rio Tinto's processes of identity construction during public hearings or labor disputes.

Rio Tinto may be abstract, but it comes to life as a rhetorical actor through different alchemical processes at its different sites of extractivism. Like copper, Rio Tinto is in constant motion as a conduit or medium for what George Kennedy has called "rhetorical energies," which is why this book embraces a form of what Elinor Light has called a "moving methodology" that looks to "movement, affect, and aesthetics as primary modes of understanding *in situ* [rhetorical] communication."[77] This methodology is used to highlight how Rio Tinto maintains consensual "distributions of sense" that normalize extractive coloniality in the Anthropocene.[78] Below I call this method secular pilgrimaging.

Secular Pilgrimaging

I approach Rio Tinto as a secular pilgrim who travels to, and seeks out, Rio Tinto's different rhetorical presences at the places it dwells: mines, visitor centers, national parks and forests, and cities. The secular pilgrim has its roots in the practice of "pilgrimaging," which involves a religious journey to certain holy sites (e.g., Mecca, Bihar, the Mormon Trail, Canterbury Cathedral) to gain increased awareness about oneself from in situ past events. The "rhetorical pilgrim," to Marouf Hasian Jr. is one who journeys to certain sacred sites to learn about the different rhetorical decisions that go into curating, designing, or assembling place-based rhetorics. In his journey to the United States Holocaust Memorial Museum, for instance, he details "interventionist practices of the rhetors associated with the museum" and also a range of "clues about the privileging" of certain "historical memories of the Holocaust."[79]

While pilgrims may be motivated by certain religious impulses, or transcendent objectives, the secular pilgrim is one who travels to those extraordinary, special, or mysterious sites without a teleological (or transcendent) objective, for example, a "religious" paradigm. For our purposes secular pilgrimaging is a practice rooted in what Edward Said has called secular criticism (as opposed to religious criticism) in *The World, the Text and the Critic*. To Said, secular criticism is an orientation toward the world that does not assume a subjective pretense about how the world is, or how it should be, based on certain theoretical commitments.[80] To assume one "knows" the world before the critical act is to adopt a "religious" orientation toward the world that, I may add, also adopts what Donna Haraway has called the "god trick."[81] Instead, to Said, criticism "is always situated, it is skeptical, secular, reflectively open to its own failings."[82] In this way secular criticism becomes "not a theory but a practice that counters the tendency of much modern thinking to reach for a transcendentalist comfort zone, the very space philosophy wrested away from religion in the name of modernity."[83] In other words, secularism is immanent, meaning it does not assume a distinct separation between rhetor and the world it studies to advance a particular "religious" objective.

My pilgrimages to Rio Tinto's different sites in the American Southwest are also informed by the immanence of participatory fieldwork methodologies, which provide a vocabulary for tracking the movements and presences of Rio Tinto as a dominant rhetorical actor that naturalizes dominant orientations toward its sites of extraction.[84] Participatory rhetoric has its roots in Middleton et al.'s germinal essay on rhetorical field methods (RFM), which has served as a touchstone for rhetorical fieldwork operating on the "intersections between [critical rhetoric], ethnography, and performance studies."[85] While not the only way to go about rhetorical fieldwork, RFM, and what has since become participatory critical rhetoric (PCR), equips rhetorical scholars with tools and sensibilities for advancing the critical rhetoric project to "live" rhetorical situations.[86]

Advancing critical rhetoric in the field is no doubt an important telos, but this author also recognizes its tension with secularism and what scholars have named immanent participation. As McHendry et al. write, and Middleton et al. affirm, immanent participation "asks what can be done in the immanent moments of (co)participation in the field and demands that such moments (and the choices they entail) equally influence our critical findings."[87] Rather than *mining* objects for discursive or material fragments, immanent participation is "a way to understand how in situ rhetorical approaches embed critics and their bodies in a web of interpersonal relationships, affective claims on the critic, potential vulnerabilities, and political choices."[88] In this way, secular pilgrimaging can be a form of immanent participation that privileges the here and now over the "proper" course for future action.

This tension between immanent and critical rhetorical fieldwork is present in these pages about Rio Tinto's rhetorical existence when it comes to naming. While naming and essentializing Rio Tinto as a colonial, racist, or genocidal actor before pilgrimaging to its sites of extraction could lend itself to important insights into how Rio Tinto functions as *that* kind of subject, I find it intellectually necessary to foremost understand how Rio Tinto works before evaluating its actions within larger moral, economic, and political frameworks. Doing so allows us to immanently study how Rio Tinto's rhetoric stabilizes particular visions, feelings, and tropes about its identity and its mines within the communities in which it resides.[89]

At the same time, we have to land somewhere. That landing happens in chapter 5, where after imminently tracing Rio Tinto's existence from secular pilgrimages to Boron, Salt Lake City, and Superior, I take up different rhetorics of social protest struggling for labor rights, clean air, and decolonization. This critical rhetorical intervention is a departure from the more immanent secularism of the first four chapters but is also necessary for understanding the fuller range of issues and identities surrounding Rio Tinto's extractive practices. Rio Tinto is a global colonial power, but we must first immanently attend to its subtle nuances, differences, and alchemies, because as we will see, Rio Tinto is also so much more.

As a secular pilgrim, I have traveled to Rio Tinto's three different mines, cultural centers, and places of rhetoric to seek out, decode, and construct different readings of Rio Tinto's rhetorical presences (and absences). Through rhetorical fieldwork methodologies these experiences have allowed me to study Rio Tinto's alchemical rhetorics in the places it dwells. For instance, over the past decade, I have visited the Bingham Canyon Mine in Salt Lake City, Utah (five times); the Borax Mine in Boron, California (one time); and the proposed site of the Resolution Mine in Oak Flat, Arizona (one time). At the mines themselves, I have apprehended the magnitude of erasure, gone on corporate mining tours, visited visitor's centers, and contemplated corporate being in the Anthropocene. Since Rio Tinto, as a sort of network, spends most of its rhetorical energies away from these mines, in the urban-scapes that surround them, I have also visited many of the places and spaces that Rio Tinto has sponsored.

Rio Tinto is an agent that consists of many different subject positions and personae (see chapter 1).[90] Since our geological epoch is defined by different hybridities that we are coupled with, including extractive companies and their mines, this work can also inform us about ourselves in these strange times. Understanding how Rio Tinto works has the potential for other critics or activists to use this book, and its concepts, as they will. As Deleuze and Guattari have put it, "A concept is a brick. It can be used to build a courthouse of reason. Or it can be thrown through the window."[91]

Why Rio Tinto?

At this point it is worthwhile stating, in case it is not already clear, why this one particular mining corporation is the focus of this book rather than a broader more comparative approach to different mineral mining companies or extractivism generally. Beyond the obvious fact that Rio Tinto is one of the largest of its kind in the world in "the age of copper," it is also indicative of the mundane and unseen, yet necessitous, nature of natural resource companies in everyday life. Precisely because of its invisibility, Rio Tinto as a rhetorical object helps us make sense of our entire world in this current geological moment defined by the ordinariness of absence. What better way to study the processes of erasure in the Anthropocene than through a mundane, yet colossal, mining company?

Because Rio Tinto's main extractive focus, from the nineteenth century to the present, has tended to be copper, Rio Tinto also has great value in the field of communication (among others) in the digital age. For environmental communication specifically, Rio Tinto reveals many of the tensions within the very idea of sustainability through green technology while also informing critics how extractive companies, not just coal or energy companies, work rhetorically.

This project can also be seen as a Wendell Berrian commitment to place (or emptiness, considering the focus on Rio Tinto's open pit mines).[92] In our changing and disposable world, there is much theoretical value and praxis in staying committed to one object of study over time. Samantha Senda-Cook emphasizes the value of this kind of concentration for "long-term field work" that can determine how the materialities of place and space, and their discursive effects on identity formations, change over time.[93] Of course a true long-term account of Rio Tinto, over the more appropriate geological time, would exceed the scope of this project (and the lifetime of this mortal); nevertheless, it remains of great importance to commit oneself to place through the objects that we study while we can.

Christine Harold has recently argued for greater attachments to objects as a form of resistance to fetishized capitalism and its culture of disposability.[94] What if we treated rhetorical artifacts the same way? I am suggesting that extraction is not just the physical action of mining land for precious mineral metals. It is a cultural practice intersected with different sensibilities, performances, language, and rhetoric that some might suggest is inescapable. All too often, objects of rhetorical analysis, like, if not as, objects of consumption, are treated by the same politic of disposability as commodities where researchers assay, extract, and dispose before moving on to the next artifact. Rhetorical texts have become commodities and then trash.

Consider what Thomas Rickert has called the "extraction model" of rhetoric that is opposed to his notion of "ambient rhetoric," which calls for more attention to environs, nonhuman rhetorics, and ways of being in the world, or the "weddedness in the world," that call out rhetoric as an extrahuman affair. Rickert notes, "We might keep in mind what the rhetorical tradition often asserts, that just as a comedian extracts what is funny from life and world to make an audience laugh, so a rhetorician extracts, via the available means, what is persuasive from life and world to motivate or transform an audience. . . . The extraction model fosters the belief that rhetoricity or comedy, being human-initiated affairs of the symbolic are exclusively human doing."[95] Whether or not it is possible to escape this kind of extractivism in rhetorical theory and praxis— possibly through a form of *strategic essentialism* or *extractivism* I discuss in the conclusion[96]—it is nevertheless worthwhile naming this practice as a rhetorical colonial tactic grafted on top of layers of extractivism from mine to computer.

Rhetoric, like geology, is not neutral. At the same time there are limits to this idea of extractivism within, or through, rhetorical criticism because of the ways criticism can give back through certain fieldwork methodologies, coalition building, and care.[97] From another viewpoint, maybe rhetoric, if anything, is more akin to photography than extraction.

These are some of the questions I work through toward the end of the book. For now, I am suggesting that we may consider spending more time with objects as "things worth keeping" while they last.[98] While there are numerous explanations for the extractivist process of consuming and disposing of artifacts in rhetorical research—for instance, tenure clocks, institutional resources (or lack thereof), allotted time, and also artifact burnout—in the Anthropocene, where geological temporalities are so rapidly rupturing place and its changing "ecocultural identities," there is increased value in sticking with objects, and their troubles, to see how they, and we, change over time.[99] This is especially true when it comes to mining companies given the pace of their "mass destruction" within our global economy.[100]

Given the global reach of Rio Tinto and the scale of its ecological costs at its numerous mines, the company deserves sustained critical analysis rather than passing glances despite the fact that our visual culture inculcates this kind of consumption. This by no means is a case for more object gazing to try to interpret truer transcendental meanings. Rather, it is a simple form of academic commitment by conducting more analyses of the same objects over time with the emphasis on difference (e.g., different readings of changed objects in constant motion). This can also become one way of challenging extractivist ideologies and their links to different colonialities in the academy (#RhetoricSoExtractive). The goal after all is not to provide the final reading but to keep the conversation going in more inclusive, polyvocal ways.

Chapter Previews

The remainder of this book is organized around Rio Tinto's different sites of extraction in the American Southwest. Before studying these mines, however, the basic, or primordial, nature of Rio Tinto's rhetoricity must first be more firmly established. That is why in chapter 1, I begin again with an ontological probing of the nature of Rio Tinto's existence as a corporate actor. In this chapter I situate Rio Tinto broadly within discourses of corporate personhood and make the case that corporations have personae. Building off the concept of alchemical rhetoric and adding to those in rhetorical communication that have conceived different kinds of personae, I read the corporate persona as an animate, and affective, force that gives corporations rhetorical presences where otherwise there are absences. Advancing work by those that have already studied different kinds of discursive persona—namely, the first, second, third, fourth, and null—I argue that the corporate, or "fifth," persona responds to questions about the nature and necessity of corporate rhetoric in the present as one way to understand the ontology of their personae at different places and spaces. To show how this works, I seek out "corporate personhood" through the spatial absences of the Bingham Canyon Mine and show that while Rio Tinto's existence is akin to these absences, it is very much alive through objects, media, and places (*topoi*) of corporate rhetorical invention.

After working through Rio Tinto's rhetorical existence, I then move geographically from west to east—and temporally from the past to the future—to draw out Rio Tinto's alchemical rhetorics and corporate personae at the Borax Mine, the Bingham Canyon Mine, and the proposed Resolution Mine. I start in chapter 2 at the Borax Mine in Boron, California (Rio Tinto's western-most mine in the United States) with a reading of Rio Tinto's rhetorical pasts by returning to the one and only Ronald Reagan. Reagan, as noted, was a spokesperson for the mine's 12 Mule Team Borax on several commercials during *Death Valley Days* when the mine was owned by the U.S. Borax Company. While Reagan was no longer with us when Rio Tinto took over the mine, the company nevertheless continues to use his celebrated rugged frontier ethos to fill the Borax Mine's material absences with cultural presences (a form of what I call "historical incorporation"). These presences are most immediately felt at the U.S. Borax Visitor Center where Reagan is a condensation symbol for all the meanings of borax in everyday life. The cultural articulations of the mine are also felt at the Twenty Mule Team Museum and Death Valley National Park, which both, in different ways, commemorate the legacy of physically hauling borax from the Mojave Desert to cityscapes using twenty-mule teams. The mine, its visitor center, and other places of rhetoric, such as Death Valley National Park (Furnace Creek) and museums, all indicate how Rio Tinto draws from vast cultural resources to build a historical, and famous, persona uniquely adapted to place.

Chapter 3 takes readers back to the Bingham Canyon Mine in Salt Lake City, Utah. This mine is a present-day example of how resource companies imbue their identities in the materialities of place. I argue that Rio Tinto embeds its identities in the materiality of places and spaces throughout Salt Lake City to create a pioneer persona that is uniquely adapted to Mormon cultural identities and memories of emigrating west during the nineteenth century. Based on years of fieldnotes, participant observations, and several personal correspondences, I follow Rio Tinto in the Salt Lake Valley and piece together a patchwork of images and narratives that stabilize Rio Tinto's persona as pioneer. My objects of study include a visitor's tour of the mine, the Natural History Museum of Utah, Daybreak (a suburban community on reclaimed mining land), and a Major League Soccer stadium that is home to the Salt Lake Real and was formerly named the Rio Tinto Stadium (now the America First Stadium).

Chapter 4 takes readers to Oak Flat, Arizona, where Rio Tinto and BHP Billiton have created a joint company, Resolution Copper, to extract one of the last largest deposits of copper in North America, which exists on land sacred to the San Carlos Apache. Through the particular methods of mining that Rio Tinto intends to use, a metallurgic method known as block caving, sacred burial and ritual sites would be decimated by a future one-thousand-foot crater-like mining subsidence. Indigenous social actors and protesters have decried Rio Tinto's Resolution Mine as an instance of cultural and religious genocide that extends a legacy of colonialism and conquest of Indigenous persons. Responding to heightened public scrutiny, Resolution attempts to stabilize a paternalistic persona that knows the needs of "the people" and provides through economic, historical, and securitized rhetorics in Superior and Oak Flat, Arizona.

Chapter 5 is devoted to the ongoing struggles of those impacted by Rio Tinto's extractivism at Oak Flat, Salt Lake City, and Boron. In this chapter I argue for a stronger process-oriented approach to extractivism that sees companies such as Rio Tinto as rhetorical actors made real through processes in constant motion. I take up different moments of dissensus—or a redistribution of the sensible—that can performatively "jam," or "monkey wrench," Rio Tinto's becomings—to shape new communities of sense.[101] I identify three possible moments of process-oriented interruptions: public hearings, organized labor, and place-based protests and occupation.

I conclude with a brief discussion of the effects of these extraction politics to the idea of "public screens," which, I hold, must be considered via theory and praxis alongside the possibilities of "image events." Not only are there severe ecological, social, economic, and colonial implications to processes of corporate world-making and -ending, but we must also ask difficult questions about our own culpabilities during the critical rhetorical act. Are critics liable for world-ending practices in Oak Flat or Bougainville when using digital technology to critique those practices? Are we not all becoming Rio Tinto? How to de-link these colonial networks, and decolonize, from copper in the Anthropocene? Again, the objective here is not to make any Kantian conclusions but to open up the dialogue for new creative possible futures as we plunge deeper into the Anthropocene.[102]

1

The Corporate Persona

One can make sense of our entire world from Utah's Bingham Canyon Mine. Located a mere thirty-five miles southeast of Salt Lake City, Utah, the BCM has been a wellspring for copper, among other precious mineral metals, for more than 150 years. While the mine started with small mining claims in the early twentieth century, advances in technology, transportation, and science have transformed this part of the Oquirrh Mountain Range into the largest open-pit mine in the world that now covers approximately twenty-seven thousand acres of land. Staring into the mine's spatial void (*kenon*) from a visitor's platform, viewers may not be surprised that the BCM has produced more copper than any other mine in the history of the planet (nearly 20 million tons).[1] As they take the visual plunge to the depths of the mine, they become lost in space and forgetful of worldly intelligibilities that constitute such facts (see fig. 3). The reasonable subject instead dissolves in an abyss that spans more than two miles in length and three miles in depth and the sublime response takes hold. Overwhelming the human capacity to reasonably apprehend the mine, the subject is caught between paradoxical feelings of terror and awe as they come face-to-shadowy-face with what Slavoj Žižek might call a "kernel of the Real" and Martin Heidegger, a "standing reserve."[2]

As visitors turn around and face the city (*polis*), however, the knowable world returns. On the ground where they stand is a surfeit of corporate texts, images, and personae that may bring them back to reality. Here, in an artificial space between mine and city, they remember that this open-pit mine—the largest in the world—is not just intelligible within the referential totality but meaningful in more ways than some. For instance, on the visitor's observation platform they see machine parts, still frames, maps, and timelines that mediate the meaning of the mine with a powerful narrative of industrialism that suggests through advances in technology, human ingenuity, and the American spirit, human and corporate alliances have conquered this mountain for the betterment of society.

Fig. 3 | The Bingham Canyon Mine. Photo taken by author.

And without copper, technology—including all of the haulers, conveyers, refin-ery, and smelter at the BCM—fails, and so too does the modern empire of com-munication that it has built. Copper is the essence of our modern existence, and this is made most clear in the nearest city to the mine, Salt Lake City, where Rio Tinto has an ineffaceable presence in the architecture of the cityscape. Through places and spaces such as a natural history museum, a soccer stadium, university buildings, and an entire suburban community, Rio Tinto, copper, and the BCM acquire added rhetorical agency (see chapter 3). Here Rio Tinto uses copper as an alchemical rhetorical resource for invention in ways that infuse the BCM, and copper, with life.

The Bingham Canyon Mine is the Greek temple of our time. As Martin Heidegger explains in the "Origins of the Work of Art," the Greek temple was the ethos of ancient Athenian society because it so perfectly embodied Greek style—one rooted in the heroic actions of Gods and mortals—that it character-ized the entire age of Greek existence. While that world may no longer be acces-sible to us, the Anthropocene also has its unique cultural mood, or ethos, monumentalized by this mine. As mountains, and their ecologies, wash away in the sand, industrial corporations like Rio Tinto emerge as dominant rhetorical actors with presences that suture these absences with meaning. While this kind of absence (and death) creates the need for new, and creative, experiences of grief, mourning, and dwelling, as Joshua Trey Barnett has poignantly observed, such absences also create a clearing for understanding how we got here.[3] Humanity's reach has penetrated the very geological strata that we have used to distinguish pasts from presents, and the world of transcendence has formally come to a close, but arguably so too has dialectics—for where is the Other, the counterpoint, the antithesis in a world wrought with human tracings on every point of its surface?

Alchemical rhetoric helps readers understand how copper becomes part of the materiality of civic life, but what about the presences of Rio Tinto? Where is it if not in the emptied viscera of the BCM? Rio Tinto, and its absences at this mine, haunt philosophy and rhetoric as much as they do the Oquirrh Mountains. Positing whether the Rio Tinto and the BCM are present or absent, material or ideal, stirs conversations with Plato, Aristotle, and the continental philosophers about the role of rhetoric, the idea of the subject, and the prospect of meaning itself. As we stare into the depths of the BCM, we encounter something more akin to rhetoric's "pre-symbolic" ontological basis.[4] Is rhetoric even capable of reading corporate agencies and performances as an extrahuman, abstract actor?

My focus in this chapter is on the idea of the corporate subject and its possible personae. Although many have necessarily displaced the singular, speaking, rational subject by attending to the manifold absences of being and approaching what was once uncritically called "the subject" as a network, trace, assemblage, or simply nonexistent rather than a fully present being (temporally and spatially), criticism has not yet taken up philosophical insight of corporate rhetoric as a post- or extrahuman affair. Since George Kennedy's important essay on rhetoric as energy, several notable scholars have expanded rhetorical agency to the nonhuman world.[5] As noted in the previous chapter, Timothy Johnson's notion of incorporational rhetoric, much like alchemical rhetoric, shows how corporations can use different texts and media to create new perceived realities within novel "rhetorical economies" and industrial aesthetics.[6] With the exception of Johnson's work and also research by organizational communication scholars such as George Cheney and Jill J. McMillan, corporate rhetoric has largely remained in the background of the rhetorical tradition.[7] Corporate beings may be hidden, or concealed, from us, but as one look at the BCM makes clear— not to mention the myriad places, spaces, and objects that corporations disclose themselves through branding strategies—they are also in plain sight. As Heidegger would suggest, sometimes things have to be invisible for us to see them. Like the fish in the water, the things that are nearest from us also tend to be the furthest.

One way to address this lacuna without assuming some glorious return of the subject—which to be clear is not only impossible in the Anthropocene but problematic in and of itself—is through the concept of the rhetorical persona, which broadly refers to the various masks that speakers and authors wear to present their"second selves" before audiences. Up to the present, personae have been used to study the different rhetorical performances of speakers and audiences, and for our purposes this concept may be capable of describing how Rio Tinto manages its different place-based identities at its sites of extraction as both a local and global actor. Corporations may not be human, but they nevertheless disclose different rhetorical identities through structures of feeling tied to their literal and figurative image. Personae, I intend to argue, are not always seen. They are also felt.

The roots of persona are found in the Greek term, *prosōpon*. Unlike more specific terms for particular kinds of masks, as revealed in dialogues such as *Gorgias* and the *Symposium*—for example, *gorgoneion, mormolukeion,* and *prosopeion*—*prosōpon* more broadly references the myriad masks Greek wore for dramas, religious rites, and rituals. Importantly, it emphasized visual displays of individuals that not until the Roman era implied revealing. *Prosōpon* as both mask and face was an embodied visual display that made present. In this way *prosōpon* was a mode of presentation that strategically simplified identities for particular audiences.

To Plato, *prosōpon* was used to describe how interlocutors engaged in meaningful dialogue through face-to-face communication, as it denoted the act of turning to present something or someone for presentation (not concealment). The ontological basis of the Greek *prosōpon* thus might be said to be rooted strongly in a Platonic metaphysics of presence where through dialogue, interlocutors could capably name objects and "favor the gods."[8] In an oral culture that privileged the presence of face-to-face dialogue, *prosōpon* was the way in which interlocutors revealed their souls.[9] To the author of *Plato's Persona*, Denis Robichaud, through the eyes, or the "organs for the soul's divinatory foreknowledge and foresight," one could engage others directly by revealing interiorities of selfhood through face-to-face communication, which was"propaedeutic for dialogue with the divine."[10] With authorship not yet a serious epistemic invention, *prosōpon* for Plato was a mode of presentation for soul-to-soul communication. While *prosōpon* in the Greek tradition was a visual, non-duplicitous mode of concealing, Plato of course also recognized how *prosōpon* could deceive as observed in his condemnation against Homer for concealing himself behind characters (*prosopopoeia*). Masks to Socrates could be used as imitations that hide the soul. This slipperiness, since Plato, began to separate *prosōpon* as face from *prosōpon* as mask, considering the term could both reveal and conceal. For this reason, the *prosōpon*, to Robichaud, is not "a simple presentation of the true individual, since the principle unification that makes one a singular individual is interiorized."[11]

During the Roman era the distinction between *prosōpon* as a mask (persona) and a face (*os, vultus, facies*) was even more discernable because of the translations of Plato during a time when the Roman culture of orality in civic and legal contexts became more phonocentric and less ocularcentric. One consequence was that *prosōpon* became translated from the audible etymology of per-sonare ("sounding through") and interpreted in terms of how "a voice resounds" through the wood of a mask placed over faces.[12] Contrary to the Greek understanding of masks as presentational—and without duplicity—the Romans understood the term, now translated as persona, as a term for concealment.

With what Foucault would call "the invention of [humans]" in the modern episteme, which can be characterized as a moment where language becomes an object rather than a representation of thoughts, came the invention (and subsequent "death") of the author and a new realm of possibilities of persona within emergent literary traditions.[13] Pioneers of this new literary style such as T. S. Eliot crafted persona as a device for separating the author, or poet, from the text. No longer was persona a matter of revealing one's soul to others in preparation for the gods or a Ciceronian form of resemblance but a literary device for separating the author from the words on the page. The invention of the subject (author, character, individual, analysand) can be read as occurring through this new persona, and many, from Erving Goffman to Carl Jung and Judith Butler, have invoked the term to broadly express various relations between the self and the social.

This mini-genealogy not only informs readers about the changing history of persona but also shows that rhetorical personae are not philosophically transcendent. The conceptual meaning of persona, through the mask, has changed over time based on different societal privileging of communicative forms—visual (Greek), audible per-sonare (Roman), literary (modern)—and with these epistemic changes have come new intelligibilities. As Donald Lowe has argued, perception itself has a history across different epistemic orders over time.[14] Temporality, spatiality, and embodiment, for instance, have had different meanings to "bourgeois societies" that privileged certain modes of perception.[15] Personae, too, have been experienced differently. In the present epoch of the Anthropocene, persona may have withered as a visual, audible, and literary device but it lives on through structures of feeling that hold together different assemblages of humans and nonhumans.

The visual is still undeniably a dominant mode of sense across hypermediated ecosystems. However, corporations, invisible subjects, condense identities through affects (as well as discourses). Understood as those "capacities to affect and be affected" in a "zone of indistinction" and "indeterminacy" that hovers between thought and action, affect is how corporations are perceived.[16] Their presences are felt, not just seen. Affects can create personae that stabilize identities otherwise networked, dispersed, and wild. This is characteristic of how corporate personae are experienced in the Anthropocene. In an epoch where nature and culture are hybridized, and Nature is dead,[17] the very notion of the subject—or the rational, individual actor behind the figurative mask—has no doubt become fragmented, splintered, torn; nevertheless, persona has survived as a rhetorical device for expressing character, ethos, goodwill.

With the ascendency of corporate agencies, persona takes on increased relevance for feeling corporate presences and maintaining the notion that we still have it together. In other words, personae are not only avenues for studying corporations' rhetorical existences, but they also give impressions that humans are still singular rational actors separate from the nonhuman world. For corporations, personae work through feelings that *hold together the idea of a singular coherent subject*. What I am suggesting then is that personae are ontological; meaning, they are not just real but part of the actor's existence as an alchemical reaction from the rhetorical resources they deploy.

Rio Tinto and the Bingham Canyon Mine force rhetoric to come to terms with the ontological basis of persona to uncover corporate disclosedness in a world beyond subjectivity and nature.[18] Rio Tinto's rhetorical presences are just as real as the absences of the mine. While various contemporary rhetorical scholars have advanced the rhetorical persona by theorizing implied and negated auditors, passing strategies, and silenced rhetors, what has not been considered, since Plato, is the ontological underpinning of persona that affect and are affected by changes in the world. How people perceive personae may have changed, but the persona itself has not. While subjects and the world have changed dramatically over the past two millennia, the ontology of personae has largely remained transcendent (namely, humanistic). In the Anthropocene, where human and nonhuman actors exist on the same plane of immanence, persona must move beyond internalities and externalities that have distinguished face from mask. To Timothy Morton, "a good reading of the Anthropocene is *There is no outside-human text*. Yet for this very reason, the nonhuman has made decisive contact with the human . . . the human is always already occupied by nonhumans."[19] One of the consequences of this shift, notes Morton, is that "without a world, without Nature, nonhumans crowd into human space, leering like faces in a James Ensor painting or the faces of Butoh dancers. The difference between a face and a mask (Greek, *prosōpon*) collapses."[20]

Morton's troubling of human existence in the Anthropocene points to the necessity of a theory of immanence for rending sensible personhood on a "flattened" world without distinctions between nature and culture. Without the certainty from a knowable world, masks and faces become conflated, and while several scholars in our field have studied different kinds of personae, their ontological basis remains untheorized. The Anthropocene forces critics to come to terms with the fact that we live in a "postdialectical" world that consists of networks and assemblages on a flattened plane of consistency.[21] From this postdialectical angle, the role of the critic is to take up the ontological task of tracing how the world works as networks, affects, and forces.

The rest of this chapter pursues a seeking of the corporate persona from the absences of the Bingham Canyon Mine, corporate personhood, and persona criticism. I begin by returning to our gaze into the Bingham Canyon Mine to seek out Rio Tinto's presences from the absences of the mine. I consider a few of the historical presences and absences that define its territory, including ghost mining towns, metallurgists, and previous owners of the mine. I then situate these presences/absences in the current context of the corporate personhood thesis and seek out possibilities for reading corporations as agentic rhetorical actors with personae. Locating the corporate persona within organizational rhetoric, this section lays the groundwork for what I call the corporate, or "fifth," persona, which I discuss as a supplement to what has been labeled the first, second, third, fourth, and null persona. The corporate persona, I argue, exists where the author, or rhetor, does not, and is mediated through affects and discourses that stabilize feelings of corporate presences where there are otherwise absences.

Rio Tinto's Corporate Personhood at the Bingham Canyon Mine

What does one see as they gaze into the Bingham Canyon Mine? Memories of ecological pasts, techno-scientific achievements, and corporate legacies may swirl around this massive hole, but to encounter the mine itself is to come face-to-shadowy-face with the scale of ecological carnage in the Anthropocene. Before considering what the mine means, we might start by asking if this hole actually exists if the goal is to seek out Rio Tinto's presence—a worthwhile analytical (philosophical) question in and of itself considering the existence of Rio Tinto largely rests on the existence of this spatial absence. Casati and Vaazi's insightful book *Holes and Other Superficialities* offers some guidance. To these authors, holes are spatio-temporally localized entities that take a particular shape, or form. They are also wrapped up in different possibilities about what they could or could not be. Processes of "reasoning about holes" involve ponderings about how holes "can be created, operated upon, and destroyed."[22] Holes are also patterned in ways that create impressions. These four "interrelated abilities" lead the authors to conclude that holes are "superficial particulars" (not properties) that "cannot exist alone," for their "immaterial bodies" depend on "the surfaces of their hosts."[23]

Following this thinking, we might say the BCM exists but only in relation to the Oquirrh Mountains (the "host") that gives it form. At the same time, while analytical philosophizing may help for mathematizing the BCM, seeing the mine's absence as the presence of corporate agency, or personhood, is something that requires continental heft. To that end we may rather say, with help from Derrida, that the presences of the BCM's absences are only apparent through the metaphysical system that stabilizes its presence.[24] Recall how to Morton, through Derrida, "There is nothing outside the text."[25]

The BCM is indelibly defined by absences. Absent mountains, ecologies, and even towns haunt both mine and body. What, though, about the presences that remain in the vestiges of past industrialism? The residuals of mining pasts, such as the presences of waste, also has an indelible mark, and it has captivated the attention of artists such as Edward Burtynsky, who featured the Bingham Canyon Mine as one of several portraits in his "Mines" collection (Mines #22). Through photography, Burtynsky reveals how chemicals from these mines have become just as prominent in our everyday lives as the commodities they generate. To Jennifer Peeples, Burtynsky's photographs are illustrative of what she has aptly called the "toxic sublime," which explains what I felt earlier while taking the visual plunge to the mine.[26] Staring into the BCM from the visitor's center, one no doubt appreciates these internal states of dissonance that push and pull the viewer between aesthetic realms to elevate consciousness about the costs of industrialism in the Anthropocene where humanity has seemingly moved beyond itself.

How does a mountain get transformed into so much absence, and what does this say about Rio Tinto's existence? Are we seeing the counterpart to techno-logical sublime of communication technology?

Consider the conjunctural processes and possibilities that created this mine. While the BCM today epitomizes what Heidegger once called a "standing reserve" (Bestand), which names anything ordered in such a way that it is desig-nated to "stand by," "be immediately on hand," "on call," the Oquirrh Mountains were not always seen as a storehouse of resources to be "challenged forth."[27] In Steep Trails, for instance, John Muir describes his time spent looking for "Mor-mon lilies" and other "trinkets" during the spring of 1877 in this region of the Oquirrhs, as he encountered a splendorous countryside replete with fragrant evergreens, luscious wildflowers, and pine-filled glacial hollows. Muir described this environment as pristine; the mountains were "without any marked charac-ter," he wrote.[28] As if to portend the transformation of the Oquirrh's, to some-thing else entirely, however, Muir noted the curious quality of the rocks during his excursion and wondered "what [they] were made of."[29] Of course, the rocks were awash with copper, and this latent discovery facilitated the transformation of this mountain into the standing reserve observed today, but at the time of Muir's musings, Nature still existed.

As a testament to the epistemic authority of nature, rather than humanity during this time, consider how years earlier, when copper was first "discovered" in Bingham Canyon by Mormon settlers in 1848, the pioneers did not even see the mineral metal as a commodity worth their time or trouble. They were instructed by leader, Brigham Young, to leave the copper alone and instead focus their attention on activities more worthwhile, such as grazing cattle and cutting timber. Not seeing the copper from what would become the largest copper mine on Earth attests to the ways nature, and not yet humanity, did the ordering, or the poetic "bringing forth."[30] Industrial affordances had also not yet enabled this kind of world view.

There were also people who once dwelled here. First the Goshute persons resided in this territory. After years of settler colonialism in the wake of new mineral "discoveries," this region was transformed to the bustling mining town, Bingham, that existed at the center of what is now the BCM. At its peak, Bingham had fourteen thousand residents, most of whom were miners that migrated to the town for work. However, as the methods for open-pit mining improved, mining became the source of the town's erasure. As the BCM expanded, the town disappeared. By 1972, the mine entirely subsumed Bingham. Lark, Utah, is another mining ghost town that vanished a few years later (1977) when juggernaut company Kennecott Copper decided to use it for overburden (waste rock).[31] As Michelle Wentling put it, "Goshute land exists only as an imaginary as the canyon of copper is scraped like the last bit of soup in the post-depression bowl. . . . A hole in the canyon remains."[32] And yet the processes of erasure that would envelop this mountain were only beginning to take hold, as it would take generations of technological advancement to industrially "challenge forth" ore that contained only 2 percent copper.[33]

How did this happen? When mining activities became widespread in the 1860s, technology was antiquated and limited to the extraction of large, veined deposits, which meant commonplace techniques such as placer mining had little long-term success when those rare deposits were depleted. When the transcontinental railroad reached the canyon in 1873, however, the conditions were set for a newer mining technology specifically designed to uncover the small deposits of copper otherwise unprofitable.[34] In *Mass Destruction: The Men and Giant Mines that Wired America and Scarred the Planet*, Timothy LeCain discusses how porphyry mining techniques—invented by metallurgist Daniel Jackling—irreparably altered the fate of the Oquirrh Mountains. No longer did miners have to dig underground to seek out those rare copper veins.[35] Instead, all they had to do was blow the mountains up. While barbaric, this open-pit method changed everything by allowing miners to sift through the ore for massive amounts of tiny granules of copper (usually less than 2 percent). After smelting and concentrating, copper was indirectly sold to the masses as a widely available, and inexpensive, material that became the basis for the modern communication technology empire. It is no surprise that by the middle of the twentieth century porphyry mining was standard practice throughout the continent. More than 60 percent of US copper was mined from the BCM alone. So began the methodical erasure of Bingham Canyon by ascendent industrial companies such as the Utah Copper Company, Kennecott Utah Company, and eventually Rio Tinto (1989).

Still these narratives are shadowed by the voids of the BCM, which remain inseparable from the evolution of the mine and its contribution to our techno-scientific world. The story of Jackling, for instance, shows how the "hidden figures" of mining normalized, and eventually black-boxed, a "culture of mass destruction."[36] While Jackling is not remembered the same way as Thomas Edison, Henry Ford, or Steve Jobs are as famous industrialists and entrepreneurs, he is no less significant for the production and consumption of wired technologies and their narrow version of (copper-coiled) human progress. The lightbulb, their powerlines, the Model T, and today, the iPhone, are all made possible by this mining method pioneered by Jackling to cheaply provide an abundance of raw material. "No other phrase [than 'mass destruction']," notes LeCain, better captures the essential traits of this transformative but often overlooked technology that was a necessary condition to the building of the modern industrial and postindustrial world."[37]

While those in Silicon Valley may wish to disavow their connections to these practices of hard-rock mining, they are in many ways just as culpable since their invented technologies only exist as a result of more than a century of utter mass destruction of the Earth's crust. This view of humans as conquerors of nature is what made the BCM, and its history of corporate successors, possible, even though its material flows are oftentimes moved to the shadows of history. "One of the defining features of modern technological society," LeCain notes, "is its tendency to distance us from the environmental first sources of our material world."[38] Like the centralization of meatpacking in Chicago, which distanced meat-eaters from the source of their food (actual animals), technology consumers have been taught to forget that their iPhone came from mountains. As William Cronon observes in *Nature's Metropolis*, "Meat was a neatly wrapped package one bought at the market. Nature did not have much to do with it."[39]

Rio Tinto exists in the wake of this "destructive" historicity and has since inaugurated a near-perfect system of extraction distantly removed from the days of placer mining. While Jackling's open-pit method is still the basis of current operations, Rio Tinto's extractive techniques have become more refined. After detonating thousands of pounds of explosives inside the earth, a fleet of massive hauling trucks move the ore to a gyratory crusher that diminishes the massive lodes of ore to ten-inch fragments. Once crushed, the ore is transported and stockpiled until it is called upon for concentration. At this stage, the precious mineral metals are separated from the ore and turned into a liquid known as a slurry. After retrieving the most valuable minerals using a floatation cell system, the concentrate is smelted, which consists of a purification process that, through a series of chemical reactions, creates massive (750-pound) copper anodes refined to 99.999 percent pure copper.[40]

As the technological sublime grew over time, the BCM increasingly became the black-boxed "other." Today the BCM today is the second-largest source of toxic release in the United States (208 million pounds), which has played no small part in making Utah the third-most-toxic state in the country (behind Alaska and Nevada).[41] Who or what is responsible for the environmental waste at, around, and from the BCM when this culture of "mass destruction" has been calcified at the BCM for more than one hundred years? Should Rio Tinto take ownership of a legacy of toxic waste that, since 1989, it only recently inherited? Is there any one singular agent with accountability?

These questions are suggestive of one of the rhetorical affordances of what I describe below as a networked corporate agency, which allows for corporate networks to "own" socially beneficial aspects of its practices while disavowing more troublesome relations. While Rio Tinto may act as though it was alongside Jackling when he invented porphyry mining technique—something I return to in chapter 3—the company can also safely distance itself from this history if and when doing so is strategically advantageous. For instance, Rio Tinto takes much credit for the history of technological progress that Jackling and colleagues pioneered at the BCM's visitor's center, but it is also quick to admit that it played no part in contributing to the BCM's legacy of toxic waste when it purchased the mine in 1989.

Between 1994 and 2008, the BCM was one of the nation's largest Superfund sites, due to nearly a century of mining activities. Water was undrinkable, land was unusable, and fish and animals were dying, as layers of toxic sludge surrounded the base of the mine.[42] Rio Tinto did its part to clean up the mess but not necessarily out of the goodness of its heart or because it accepted full responsibilities for environmental sins before its ownership of the mine (how could it?). Rio Tinto simply complied with the EPA's mandate to clean up the site.[43] From a rhetorical viewpoint, though, Rio Tinto also used this environmental situation as an opportunity to boost its corporate ethos as a caring corporate citizen with goodwill. Today Rio Tinto touts itself as an environmental steward by using this environmental history to promote its land reclamation practices. For instance, the site of the former Superfund Zone exists today as a suburban neighborhood where thousands of people live, known as Daybreak. Rio Tinto successfully turned what was a sacrifice zone, due to years of mining before it even owned the BCM, into a home (see chapter 3). Whether or not this is an example of the (im)possibilities of corporate accountability, Daybreak is a premiere example of alchemical rhetoric and networked corporate agencies in the Anthropocene.

These forces of science and technology (and waste) are characteristic of the presences and absences in the Anthropocene. While the origins, and geological basis, of this epoch remain contested, it nevertheless designates a worldly transformation where humans have become "a geological force" so powerful, and dangerous, that it has created a tailspin of events rapidly leading to a sixth mass extinction.[44] Rio Tinto, Vale, BHP, Glencore are some of the names tied to these ecological transitions. With such dramatic changes for Being-in-the-World, absences have become more literal. The erasures of species, ecologies, mountains, subjectivities are characteristic of our age when coping becomes a mode of adaptation and dwelling a form of survival. This is why the BCM is a monument to this strange new world and its irreparable rupturing of the fourfold (earth, sky, divinities, mortals) and its presences and absences define the mood of our epoch.[45] In this age, the BCM stylizes our Being.

What we are seeing at the BCM is thus our entire world in this unique moment of time where humanity has exceeded itself in an epoch defined by irrevocable environmental disrepair. Humanity's separation from nature no doubt enabled this transition, but is it also not the forces of extractivism that continue to methodically dig deeper into the heart of the mountain that act as a chronotope for the Anthropocene? Where is Rio Tinto if not in the vacuous bowels of the Oquirrh Mountains? Like, if not *as*, the BCM, Rio Tinto is defined by its metaphysical absence. No body. No soul. No flesh. Yet it exists. And it does so as one of the most powerful forces in the history of humanity. Rio Tinto, like other corporations, is an exemplar of the poststructural subject that is defined by absences and multiplicities just as much as presences and singularities.

The Bingham Canyon Mine is Rio Tinto's corporate personhood in the Anthropocene, which is rife with all sorts of absences that define our age: metaphysical, historical, ecological, subjective. If this mine is Rio Tinto's personhood, where is the persona? Must persona assume a human person that exists as an author, speaker, or subject?

Rio Tinto as a corporate person may be absent, but it garners subjective force through a relational sociology that is illustrative of how corporations shift, transform, and propagate immanently among swarms of objects both organic and creative. As such, corporate personhood, or even subjectivity, is a relational multiplicity, a "happening born," that produce affects, forces, and networks stabilized by an image or personality.[46] In this way, corporations rhetorically construct their own identities through material and semiotic relations in public fora and places and spaces. This rhetorical accomplishment involves the ephemeral creation of a singular persona to achieve specific, but potentially unintended, rhetorical consequences. While this persona may be considered a networked example of what has been referred to as the first persona, or "the author implied by the discourse," such a consideration risks reinforcing a singular speaking actor as the basis of subjectivity.[47] Thus the specter of another persona, as the product of a multiple subject, potentially lurks behind every space and place of rhetoric.

The following section embarks a search for the corporate persona—a search that began when J. J. McMillan once pursued the "organizational persona" and is one that continues here. To seek out this corporate persona while adding to those in rhetorical communication that have extended the classical personae to a range of rhetorical situations and subtexts, I take up the pursuit of the corporate persona within the canon. As I argue, the corporate persona takes into account the forgotten ontological dimensions of persona criticism. In the Anthropocene where Being-in-the-world has fundamentally altered our mode of existence, ontology is a crucial component of criticism, as the assumptions we hold about our own existence directly affect the possibilities and restraints for any rhetorical act, especially persona. In this epoch, humans are constantly crowded by swarms of nonhumans, including corporations. Like Reagan, we are never quite ourselves.

The Search for the Corporate Persona

In *Rhetorical Criticism: A Study in Method*, Edwin Black states that the foundations of rhetorical criticism lie in the shared commitment to study human activities, for that is what separates criticism from science, which, to the contrary, is doled the task of studying natural things by empirical observation. "The subject of criticism," says Black, is a "humanistic activity" that "consists exclusively in human activities and their results."[48] Criticism is thus defined as the "discipline that, through the investigation and appraisal of the activities and products of [humans], seeks as its end the understanding of [humans themselves]."[49] Free from the tyranny of what was called neo-Aristotelianism—which restricted critics' ability to appraise rhetoric within the narrow scope of the text—Black helped expand criticism beyond scientific observations of texts, which enabled critics to interpret different relations, and dimensions of power, between rhetors in relation to their audiences.

Rhetorical scholars have since considered who gets to speak, what they can and cannot speak about, and those that are affirmed and negated through speech.[50] This range of rhetorical presence has been considered the second, third, fourth, and null personae within rhetorical theory. Each of these advancements in persona criticism have greatly expanded the scope of rhetoric beyond the speaker's individual intentions. What appears to be missing, though, is how nonhuman, namely corporate, actors construct personae to deploy rhetorical strategies as subjects. For instance, when Black said, "Discourses contain tokens of their authors" as "external signs of internal states," he debarred corporations because "the author" is assumed to possess a singular, intentional actor, whereas corporations exist as networks.[51] Black is also careful to note, however, that criticism is unique to the "results" of "human activities," which may be said to include the concrete and abstract creations of humankind, such as technologies, rote commodities, and, what may be considered the creative magnum opus of humanity: corporations.

Even if critics were to accept Black's definition of what counts as an object of criticism, corporations still qualify as "products" of humanity that can teach us how rhetoric and subjectivity work as poststructural networks and forces.[52] But as George Cheney and other organizational rhetorical scholars have argued, rhetoric needs to move beyond its "individualistic bias" to more critically embrace corporate rhetorics and their possible "organizational persona" which exceeds individual human subjectivity.[53]

Given the prolific work on rhetorical subjectivity and persona since Black, which has been enormously influential, not to mention the recent surge in research about nonhuman rhetoric, critics are now in a position to expand persona criticism to the realm of corporate actors.[54] In a way, personae have always been about the nonhuman, multiple subject in the abstract since they exist as imagery constructions. Black, for instance, defines the first persona as follows: "the author implied by discourse is an *artificial creation*: a persona, but *not necessarily a person*."[55] At the same time, does not persona also assume a human subject behind the mask? Looking behind Rio Tinto's mask at the BCM, there is nothing but absence. How is it that this mine, then, can be the face of corporate subjectivity?

Rio Tinto is a sort of network, not a subject, so if personae must assume a subject, then Rio Tinto is plainly left out as a rhetorical actor. But how can this be when it is still a legally recognized corporate person that exists at museums, stadiums, and suburban communities, and adopts many of the same rhetorical strategies as coal companies? How else to explain the corporate rhetoricity of Ronald Reagan? Yes, Rio Tinto dons the mask, but its personae tend to alchemically reveal rather than conceal. As noted in the previous chapter, Rio Tinto uses its resources to create feelings attached to its networked identity, and those alchemical reactions are no less real than its face at the BCM. Rio Tinto's personae may be "creations," in Black's terms, but they are not necessarily "artificial." Alchemical transformations are real and material. In a strange way, then, personae also *are* persons in a post–*Citizens United* world. Persona has never been more important, but it must be adapted to the Anthropocene. Before considering the presence of another, and possibly "fifth," persona to meet the needs of studying corporate rhetoric, let us foremost consider extant theorization of personae of speakers, particularly the first, fourth, and null.

As noted, the "first persona" is commonplace within the rhetorical tradition: the rhetor's "second self." This idea dates back to ancient Greece when different masks were worn as social performances. As noted earlier the concept has its own genealogy with different implied subjects and modes of perception up to the present. In rhetorical theory, the first persona broadly includes this historicity. In the "Second Persona," written five years after *Rhetorical Criticism: A Study in Method*, Black implicates the first persona when he says, "The author implied by the discourse is an artificial creation" that "amounts to something, that the implied author of a discourse is a persona that figures importantly in rhetorical transactions."[56] This persona may be assumed in Black's essay to help him make his case for the "second" persona, but it is nevertheless the basis of persona criticism. Potentially, the corporate persona is an example of the first persona. At the same time, does not this persona assume that the "real author," that is to say, the subject, is human? Moreover, is not this subject not a singular, rational, male subject that is also, in all likelihood, white and masculine? After all, Black's example of this persona—and its "disparity between the man and his image"—comes from Gore Vidal's report on none other than Ronald Reagan in the 1968 Republican convention.[57]

Consider the fourth persona. Charles Morris III adroitly argues that rhetorical discourse can appeal to multiple audiences and as such can be adapted in such a way that allows certain "invisible audiences" to decode ideological messages without revealing their commitments. In other words, the fourth persona is a form of "passing" that is characterized by the "wink."[58] To Morris, the fourth persona is "a collusive audience constituted by the textual wink. Similar to its counterpart, the second persona, the fourth persona is "an implied auditor of a particular ideological bent."[59] As an invisible audience that occupies "two ideological positions simultaneously, one that mirrors the dupes and another that implies, via the wink an ideology of difference," the fourth persona takes on the performative dimension of "passing," which involves "the dupe" and the "in-group clairvoyant."[60]

Morris's example is J. Edgar Hoover's "pink herrings" in the 1930s, which manufactured a "moral panic about sex crimes" to reinforce dominant gender norms and distract publics from his own queerness.[61] Others such as James Sanchez have used the fourth persona to study Trump's "dog whistles" through appeals to "patriotism," "heritage," and "security" to the Ku Klux Klan as a form of "rhetorical versatility."[62] Recently Michelle Gibbons has taken the fourth persona to digital spaces by attending to "persona 4.0" where web designers craft "algorithmic address" to search engines that affect web-traffic, not just users.[63] Considering the copper that runs through these devices and their platforms, such as X (formerly Twitter), is it possible Rio Tinto adopts the fourth persona to code rhetorics to technologies, programmers, or shareholders?

The fourth persona is perhaps the most vital to the corporate persona because it recognizes the performative dimensions of rhetorical situations. While the focus for Morris is on the way rhetorical address can involve multiple audiences, it also progressively implies the rhetor is subjectively fluid as they can occupy multiple playful positions when crafting their messages for secret audiences. From one end, we can say that Rio Tinto, as an environmental, social, and economic actor frequently adopts the fourth persona before all sorts of "collusive audiences" such as politicians, investors, and other audiences that share ideological commitments beneficial to the company. For instance, Ronald Reagan's role as corporate ventriloquist dummy is arguably an instance of the fourth persona given the ways he implicitly promoted copper in his address at Guildhall. Whether or not he deliberately colluded with Rio Tinto to "rig" the market in its favor (unlikely), he nevertheless became a sort of technological clairvoyant for Rio Tinto by assuming the mass availability of certain resources, namely, copper.

THE CORPORATE PERSONA   47

More generally, corporations speak to investors all the time—both directly and indirectly—through sales, products, and social conditions that affect the company's future pricing indexes for their stocks. Corporate greenwashing or green marketing tactics can be a fourth persona because of the way those messages are designed to "pass" as environmentally friendly before publics while perhaps signaling otherwise to ideological allies.

On the other hand, Rio Tinto's corporate persona is not always designed to dupe or mislead the masses. Corporate rhetoric, from an alchemical standpoint, is not necessarily ideological. While there is no doubt corporate rhetoric can and has been read ideologically, alchemical rhetoric, recall, is a creationist use of resources, or base metals, that establishes very real social presences and materialities where otherwise there are absences.[64] As the rest of this book shows, Rio Tino adapts its identity to meet the needs of certain communities in which it dwells, so in a way all of Rio Tinto's corporate rhetoric can be seen as extensions of the fourth persona. Still unanswered, however, is the question of ontology concerning the author and their persona.

Consider also what Dana Cloud aptly calls the "null persona." Extending specifically Philip Wander's "third persona," Cloud understands the null persona as a strategic silence that points to larger extradiscursive constraints and the "relations of power" that inhibit speech and agency. Analyzing transcripts from the *Uprising of '34*—a documentary about the massive strike by cotton mill workers in the South who were "beaten, shot, discredited, and evicted from their homes in company-owned towns"[65]—Cloud draws out the material interconnections between racial, gendered, and labor inequalities that barred many from speaking out. As she notes, "For many of the workers interviewed in the documentary, the primary lesson of the strike was to keep quiet . . . the silence about the strike is linked fundamentally to a system of combined race-, gender-, and class-based oppression and exploitation, in which an ideology of paternalism, alongside the threat of racist violence, made for a muted, though debilitating, segregation."[66] The null persona importantly highlights the importance of considering extradiscursive forces that shape the possibilities and constraints of speech and also how silence can be used strategically among marginalized communities. This is useful because it helps critics track the material conditions, and consequences, of corporate action. Rio Tinto, like the Piedmont cotton factory, is the dominant capitalistic actor that shapes the extradiscursive system of power from which null personae stem. From a Marxian sense, Rio Tinto is the dominant ideological actor that shapes who can and cannot speak and what can be talked about.

Since Black's *Rhetorical Criticism: A Study in Method,* Wander, Morris, and Cloud have advanced the field of rhetoric beyond measure by creating spaces for studying unseen, unheard, and unknown relationships between speakers and audiences, the identities that lie betwixt and between rhetorical subjects and their implied audiences have taken on new dimensions in criticism. From ideological criticism sprung possibilities of reading texts with moral certitude no longer restricted to the limits of neo-Aristotelianism, which barred critics from reading texts as anything other than scientific data.[67] Persona criticism nevertheless remains committed to a logocentrism that assumes discourse, or lack thereof, is the main vehicle for crafting different rhetorical identities (and their negations). Corporate ventriloquism shows how corporations speak through other entities, such as front groups like Friends of Coal, to present publics with an alternative ethos, and increase the "plurality of voice," but they do not, and cannot, speak as individual actors. Yet as constitutionally protected subjects, they also have rhetorical capabilities (e.g., money/speech, affect). How can they function as personified persons when their actual existences are characterized by the howling silence of the Bingham Canyon Mine as well as their public relations agencies, corporate statements, and advertisements?

All of this is to say that we have overlooked the ontology of personae. While Wander and Cloud recognize the possibilities of non-Being through language, the Being behind the rhetor's mask remains unquestioned. Corporations, like the poststructural subject, exist within the voids of the Bingham Canyon Mine. Since the corporate persona is both discursive and extradiscursive, and is derived from a subjectless nonhuman author, it exists beyond the first, second, third, fourth, and null personae and must be characteristic of another "self" that we can call the fifth.

The Fifth Persona

Contributing to the corpus of work on personae criticism, the fifth persona recognizes the need to study corporations, and their rhetorical strategies, as networked actors that construct singular identities in public arenas. As a derivative of the relations established between and among human and nonhuman networks that give them agency, the fifth persona is the image of the rhetor implied by discursive and extradiscursive forces. Said otherwise, it is the affective and discursive presence of an invisible rhetor where the speaker/author/subject *becomes* the persona. As such, the fifth persona is located in objects, affects, and forces that stabilize literal and metaphoric images of a singular author as condensations of multiplicities.

Animated by personae null through 4, but especially those regarding the rhetor (e.g., null, first, and fourth) the fifth persona understands the rhetor—and not just the audience—as an invisible multiplicity that constructs a sort of "passable" material identity in public places and spaces to advance rhetorical motivations. With corporate actors specifically, but not exclusively, in mind, the fifth persona accounts for corporate privileges and resources that enable corporations to use their networks to stabilize a figurative and material image of an author where that author is otherwise multiple, abstract, or as Barthes would put it, "dead."[68] That figment of the author may then, and oftentimes does, activate other personae afforded by its constructed subjectivity (e.g., greenwashed audiences, negated mountains, tipped shareholders, silenced laborers). All personae are networked. Read another way, the fifth persona is a networked take on the first persona that accounts for both discursive and extradiscursive forces from a multiplicity of human and nonhuman actors.

The fifth persona opens new doorways for studying corporate rhetorical advocacy in public and political affairs. If the first persona is the speaker (grammatically, the "I"); the second, the implied auditor (the "you"); the third, the negated audience (the "it"); the fourth, the invisible and "collusive" audience (the masked "you"); and the null, the strategic silence that points to extradiscursive, or material, relations of power (the "not I"); the fifth persona involves the complex multiplicity of the "we"/"us"/"it"/"it" subject/object pronouns in the third person and first person plural.

The fifth persona most directly challenges the Cartesian "I" of the first persona, which since antiquity has assumed actors/subjects/authors/speakers are singular, sovereign, and rational actors capable of deliberately crafting persona to meet certain rhetorical situations. On a plane of immanence, speakers are always speaking from and through other entities. Rhetorical addresses are moments of corporate ventriloquism all the way down. But rhetoric, and the possibilities of personae, are not just spoken. They are also, if not primarily, felt through presubjective affective sensations. The world is flat to Latour and Deleuze and only consists of objects, forces, affects, and relations. As nonhuman, subjectless actors that exist within the human-made chasm of the BCM, corporations *are* their personae. To find them, though, we must look away from the BCM and toward the city in a sort of choric relation between country and city that mediates corporate existence.[69] For Rio Tinto that existence is alchemically mediated through natural resources such as copper.

The fifth persona adapts rhetoric to a networked perspective on subjectivity that recognizes how networks and assemblages produce subjective singularities that rhetorically engage networks by affect and force. These personae open doors for studying how corporations engage in public debates and controversies; it also, more broadly, enables rhetorical inquiries of subjective multiplicities (including human).[70] The fifth persona further decenters the individual speaking subject by generally attending to the way organizations maintain identities, speak, and advocate in public affairs. Although the cultural significance of the individual, especially in a neoliberal governmentality, has predominated much of Western society for several generations (perhaps since World War II), the corporate persona reminds rhetoricians that rhetorical processes of identification are themselves networked achievements that already assume the displacement of the individual for attachments with a shared collective identity.

As an alternative to the hegemony of the singular rational speaking subject, the fifth persona is a *topos* for the vast, and oftentimes unruly, networks of global and posthuman societies. The conceptual utility of this persona is that it allows critics to analyze how corporate subjects alchemically build material identities, or corporate temperaments, faces, images, that more or less have voice in society. For Rio Tinto, the corporate persona helps us understand how this international mining company crafts different localized identities at the places it mines in front of audiences that may otherwise disagree with the practice of mining. Much like "the frontier of science metaphor" that Ceccarelli wrote about, the frontier of mining becomes a way that companies, spokespersons, and politicians deflect criticisms that could meaningfully, and necessarily, challenge some of the more troubling implications of this trope.[71] The corporate persona helps explain how Rio Tinto writes its arguments on the surface of the planet.

In sum, the corporate persona is a conceptual heuristic for studying how human corporate actor-networks engage rhetorical discourse and produce rhetorical subjectivities and identifications in public spaces and places. It can be found in the margins of extant research about corporate rhetorical advocacy, places and spaces of material rhetoric, and even public addresses, but bringing it to the fore enables critics to hone in on those material, affective, and discursive networks that give form to the figure of a singular subject that deploy rhetorical strategies in public spaces and places. This persona broadens our view of rhetoric, subjectivity, and social change.[72] All this is to say what we have called the corporate persona is another, and simpler, name for the fifth persona (herein out, "corporate persona").

Following Rio Tinto's Corporate Personae

This chapter has argued Rio Tinto's existence is located via personae. What I am calling the corporate persona is how Rio Tinto, as an abstract corporate actor, exists rhetorically at many different places and spaces. In the Anthropocene where distinctions between humans and nonhumans are no longer discernable, and extractive companies such as Rio Tinto thrive off ecological absences as large as the BCM, personae no longer conceal subjects as speakers, authors, or faces. Persona must be recognized as an affirmative revealing of "tokens," or traces, of what remains: wild assemblages without remainder.[73] In Morton's words, again, "*There is no outside-human text.*"[74] Hence the importance of affect for reading these personae.

The following three chapters analyze Rio Tinto's personae at its three different sites of extraction: Boron, California; Salt Lake City, Utah, and Oak Flat, Arizona. Based on several different visits to these locations, I offer critical analyses of how Rio Tinto creates different, and even competing, personae that rhetorically manage its abstract identity. Even though Rio Tinto's headquarters are in both London and Melbourne—thousands of miles away from any part of the American Southwest—Rio Tinto nevertheless creates disparate place-based identities of goodwill to "pass" as a reasonable member of the community (i.e., ethos).

Rio Tinto's presences at the Borax Mine, the Bingham Canyon Mine, and Oak Flat are all illustrative of how the company alchemically forges different personae from the resources it extracts. These personae stabilize the rhetorical presence of a singular actor that is otherwise absent and multiple. Importantly, as instances of the corporate persona, these personae are not elusive images, ideologies, or simulacra of some shrouded figure behind the mask. These personae *are* Rio Tinto.

2

Historical Extractivism at the Borax Mine

Death Valley National Park may seem like an unlikely place to begin our search for Rio Tinto. After all, Death Valley is one of the hottest, driest, and lowest places on Earth. Temperatures in the summer months regularly top 120 degrees. It gets so hot that batteries melt and life has to hide under rocks until the early morning. Annual rainfall is fewer than two inches. Death Valley is a place of extremes. Even in this valley of death, though, life persists even if it is not made apparent on the surface: Joshua trees, desert candles, lizards, crows, and for our purposes, mining companies. In this most inhospitable of places, Rio Tinto not only exists but thrives. Is it any accident that US mining legacies have taken form in this strange and hostile environment? Is this not Rio Tinto's natural habitat?

Secular pilgrims must also take into account DVNP's inaccessibility. Four hours east of Los Angeles, the park is as remote as it is hot. Traveling to these hinterlands is thus not unbiased to privilege, as it requires substantial monetary, and temporal, commitments, in addition to the racial privileges that continue to code this land, and its peoples, as extractible property.[1] Dependable air conditioned transportation is of no less importance, not to mention considerations of fuel, food, and water—all of which are matters of survival.

For those able to safely venture away from energy hubs, the drive can be exhilarating. The trip to DVNP was once even a "fabled drive" for Angelenos that wanted to "see the wild desert." In a way, as Char Miller argues, Los Angeles "invented what we now know as the contemporary Death Valley."[2] Those who make this difficult trek must be searching for something, but what can they find in the desert that they cannot in Los Angeles? Freedom, absolution, Zen? Buried treasure?

I went searching for Rio Tinto and its corporate persona, no less, in mid-August—perhaps the most dangerous, yet privileged, time of year to make this trip. On these 120-degree days, few people, animals, and plants are out to play.

As I moved from the city to the country, I became part of a fluid process that carries resources, persons, and energies to and from city and desert via pipelines, railroad lines, automobiles, telephone lines.[3] These continuous flows of extraction, transportation, consumption, and disposal define the landscape. They are also characteristic of what E. Cram has recently labeled metaphoric "landlines" that indicate how "political and economic actions tether, or forge connections, between domains of sexuality and land use in settler colonial North America, inclusive of enclosers, appropriation, sacrifice zones, and labor."[4] Even, if not especially, in the most remote of places (i.e., the Mojave Desert) there are clear markers of humanity's historical and contemporary desire for extraction, exploitation, and consumption.

This part of California is intimately part of the public imaginary of the American West, and as many different scattered mining artifacts, museums, and visitor's centers make clear, is characterized by different places of public memory that have shaped, and continue to shape, the mythos of the American frontier and its different rhetorical tropes in public and scientific discourse.[5] To Dickinson et al., among others, places of public memory are profoundly rhetorical.[6] Through material, symbolic, and affective appeals, places of memory can narrate "common identities" and "sense[s] of belonging" (i.e., "public") in response to certain "concerns, issues, or anxieties of the present" (epideictic rhetoric).[7] As a pilgrim, I have traveled to this part of California to search for Rio Tinto and its corporate persona at different places of memory. Like SLC, a place I return to in the following chapter, Death Valley is a kind of distributed, material rhetorical place alchemically transformed by Rio Tinto. On my pilgrimage, I passed factories, refineries, mills that carried minerals to urban centers via the media that followed my path: railroads, pipelines, highways. I smelled chemicals and rolled up the windows. Polyvinyl chlorides? Nitric oxide? Methane? The toxic waste inventory for Searles Valley and Trona—where this smell was most noxious—turns up dismal results. Besides a few pounds of naphthalene—a compound used for mothballs—there are no reportings of air chemicals from what appears to be Searles Valley Minerals. The land, however, contains 4,007 lbs. of lead and lead compounds, which all things considered is not that much.[8] Just don't eat the Mohave prickly pear (*Opuntia phaeacantha*). What then am I smelling? Are my senses wrong?

As one moves further and further from the urban center, nature/culture distinctions become even more unclear. Am I touring a toxic wasteland or a national park? The fragilities and inhospitalities of this desert landscape suggest neither, for why pollute something already so delicate or make a park somewhere so hostile to life? Something else is happening here, and it takes the form of crystalized minerals called borates that help explain the industrial presences in this desolate area, not least of which, Rio Tinto.

Borates are one of Rio Tinto's basic elements of existence. Borates are crystalized salts that contain elements of boron—an element commonly found in different types of technologies, including renewable energy technology such as windmills and solar panels and also communication technologies requiring heat resistant glass (e.g., smartphones). Borates are also used for fiberglass insulation, fertilizers, and even space shuttles.[9] These particular salt-bearing borates (evaporites) are precipitated by the chemical effects of evaporation in impermeable (nonporous) basins such as deserts. Because of their extreme surface temperatures, low elevation, and minimal rainfall, Death Valley and the Mojave Desert are perfect geological candidates for finding these crystalized minerals. No wonder this area, known as the Kramer district, has become the locale for one of the largest deposits of borate minerals in the world, with enormous deposits of kernite, borax, colemanite, and ulexite.[10]

These minerals are so profusely distributed in this area that they are even visible from the car as one enters DVNP. Blanched from years of unremitting sunlight and evaporation, these minerals almost resemble a thin layer of freshly coated snow that can trick the mind into thinking they are somewhere else. Until, of course, they roll down the window and feel the heat.

Throughout this massive park drivers pass many artifacts and displays about mining pasts. One such location, also on the National Register of Historic Places, is the Harmony Borax Works (see fig. 4). One of the first mining operations in Death Valley to extract and transport borax deposits, Harmony Borax Works is commemorated for its contribution to industrial America. After obtaining several mineral claims, the company undertook the first initiative to profitably mine borates from 1883 to 1888, which made it possible for future mining companies to operate at industrial scale. Located just outside of Furnace Creek, this exhibit consists of a smelter apparatus and various signs detailing the extractive process. Most prominently told is the narrative of how miners using twenty-mule teams would haul ten short tons (nine metric tons) to the nearest railroad in Mojave, California. Crossing 165 miles of rugged mountain terrain, mining teamsters would endure the harshest of environments to ensure their loads of ore were successfully transported from the hinterlands to the South Pacific terminus that would supply the minerals to the

Fig. 4 | Harmony Works Borax. Photo taken by author.

sprawling American cities throughout the United States. That is, until the Pacific Borax Company, under the leadership of Francis Marion "Borax" Smith, purchased the mining claims in 1890, which brought to fruition the prospect of "large-scale" mining.[11] Important for the latter part of this story, one of those claims was located on what is now known as Boron, California, at the former Baker Mine.

Those who visit this Harmony Works Borax exhibit learn about the historical significance of early mining pioneers that endured this harsh environment—something also felt on visitors' bodies as they read the different placards—and its contribution to the evolution of mining. Yet Rio Tinto is still nowhere to be found. If not here then where is Rio Tinto?

As the previous chapter showed, Rio Tinto is an abstract corporate actor that is empty in the flesh but alive with rhetorical personae. Looking into the Bingham Canyon Mine we saw the expanse of those absences. Yet we also saw how Rio Tinto is made real and concrete in the city. What then when there is no city for hundreds of miles? Does it not make sense to find Rio Tinto across the desert sprawl of sand, stone, and heat given the global intensities of its mining operations. Where can Rio Tinto, that is, its corporate persona, be found?

Cultural narratives surrounding this place offer clues. If we listen, we can hear stories of Rio Tinto's historic existence told by no other than Ronald Reagan. Before serving his two terms as California's governor, Reagan hosted the hit radio and television program *Death Valley Days* (1964–66), as his last job in his acting career.[12] The show featured heroic tales of the Old West, particularly in the Death Valley area. Taking over for "The Old Ranger," Stanley Andrews, Reagan introduced audiences to many different stories about settler colonialism, confrontations with American Indians, and mining.[13] He also acted in twenty-one different episodes, frequently playing the role of pioneer, miner, or businessman.

As host, Reagan would conclude each episode with a few words that reinforced the significance of certain events, explained moral dilemmas, and reminisced about the old frontier. Mining was a dominant theme of the program, which coincided with myths about "how the West was won." While not the explicit focus of every episode, mineral and metal mining were always present throughout the entire program, not least of which were the narratives surrounding the twenty-mule teams commemorated at Harmony Borax Works. It should be no surprise, then, that the Pacific Coast Borax Company—later renamed U.S. Borax—sponsored the show. Reagan became its primary sponsor as "Borateem-pitchman."[14]

In more than a few advertisements, Reagan promoted the wonders of borax for the U.S. Borax Company's most well-known products, such as the laundry additive, 20 Mule Team Borax, the laundry detergent known as Borateem, and Boraxo, a powdery hand soap (now all owned by Dial). Promoting the new and "exciting" waterless Boraxo hand soap in one of his *Death Valley* commercials, Reagan delivered an important message to audiences tuned into the show in 1966. While standing in front of the *Death Valley* set in his Western garb, Reagan and his daughter, Patti, had this to say:

> **Reagan:** When we're on a *Death Valley* set and water is not handy, Boraxo waterless hand cleaner really cleans up. Just a dab removes paint, grease, tar, carpet, ink, even plain dirt—anytime, anywhere without water. The whole crew swears by Boraxo waterless. So will you. Meanwhile, back on our ranch where there is plenty of water, our daughter Patti has another tip for you.
>
> **Patti (*in house*):** Marvelous, Daddy. Boraxo powdered hand soap. Looks like this on your grocery shelf (displays Boraxo). It's so pretty like this

(*takes off label*) on your kitchen or bathroom sink. Powdered Boraxo:
washes the whole family's hands and leaves them soft and smooth.

Reagan: So in the workshop, on the road, wherever water is not handy,
make sure that Boraxo waterless is.

Patti: And for everyday handwashing, remember Boraxo powdered hand
soap.

Reagan: Two fine hand-cleaning products from U.S. Borax. Keep them
both handy.[15]

Reagan was both the face and the mask of U.S. Borax. Attaching his straight-shooting Hollywood ethos to U.S. Borax, Reagan's familiar face became a visual condensation symbol for corporate America. In this same way, Reagan was also the mask, or persona, that animated the life of a company otherwise distantly removed from the *Death Valley Days* scene. Like his previous role as host for *General Electric Theater*, Reagan once more became a spokesperson for America Inc. on public screens.[16]

A year after Reagan left *Death Valley Days* to become the thirty-third governor of California, Rio Tinto bought U.S. Borax (1967).[17] With this acquisition, Rio Tinto inherited all of the histories of borate mining at Death Valley, from Harmony Borax works, Pacific Coast Borax Company, to U.S. Borax—inclusive of all the cultural narratives, and memories, attached to twenty-mule teams and *Death Valley Days*. While Rio Tinto was not in Death Valley when these cultural attachments were being formed, it nevertheless incorporated the entire history of borax mining in this region and has since used it as part of its current corporate persona (historical incorporation).

Rio Tinto exists in Death Valley as a *Geist*-like actor imbued within the materialities of countless mining artifacts—large and small—scattered throughout this vast 1.3-million-acre landscape. Harmony Borax Works is just one example. As memories of mining camps swirl around like tailwinds across this vast desert, and narratives of the Old West crystalize in its basin, Rio Tinto extracts borates around the clock in the small town of Boron, California, located 150 miles southeast of the national park. Here Rio Tinto owns and manages the second-largest mine in the United States and the largest in California: the Rio Tinto Borax Mine. Staring into the mine from the U.S. Borax Visitor Center, Rio Tinto, like its existence at the BCM, is located in the spatial absences of the earth. What is different, among other things, is its presences that fill this mine with meaning. A far cry from a valley of more than 1.2 million people (Salt Lake Valley), Boron is a town of 1,200 people in the middle of the Mojave Desert.

At different places and spaces throughout Boron and Death Valley, Rio Tinto exists through U.S. Borax's memories of mining pasts. While Rio Tinto was nowhere to be found in North America 130 years ago, Rio Tinto nevertheless draws from this rich history, and the cultural experiences tied to it, to create an image, or mirage, that it was part of the twenty-mule teams as they hauled borax from the valley.

This chapter thus shows how Rio Tinto can alchemically transform selective cultural, communicative, and physical labors of industrial pasts into powerful corporate rhetorics in the present. This corporate ability to subsume historical events they played no part in is a form of *historical extractivism* and *incorporation*, which involves extracting historical and cultural fragments and alchemically using them as part of their corporate persona. For instance, when one visits the town of Boron, California—home of Rio Tinto's Borax Mine—it is almost as if Rio Tinto has been there all along. No less, DVNP is haunted by the presences and absences of a company that appropriates the histories and memories of borax mining without ever stepping an extractive foot in the valley. This is why Rio Tinto also goes by the names of U.S. Borax, and also simply "Borax," as a sort of passing pseudonym on its website www.borax.com.

Extractivism is also a selective process that ignores greater ecological complexities. Such historical extractivism draws from only what is useful, or valuable, to Rio Tinto's ethos, and by effect leaving out darker historical realities of labor struggles and toxic waste both in Boron and at other Rio Tinto mines. As we will see in the following chapter, this is also how Rio Tinto exists at the BCM—another place full of the kind of histories people have built entire identities around that Rio Tinto extracts and incorporates as its own.

The remainder of this chapter follows one of the trails twenty-mule teams took when hauling loads of borates from Death Valley to the South Pacific railroad. Starting with a trip to Boron, California, I detail Rio Tinto's alchemical rhetorics that both extract and incorporate select histories as a politic of revealing/concealing. I argue that Rio Tinto is part of a history that has created not just material corporate presences through, say, mining artifacts but also established the entire town of Boron—a corporate town *par excellence*. Boron is a material extension of the mine and shows how corporate rhetorics take hold on communities in the most unlikely places.

The mutually constitutive rhetorics of mine and community create a powerful hybrid of corporation, town, and history. This is particularly evident at the Twenty Mule Team Museum, which tells the story of Boron as perhaps the most famous towns visitors have never heard of. The celebrity status of Boron—through figures such as Reagan—serves an ego function despite lingering labor problems and environmental problems that lie beneath the surface.[18] This only solidifies Rio Tinto's historical extractivism and its corporate persona. After visiting this place of corporate memory, I take readers to the Borax Mine's visitor center, where Rio Tinto incorporates the narratives told at the Twenty Mule Team Museum and articulates its persona as a philanthropic celebrity. I then trace Rio Tinto back to Death Valley to point out how this national park is a "corporate park" that exemplifies "industrial tourism."[19] Like Boron, DVNP exists *through* Rio Tinto. I conclude with a discussion about some of the labor and environmental issues that exist below the unextracted surface.

Incorporating History at Boron

Boron is a strange but charming corporate town. Arguably an example of what Michel Foucault has called a heterotopia it consists of many different, and not altogether coherent, emplacements.[20] Not only is it in the middle of the Mojave Desert, 120 miles northeast of Los Angeles, but it is also adjacent to the Edwards Air Force Base (EAFB) and testing site, which is audibly present as fighter jets rip through the sky, sometimes breaking the sound barrier. In fact not far from here, in what was once called Muroc, is where Chuck Yeager broke the sound barrier in 1947.[21]

Hearing these sounds for the first time, auditors may think they are in the midst of a nuclear blast. It is no surprise that some Boron residents have charged the EAFB with breaking windows. In a split second, however, the cacophony subsides and one is left once more with a whole lot of nothingness, except for the cacti, evaporites, a dried lake, and desert remains.

As one meanders through oceans of Joshua trees, creosote, and cholla, sometimes dipping through dried water beds and gulches, they notice the vestiges of what was: abandoned buildings, foundations, water tanks. As wild and capacious as this place is, there are also many restrictions. While driving through the EAFB, there were several warning signs that read RESTRICTED: No off-roading, no photography, no videography. So restricted is this environment that it once housed a federal prison managed by the EAFB (Boron Federal Prison Camp). Before closing down in 2000, this was a "prison without walls" that contained 540 inmates.[22] Now it is one of the many abandoned sites in this desert area. Even before travelers who have taken this route reach Boron, they get the feeling they should not be there.

So it seems. As one approaches the small town of Boron, they see a mound in the distance that resembles a landfill. But no. As they get closer, they cannot deny this mini-mountain as the acclaimed Borax Mine, which puts to rest feelings about the inhumanity of this place. This part of the Mojave Desert may not be where its borates are consumed, but it no doubt is where they are hailed by extractivism. As desolate as this place is, people, at least some, *must* be here to "pioneer the elements of modern living."[23] To understand the rhetorical presences of Rio Tinto and its mines, we must look to the city, so we go there first.

Entering Boron feels like riding into a one-horse town in an old Western movie, or the *Death Valley Days* set from which Reagan spoke when promoting Boraxo. Make no mistake this place exists exclusively to service global flows of extraction, production, and circulation as the giant borax mine sitting in the backdrop of this corporate town attests. So too does the railroad with tracks that run parallel to main street, 20 Mule Team Road. "Welcome to Boron: 'Borax Capital of the World,'" reads the welcome sign (with "welcome to" faded away; see fig. 5). Embracing the strange heteronomies felt on the way to Boron, the sign illustrates an old directional sign pointing to the "World's Largest Borax Mine" (left) and "Missile Test Site Edwards A.F.B," which is also sometimes referred to as the "world's largest natural air strip."

As one drives through town and glances at the abandoned buildings, rusty artifacts, or the town pump, they would be hard pressed to not notice the way memories of the twenty-mule teams that once rode through here are instantiated through naming practices that codify this place as historically significant: 20 Mule Team Road, Café, Museum. These places, along with their iconic images of actual twenty-mule teams, give meaning to a town that, without the mine, would probably have had the same fate as many other mining ghost towns in the Mojave Desert area (e.g., California City, Ryan, Keeler).[24] At the 20 Mule Team Café, for instance, kitsch objects—mining figurines, toy trains, and portraits decorate the interior—giving cultural meaning (and outstanding food, especially for the wary traveler) to a place perhaps remembered more for its pasts than its

Fig. 5 | Boron Welcome Sign. Photo taken by author.

presents.[25] Is Boron an example of what Morpheus in *The Matrix*, through Jean Baudrillard, would call "the desert of the real" or are these cultural memories and artifacts powerful enough to function as "precessions of simulacra engende[r] the territory?"[26]

Memories and naming practices alone do not keep Boron alive. Rio Tinto Borax (aka U.S. Borax) has 1,600 employees helping the company generate more than $550 million in annual revenue.[27] If, as we determined in the previous chapter, Rio Tinto exists through material personae in the places it occupies, where in the name of Boron is Rio Tinto? Surely, the mine should be a dwelling place of Rio Tinto—a site we will visit soon—but should not Rio Tinto's presences also be felt here?

Things, both large and small, help. For instance, adjacent to the 20 Mule Team Café is a massive "Lectra" hauling truck in what is named "Pioneer Park" (see fig. 6). Surely, we are getting close. The size of this hauling truck dwarfs the small plot. There is no doubt this truck was once used for mining activities at the nearby Borax Mine, but can we be sure it was Rio Tinto's? Does it matter?

Across the street is the Twenty Mule Team Museum. I go there next for possible answers (see fig. 7).

Fig. 6 | Hauling Truck at "Pioneer Park." Photo taken by author.

Touring the Twenty Mule Team Museum

Sitting next to the Saxon Aerospace Museum, the Twenty Mule Team Museum is a small place of memory with large significance. In telling the story of borax through countless artifacts, this museum offers important clues about Rio Tinto's rhetorical being. Before even entering the museum, visitors see dozens of old rusted mining parts scattered about within a fenced area and a small amphitheater named "Amargo Theater." While Rio Tinto's current mining technology has surely progressed since these nineteenth-century tools, they nevertheless seem part and parcel of an evolutive story of borax mineral mining that is likely told at the amphitheater.

Posted on the museum is an ad from the chamber of commerce promoting its town: "Boron is . . . Many sights to see!" The paper reads, "Due to the expansion at the Federal Prison, Edwards Air Force Base, and LUZ solar plant, the growth of Boron is inevitable . . . COME JOIN US in the greatest little community on the High Desert!" The post comments on the significance of the Borax Mine to the world, the mine's employees, and the town. "This open pit mine and refinery is the major source of borates for the entire free world." Between the Borax

Fig. 7 | Twenty Mule Team Museum. Photo taken by author.

Mine, the "clear, dry and warm climate" and the "many sights to see," Boron is a strange utopian space with global significance.[28] If not what Schneider et al. call an "energy utopia"—or a "set of rhetorical appeals that position a particular energy source as the key to providing a 'good life' that transcends the conflicts of environment, justice, and politics"—then Boron might be a *chemical utopia* with similar functions.[29] Then again, as a place with many different "emplacements," perhaps Boron is better read as a chemical heterotopia with many different incompatibilities (e.g., mine, desert, prison, museum).[30]

Entering the museum, visitors find themselves immersed in a cultural space that makes meaningful Boron's existence through countless cultural fragments about the history of borax, the mine, and the town it has created. All kinds of merchandise is for sale, yet there are so many different cultural and geological objects it is difficult to tell which objects are for sale and which ones are for display. Some artifacts, such as the "I Dig Borax" mining helmets, T-shirts, books, and postcards, no doubt are purchasable, but others, such as the many different borate rocks, Lectra Haul replicas, and paintings are unclear. Regardless, this space, and its myriad objects, is key for understanding the significance of Boron.

Since 1984 the museum has served as the archive of Boron that tells visitors about all the significant historical events, people, and stories that have put Boron on the map. Funded by Boron's Chamber of Commerce, Boron is free to the public (but accepts donations). I also learn that Rio Tinto has contributed no small sum to the museum.

I wrote my name in the visitors log and gravitated to the front desk where an employee named Harold welcomed me to the museum.[31] Excited that I was the fourth visitor of the day, he happily made himself available for my many questions about borates, the mine, and particular objects. He even told me some humorous personal stories about his experience at the mine when he worked as an engineer, which had to do with a few pranks that he and coworkers played on their boss at the time, life on the mine, and also matters of borax and its many uses.

The uses of borax are clearly illustrated in an exhibit of a midcentury American kitchen (ca. 1950). The panorama includes everything that a modern kitchen, at least during the time, would contain, including an icebox, milk jugs, a proof box, plates, pans, a rolling pin, scale, and, of course, 20 Mule Team Borax detergent. All of the objects were made possible by borates, which are of particular use in the kitchen because of their high durability to heat. "Home Sweet Home" reads a knitted decoration above the stove and proof box (see fig. 8).

More pictures are framed on the wall, including self-promoting material for both the Twenty Mule Team Museum and the U.S. Borax Visitor Center. "Discover hidden treasure" reads an ad for the visitor center. Adjacent to this is another for the Twenty Mule Team Museum: "Travel back through time." The mine, which is "today one of the largest open pit mines in the world," is "well worth a visit" reads another visual fragment. Juxtaposing images of twenty-mule teams with that of the open-pit Borax Mine—and all of the stories during this transition—is suggestive of how borax mining has evolved alongside Western civilization. It is clear that this museum and the mine cannot be separated.

I enter the next room and see many historical objects: an old fire extinguisher on wheels from the Boron Fire Department, borate rock displays (large and small), newspaper clippings of original homesteaders, vintage signs, and countless images of the Borax Mine, space shuttles, settlers, maps, and all the affordances of borates in food, soaps, and other commodities, not to mention twenty-mule team simulacra (photos, paintings, figurines; see fig. 9).

Fig. 8 | American kitchen. Photo taken by author.

Fig. 9 | Displays at the Twenty Mule Team Museum. Photo taken by author.

The Twenty Mule Team Museum ties Boron's past with its industrial presents in powerful symbolic ways. One pamphlet describes the symbol of the
twenty-mule team as "one of the world's best known and most recognizable
trademarks." As a condensation symbol for the invisibilities of all the mineral
metals, and the companies that extracted them, the twenty-mule team icon
makes visible, and felt, the histories of extraction, production, and circulation.
It is the image of corporate America. One ad lists twenty-mule teams' different "promotional appearances" in world fairs, Woodrow Wilson's presidential
inauguration, parades, and dedications. Images of Reagan supplement this
trademark as the "20 Mule Team Days Spokesperson." "For many years, millions and millions of people have heard the clarion call of the popular television program 'Death Valley Days' and have seen the 20 Mule Team . . . a living
corporate signature." Is it any accident Reagan became the fortieth president
of the United States? Was he himself not a living corporate person?

More promotional rhetoric for the "many uses of borax" circulates throughout the room. One poster reads how "boric acid, borax and other compounds of
boron are used in almost every major industry and are essential to modern agriculture. A complete list of all the uses of borates would be much too long to
include here, but some of the principal industrial uses are given below." The text
goes on to describe these uses for glass, ceramics, porcelain enamel, and building
materials.

Borates are also quite literally consumed. Not only key to agriculture through
fertilizer, but their chemical compounds can be extracted and mixed for medici-
nal uses. One display of particular interest is a medicine cabinet full of different
drugs made possible by different borates. Bottles of powders, liquids, and pills
stock the cabinet with names such as Milk of Magnesia, bismuth subgallate,
boracic acid, propylene glycol, calcium lactate, and more—all of which are part
of their own pharmaceutical assemblages: Merck, Phillips, Natco. Borates and
their compounds, it seems, run the world. From medicine and agriculture, to
nuclear energy, aircrafts, automobiles, and cosmetics, borates are the basis of
almost all commodities. "The Amazing Borax," reads a nearby ad. "You would
never guess how often you use it!"

There are countless stories attached to different fragments. One prominent
narrative, told through an exhibit entitled "The Corums and Early Muroc," is
about original homesteaders Ralph and Clifford Corum who settled on Rogers
Dry Lake in 1910 (passed en route to Boron). The Corum family named the lake
and settlement Corum spelled backwards, "Muroc," and found work drilling water

wells for fellow settlers. Ralph also was in a syndicate that discovered large deposits of borates at the former Baker Mine in 1925, which was the first borates mine in the Boron area located on U.S. Borax grounds.[32] In 1926, the syndicate sold their claims to the Pacific Borax Company, and the Corums left the desert. Now owned by the EAFB for testing and training, Muroc is one of many ghost mining towns in California preserved only by memories of adventure in the not-so-old West. The Corum's desires for riches, and willingness to endure difficult climates with little resources, lives on in the public imaginaries as examples of the possibilities of settlement, discovery, and extraction at places such as Muroc, Kramer, and "Mud Camp," now all dried up. Like the borates, these places are extracted for commodity value until their uses are exhausted, depleted, and abandoned. Remnants remain as tokens of possible pasts behind these exhibits, which themselves are valorized as rarefied commodities. Not least of which includes the "last and only crystals recovered from the Baker Mine" before it closed.

This process of cultural extraction explains alchemical rhetoric. These places are used up and abandoned, but Rio Tinto's U.S. Borax still uses them, and their place names, stories, and imageries, as cultural resources for its rugged corporate persona in places such as this museum. These resources, in other words, are continuously and endlessly mined, by the corporate persona. Unlike material things, symbols can be extracted in perpetuity without ever entirely being used up. Hence, this process as alchemical: it transforms base things into glittering golden ideals.

Stories of hardy individuals such as the Corums illustrate the timelessness of this alchemical process by keeping these extractive memories and desires alive for future generations. Some of these alchemical rhetorics do even have to do with mining, directly. For instance, in the 1920s and '30s, the Muroc Dry Lake became the "booze capital" after the discovery of water. With "Yankee ingenuity," powerful syndicates built underground stills in washes to supply Los Angeles with its demands for booze during Prohibition.[33]

More stories of famous persons and events abound as visitors walk through the remaining two rooms—both of which are full of newspaper clippings, images, and objects that create the feeling that one is walking through a scrapbook. While some, if not many, of the artifacts surveyed up to this point were surely donated by U.S. Borax, which has contributed to this museum through donations of ads, objects, minerals, and money, it is also clear that actual people—not just a famously trademarked corporation—poured many hours into arranging these displays. People no doubt care about their town and want visitors to know its history, stories, and moments of fame. Boron might be the most famous place one has never heard of, but it is no less meaningful to residents.

Consider a couple of famous persons prominently remembered in the museum. Perhaps readers are familiar with the "legendary" "Walking George" Swain, who earned his nickname by walking everywhere he went, including the Borax Mine where he worked as a chemist. With no automobile, or for that matter house, "Walking George" is remembered as a "Boron 'Real People'" and "one of the unique personalities who live in Boron." Nobody quite knew where he lived—some say it was "in a hole in the desert"—but everybody seemed to know him as he regularly attended "local events and often taught and played piano for entertainment."[34] In a place defined by its global contributions to the movements of commodities, Swain shows how not all embraced the capitalistic ethic of (hyper) mobility. As fighter jets, trains, and automobiles sped to their destinations, Swain was content walking, which Thoreau reminds us can be a transgressive act in and of itself.[35]

Other perhaps more well-known persons, such as Ronald Reagan, Julia Roberts, George Peppard, and William Shatner are also commemorated here for their roles in Hollywood movies and shows filmed in Boron. In addition to *Death Valley Days*, Boron was the scene for *Erin Brockovich*, *The Carpetbaggers*, and *Star Trek* (original). These cultural memories create a sort of Hall of Fame for those who have historical attachments to a place otherwise banal. Much more than a mere mining town in the middle of the desert, Boron is significant in more ways than some, and U.S. Borax, from its evolutive pasts that began with the twenty-mule teams and the railroad, put Boron on the map as a living example of the possibilities of industrial alliances not just for commodities but communal life.

The Twenty Mule Team Museum ties the history of borate mining to place. Responsible for the genesis of this corporate town, U.S. Borax is associated with all the famous persons, heartfelt stories, and romantic feelings attached to homesteading, all with global implications. Through their powerful historical alliance, U.S. Borax and Boron are made of all-American celebrities that crave recognition. Perhaps since *Death Valley Days*, U.S. Borax has emerged as one of the most successful public relations companies in the country, having mastered the ability to integrate its identity, narrative, and products in popular culture through branding and advertising. By default, its corporate town, Boron, has carried with it much of that same recognition. No wonder the original casts, actors, and spokespersons of *Death Valley Days* are enshrined on the wall: Robert Taylor, Rosemary DeCamp, Dale Robertson, Stanley Andrews, and Ronald Reagan.

Time to go to the U.S. Borax Visitor Center. After purchasing a few kitsch items—postcards, a coffee mug, and a Rio Tinto coloring activity book—I head outside to visit the old mining artifacts scattered across the yard, but not before Harold stops me and asks if I am prepared for the Rapture. Attempting to save my soul so it is not "left behind" (apparently "just like the movie"), he hands me a small flyer by Billy Graham entitled "Don't Be Left Behind." Feeling uncomfortable, I cut the conversation short and head for the yard, thinking this really is a place of extremes.

On my way out I take more notice of the dozens of old, rusted mining apparatuses dispersed across the sandy earth. For those visiting during peak summer, this might be an area that most skip. This place is nevertheless important not only because of its mining artifacts that graft histories of extractivism onto the architecture of place, but it also is a point of public assembly for the annual 20 Mule Team Festival, which consists of a parade, historic reenactment, and other related events. Promoted on the U.S. Borax website as a "day-long celebration of the town's mining heritage and bright future," the festival is one more example of how mine and town are mutually constitutive.[36] This theater is not just symbolic but materially used as a public space for amplifying Borax's voice.

I walk around the outdoor exhibits, encountering a range of historical artifacts used during the pioneer days of early homesteading and mineral mining. Old bulldozers, conveyer belts, a wheelbarrow, a wagon, mining headframe, and even a replica of a bunker house at the former Baker Mine. Each exhibit has a number attached, which surely corresponds to its respective name, but I am too tired, and hot, to ask Harold for the key, which may also put me at risk for more proselytizing. As I contemplate leaving, I come across one last exhibit: a mining cart full of rocks in a wooden mining shaft. In red, "Rio Tinto" is inscribed at the top (see fig. 10).

This is one of few objects that bears the name Rio Tinto rather than U.S. Borax. Why is it here? Rio Tinto, after all was located thousands of miles away in the Spanish province Huelva when twenty-mule teams hauled borates from the Mohave Desert in the nineteenth century. As a form of historical extractivism, Rio Tinto appropriates the historical significations of this site—inclusive of all the stories about settlement, labor, and fame—to boost its ethos in a discreet, mundane way. In fact Rio Tinto does not even have to do much historical work as the histories of twenty-mule teams are already etched into the fabric of

Fig. 10 | Rio Tinto mine cart. Photo taken by author.

town. It is the people of Boron—the locals, the miners, and visitors—that do the memory work for Rio Tinto as they work, play, and commemorate (e.g., 20 Mule Team Days). All Rio Tinto does is build relations with these stories in ways that do not deny historical realities.

To be sure, we must visit, alas, Rio Tinto's Borax Mine. As I head to my car, I cannot help thinking about the powerful spatial juxtaposing of this historic museum of mining pasts and the contemporary mining technologies used at the mine that we head to now.

Rio Tinto's Alchemical Rhetorics at the Visitor Center

Driving to the visitor center, one feels like a twenty-mule team. As I approach the mine, I encounter a billboard promoting Rio Tinto's visitor center with an image of a mule and the company's red-and-white logo. "Celebrating 90 years in Boron. Thank you to the team past and present," reads another from 20 Mule Borax (1872–2017). There are also strange speed limits that begin as soon as one enters the gate: 37½, 14, 23. While I later learn Rio Tinto does this to "make people especially aware of the need to drive carefully," I cannot help but wonder if these were the speeds of twenty-mule teams. Of course, those teams were much slower—only traveling a total of fifteen to eighteen miles per day—but still, after our visit to the Twenty Mule Team Museum, and corresponding images of twenty-mule teams here, I almost feel like a teamster as I enter the gates to the mine.[37]

Other road signs emphasize Rio Tinto's apparent commitment to safety and security: "Caution: Slow Down. Road Curves Ahead"; "Warning: Slow Down"; "Critical Risk: Recognize, Control, Verify—Critical Risk Management"; and "days since last incident" (13) and "medical treatment" (63). All are branded by Rio Tinto, which has a police-like presence in this securitized space.

Following the signs for the visitor center, drivers pass large processing plants, storage units, and a natural gas generator, and find themselves climbing the hill observed earlier from the main highway. On top of this mound sits the Rio Tinto Visitor Center that provides a great view of the Borax Mine. Before one even enters the visitor center, one sees mining objects that allude to the story that will be told inside: another massive hauling truck, headframe, other mining tools, and sample borates. There is also a life-size replica of a twenty-mule team beside the visitor center. No doubt we are at the right place.

From the outside the visitor center looks like the side of a twenty-mule team, with two wagon wheels, and their spokes, slightly protruding outward above the museum's façade (see fig. 11). This simple, but effective, design creates the impression that the twenty-mule team standing beside the visitor center has melded into the visitor center (and Rio Tinto) itself—perhaps an architectural example of how history has become part of the present.

As I enter the visitor center, I feel as though I am in a hangar used for any one of the Air Force jets that are part of this place's soundscape. Rather than stowing aircrafts, or even twenty-mule teams, the visitor center houses historic and contemporary images, placards, artifacts, rocks, and other media that tell the story of U.S. Borax and its massive mine. I am welcomed by a sign that says "Not far from where you're standing lies one of the biggest and richest deposits of borax on the planet. Borax is a mineral, formed over millions of years and treasured since ancient times. Borax is also a company, born in California in 1872. We now supply nearly half the global need for the mineral and are part of the world's largest mining concern, Rio Tinto. The men and women of Borax welcome you to our Visitor Center. Come learn more about our lives as miners and the important role miners play in yours." Giving the impression the visitor

Fig. 11 | Borax Visitor's Center. Photo taken by author.

center is of international significance, with many different global pilgrims that travel to this site, another sign "thanks" visitors for their support in many different languages: *"tak," "danke sehr," "mahalo," "gracias," "dankjewel."*

The visitor center comprises different sectional displays that narrate the transformation of borate mining from its "Death Valley days" to the present. Walking through a tubular passageway to the adjacent hangar, and beneath what from the outside looks like a twenty-mule team wheel well, visitors may get the feeling that they are navigating through an old mining shaft full of historical mining activity in the form of photographs, newspaper clippings, and vintage cultural artifacts on the walls. Visitors are simultaneously immersed in a borax-related gift shop where they can purchase T-shirts, coffee mugs, borates, postcards, stuffed animals, hats, magnets, jewelry, and other "earthly treasures." Many of these things are only made possible by borax, especially the more name brand commodities, such as the 20 Mule Team detergent. Like the Twenty Mule Team Museum, this section serves an important rhetorical function of making visible all the ways borates influence commodity consumption. Perhaps this is why for most visitors, the tour starts here.

The first sectional display, "Heritage," begins in this hangar. To my surprise, the story of borax begins not with Harmony Works Borax but with the "beds of ancient lakes" eighteen to twelve million years ago. On a timeline of "the story of borax," visitors see how Rio Tinto is just as historical, and as much part of the earth, as borax itself. Both are global historic travelers. Borax begins with ancient civilizations when Egyptians, "according to legend," used the minerals for mummification before it was used for "refining and soldering" by gold and silversmiths in the eighth century. The timeline then walks readers through the uses and movements of borax—such as its use in ceramic glazes in China's Liao dynasty in the tenth century and its trade routes with Marco Polo in the thirteenth century—before it became transformed by European chemists and industrialists in the eighteenth and nineteenth centuries. Then in the late nineteenth century, readers are told how Harmony Borax Works came into the picture when borax was discovered in Nevada and Death Valley, attracting gold prospector F. M. "Borax" Smith and his employee W. T. Coleman. In 1925, the world's largest deposit of borax was discovered south of Death Valley, right here in Boron.

Since the twenty-mule team days, borax has had several different owners—Borax Consolidated Ltd., Pacific Coast Borax, Dial—until Rio Tinto Zinc Ltd. (now Rio Tinto) purchased Borax Consolidated and its "sister companies" in 1968. Soon after, this division of Rio Tinto—just referred to as "Borax"—spread its global reach to Italy, Spain, Japan, England, and Singapore. Beneath the timeline is a display of a miniature twenty-mule team: "One of the most enduring and endearing symbols of our company is the twenty mule team. From 1883 to 1888, teams of two men, two horses and 18 mules carried more than 20 tons of borax per trip from Death Valley to the nearest railroad in Mojave." Rio Tinto may be part of these global historical travels, with operations in almost every continent, but it is localized by the many different cultural narratives surrounding the historic twenty-mule teams. That is why this "Heritage" section also includes many different cultural fragments of actors in Death Valley Days, such as Clint Eastwood, Carroll O'Connor, Tom Skerritt, June Lockhart, and Ronald Reagan, not to mention three of the Star Trek cast members—Spock, Sulu, and Bones—who "got their start on Death Valley Days." Again, mining borax is made culturally significant, even famous.

What is unique about this part of the visitor center, as opposed to the Twenty Mule Team Museum, is that it also tells alchemical tales of how Borax turned into a touristic destination years after most mining activity moved south of the valley in Boron. For instance, Borax offered visitors on train rides through the park on carts that once hauled ore from the mines. Even though Borax sold these real estate properties in the 1960s, it continued to promote the desert to tourists "in search of Death Valley's romantic past" and "scenic beauty" by repurposing old bunkhouses into hotels and building "the luxurious" Furnace Creek Inn. To this day, this "four-star hotel" (now called "The Oasis" and owned by Xantera) continues to exist as a top tourist destination for Death Valley.

Borax also led an initiative to include Death Valley in the National Park System. In 1927, representatives of the National Park Service, Union Pacific, and Borax met in Death Valley to discuss the possibility. One of Borax's employees who "played [a] starring rol[e]" in this proposal was Stephen Mather, who suggested twenty-mule teams be used to promote Borax, and tourism, in the Death Valley area. As a premiere example of what would eventually become part of Rio Tinto's alchemical rhetoric, the company, through Borax, effectually "created nature" when Herbert Hoover created Death Valley National Monument in that same year and Mather became the first director of the National Park Service. Six years later, his assistant, Horace Albright—another former Borax employee— became the second. Meanwhile, twenty-mule teams paraded around the country as famous icons, promoting both Borax and Western tourism.

The connections between Borax and Death Valley are not accidental, as they point to how this part of the Wild West was the origin of the company and its extractive ambitions. Nature first had to be conquered before it could be invented and preserved.[38] Akin to the ways Southern Pacific forged an "unholy alliance" with John Muir to protect Yosemite National Park in the nineteenth century, Borax (and Union Pacific) advanced their mutual interests to protect Death Valley as a National Monument, and in 1994 it became a national park. Even still, as the following section shows, this is no ordinary national park because of its climatic extremes. As one of the placards says, "The Mojave Desert was a hostile unchartered wilderness." Describing Death Valley at the end of the nineteenth century, Florence Smitheram—the wife of a Borate mine superintendent—said, "We thought we had come to the end of the world."

Before pilgriming to Death Valley, we must foremost tell the rest of the story of borax by determining how Rio Tinto has evolved from the iconic twenty-mule team to the industrial empire that has made possible the colossal open-pit mine behind the visitor center. As we continue our tour in the first hanger, we follow a geological narrative of Mining, Processing, Use, Distribution, Environment, and

Community. Passing from the twenty-mule team days—which is all detailed in great description—to the present we come to know how the Borax Mine exists as the largest mine of its kind in the world. With pictures of the mine throughout the visitor center—not to mention front-row seats to the mine in the back of the visitor center—visitors see and feel how this mine was not just made possible but necessary.

In the Mining area, the visitor encounters numerous photographs of the hauling trucks already encountered at Pioneer Park and the visitor center parking lot. Here Borax details the scale of operations at the Borax mine with images of electric shovels, hauling trucks, and water tanks that tower behind life-size persons. "Mining started in the Stone Age," says a descriptive sign on "how deposits are mined": "In California, Native Americans were the first miners, using minerals to make everything from arrowheads and tools to pottery, paints and jewelry. But when most people think about mining, they think of the Gold Rush. That's when 200,000 people came from all over the world to California to become miners . . . and to strike it rich. Mining methods have come a long way since then. Instead of pick-axes and pans, we use satellites, computers and some of the biggest and best equipment in the world." Nearby are several maps that show the geological significance of the Borax Mine and its different historical lava flows, depression from hot springs, burial, uplift, and erosion that have created perfect conditions for the world's largest deposits of borax, as illustrated in contemporary cryosections, core samples of the different layers of rocks beneath the earth's crust and particular mineral deposits they possess.

There is much geological information to learn in this section. Rhetorically, these maps and displays establish that the earth, and all of its rocks, minerals, and histories, are *knowable*. Separate from one's capacity to think, geology *prima facie* operates off a separation between nature and culture that allows for its domination.[39] What is more distant, and othered, than rocks and minerals? Even though many have argued how geology—including the idea of the Anthropocene—is not just rhetorical but inseparable from histories of colonialism, slavery, and racism, geology here is presented as a rote set of facts that almost "hails" Rio Tinto—giving life to its industrial processes of extractivism through its sole existence for humanity's uses.

Those uses are detailed adjacent to this Mining section where the visitor center puts on display of many different modern-day commodities made possible by these geological feats. In a "Borax at Home" exhibit that resembles the "American Kitchen" display at the Twenty Mule Team Museum, the visitor

Fig. 12 | Borax at Home. Photo taken by author.

center shows the many taken-for-granted things that rely on borax. From desktop computers, cell phones, fertilizers, and pots and pans, to Play-Doh, fiberglass insulation, engine oil, and of course laundry detergent, borax, it seems, is an indelible part of modern human existence (see fig. 12).

The "major uses" of minerals such as borates are detailed in an exhibit behind this display: "Life would be totally different without minerals. Did you drive in a car to get here? That took about 15 different minerals to make. Did you watch TV last night? You were watching about 35 minerals. . . . Think about it this way: if something can't be grown (like plants or animals) it has to be mined. So it's not surprising that each American needs an average of 40,000 pounds of minerals each year." Pictures of different categories of these uses and other "special assignments"—glass, detergents, agriculture, ceramics and enamels, surfing, fireworks, "homesteading," and pool "splashing" and bug "squishing"—are displayed throughout this area. Borates, like Rio Tinto, may be invisible to the naked eye, but they are everywhere and of critical importance for modern human existence.

Borates do not come "fresh out of the ground" to one's home.[40] They must be refined. The Processing section shows how this works as a six-step process that "transform[s] our ore into products that other industries use to make products you use every day." In a step-by-step display, this section walks readers through, with great scientific acumen, the processes of dissolving, settling, crystalizing, filtering, drying, and conveying. All this is done through a display of the specialized equipment that is replicated, in miniature form, on a table for closer examination. An example of what David Nye has called the "technological sublime"—which produces a sense of awe and wonder about certain technological forms or achievements—this part of the visitor center shows how the sophisticated process of refining borates post–extraction is a bewildering feat that for the technical-skeptic can even be terrifying.[41] Are we looking at the chemical sublime?

Of equal significance to the global consumption of borates is distribution. On a posterboard with this label, visitors see images of shipping yards, cargo ships, and trains. A label details "how borates are distributed": "Ever since the days when the twenty mule teams were running, transportation has played a major role in the borax business. Today instead of twenty mules, we use an enormous fleet of different vehicles to move our products out of the desert and to customers in more than 80 different countries." The story of borates has always, it seems, been all about transportation, and this section brings that story full circle by reminding viewers of the significance of hauling these minerals from the middle of the Mojave Desert to global consumers. With modern technology, borates are able to travel to virtually every corner of the world. Thanks to Rio Tinto, this narrative goes, the legacy of borax since the days of twenty-mule teams is not only preserved via historical incorporation but advanced to meet twenty-first century needs.

Such efforts are celebrated as visitors learn about the company's volunteerism with local sports teams, public schools, and 20 Mule Team Days. These activities are all commemorated through hundreds of different awards, letters, and plaques that express appreciation for Rio Tinto's / Borax's service to local and global communities. Given by politicians, including California governors, senators, and representatives, and also members of the community (including many from kids), these awards show how Rio Tinto is valued as a local actor not just famous but appreciated. One of these is a charming painting from the West Boron Elementary School that shows trucks hauling ore from the mine to its processing center along with miners happily blowing up and hauling material in a cart as the Santa Fe railroad passes by with a full load.

Visitors finished with their tour are encouraged to walk outside and see the mine for themselves. Coming face-to-face with the object of everything they have

Fig. 13 | The Borax Mine from atop the visitor's center. Photo taken by author.

learned up to this point, they can see haulers and shovels mine ore in real time as the mine becomes deeper and wider before one's eyes for the betterment of global societies (see fig. 13). In the background one can see all the processing technologies described earlier for refining the borates. From the celebrated ethos of U.S. Borax and its twenty-mule teams to the many different uses, movements, and stories of borax itself, visitors see the mine not as a "desert of the real" but as a historically famous, and much needed, Borax Mine that is deeply informative of how the West was won. The mine is no longer a hole in the earth but a symbol of American progress through corporate America. This cultural encounter fends off the sublime, making the visual experience of this mine less horrifying and ineffable than knowable and appreciated. How this happens is through an alchemical process wherein Rio Tinto, through U.S. Borax, uses its borates as resources for rhetorically inventing its own existence.

Rio Tinto altogether has extracted from the historical twenty-mule team days to create a powerful image, or persona, of a meaningful rhetorical actor that is far from the global industrial giant headquartered thousands of miles away in London. Rio Tinto is localized as an important member of the community that is also rooted in a legacy of mining with cultural attachments for many of its members. Environmental criticisms are deflected not only by the fact that they apparently rely on Rio Tinto's minerals for everyday use—an example of what Schneider et al. call the "hypocrite's trap"—but also all the "responsible" environmental practices Rio Tinto takes up at the mine, starting with safety measures that drivers themselves encountered on their way to the mine.[42] Additionally, Rio Tinto apparently cares for species and reclamation efforts. "Mining, by its very nature, disturbs the environment," says a posterboard that details Rio Tinto's environmental commitments to responsibility through land restoration, air quality monitoring, and species protection by its special environmental and animal teams.

Rio Tinto's largest environmental claim, however, is the one that is already part of the dominant narrative of the twenty-mule teams at DVNP. Through historical incorporation, it has invented nature/culture, which visitors are encouraged to experience at Death Valley.

Rio Tinto's Hiddenness at Boron and Death Valley

Visiting Boron has revealed many strange, and partial, disclosures of Rio Tinto. In a place defined by its many different extremes, Rio Tinto is less present than the pasts of its former company U.S. Borax. Even though Rio Tinto acquired the company in 1967, becoming the parent company of the Borax Mines, cultural memories attached to U.S. Borax—from its twenty-mule team days in Death Valley to its connections to Hollywood—continue to define this place as a landmark of corporate America. Far from an arm of the British company Rio Tinto—which is as distant from the minds of locals as it is in reality—Boron remains a corporate town in the hands of those such as Ronald Reagan, Julia Roberts, and Spock.

Rio Tinto in this way remains hidden behind its own incorporated history. Although Rio Tinto was not at all part of the *Death Valley Days* sets, it strategically builds alliances with those memories as if it were the teamster of the twenty-mule teams. Again, this is less appropriative than it is associative. The architecture of mining pasts are already built into the landscape of this corporate town, so Rio Tinto simply affirms what is already there.

Where then is Rio Tinto? Is it hidden behind some rock, perhaps a borate, like a Mojave fringe-toed lizard during the day? Or is it burrowed in some secret desert hole, like "Walking George" Swain?

Rio Tinto is in plain sight. If Rio Tinto *is* its persona, and that persona is tied to the lore of twenty-mule teams, then Rio Tinto is not *just* the teamster but also all of the other components of this cultural machine that link mining to desert to town: 20 Mule Team Road, Café, Museum; the hauler at Pioneer Park; the American kitchen, the Muroc family, "Walking George" Swain; Death Valley National Park. Reagan may have been one of the most famous spokespersons for U.S. Borax, but the affective attachments to all of these names, places, persons, and things also do work for Rio Tinto in the present. At the same time, Reagan and the twenty-mule team he rode in on have also made this corporate town, and *de facto* Rio Tinto, famous, which is why they continue to serve as powerful condensation symbols for all the many different elements that make this place meaningful, and not just a giant hole in the earth.[43]

But then again, in the Anthropocene these kinds of holes have changed what it means to be human. One look at the Borax Mine tells us how costly our reliance on commodities are for the environments we share. No longer can we deny our ecocultural entanglements with the nonhuman, including corporate, world.[44] If Reagan is Rio Tinto, are not we too as we consume borates on a daily basis? While not as famous as the fortieth president of the United States, we are nevertheless just as ecologically connected to Rio Tinto, and its Borax Mine, as he was when promoting Boraxo.

Back at Harmony Works at DVNP, traces of Rio Tinto's fictional pasts continue to tell stories about the early days of borax mining in temperatures that are more than 130 degrees. Wrapped in narratives of frontierism, brave visitors that venture from their cars in this heat can witness the origins of what has become a mineralogical empire. As they see the old boiling tanks and crystalizing vats, perhaps before heading to the Oasis at Furnace Creek (formerly Furnace Creek Inn), they may themselves feel the abject hegemonies of settler coloniality, masculinity (man/nature), and whiteness.[45] Subjecting oneself through environmental hardship, especially in August, to learn about borax—or even go on a hike—is itself a way of affectively attaching oneself to the romance of the past, when workers, teamsters, and swampers endured the intensive heat for, visitors are told, the betterment of civilization. Through these embodied hardships, the narrative goes, man and industry heroically conquer nature. Only from nature's defeat can humans (re)invent it as a monument to romantic pasts, perhaps best enjoyed at the nearby Oasis.

What about the Timbisha Shoshone that have, and continue to, live here? The lives of the Chinese laborers that worked the vats? Or the slaves that built the transcontinental railroad through the Mojave? Are these persons and events also not part of Rio Tinto's existence?

Such questions remain below the surface of Rio Tinto's persona, in the under-lands of history. For our purposes here, we have followed Rio Tinto's dominant persona to determine how it exists as a corporate actor. We have seen that Rio Tinto's dominant persona is rooted in famous historical persons, objects, and events that allow the company to hide in plain sight. At the same time, many issues of race, class, colonialism, and labor exist below the surface as undisturbed matters of environmental injustice.

As will be discussed further in chapter 5, one of those issues at Borax involves labor. As detailed in the documentary film *Locked Out*, Rio Tinto drastically cut worker benefits when its union contract expired. Unanimously agreeing to refuse the contractual changes, union laborers were locked out of work for 107 days and during that time learned about many of Rio Tinto's global human rights violations and environmental destructions in places such as Michigan, Australia, and Bougainville. Putting this history into perspective at Boron, one worker said, "This is a microcosm of what is happening throughout the country." Another plainly called it "economic terrorism."[46]

For those privileged enough to visit DVNP or stay at the Oasis at Furnace Creek, such matters are likely the furthest thing from visitors' minds as they enjoy the romantic splendors of this former mining colony. After all, this hotel was once owned by U.S. Borax and used to attract tourists to Death Valley's "romantic past" and "scenic beauty." For instance, before taking a dip in the temperature-controlled outdoor pool, visitors may stop by the Borax Museum a few hundred yards away to encounter some of the sixty-six different mining artifacts scattered across the ground (see fig. 14). Each one has its own unique history in the story of borax that defines this place. Visitors may also visit the nearby Zabriskie Point for incredible sunsets and sunrises across the badlands. This iconic place was named after the vice president and general manager of Pacific Coast Borax, Christian Zabriskie, who turned this area "from [a] waste-land to a wonderland" since opening the Furnace Creek Inn in 1927.[47] When done, visitors can return to the Oasis and have a burger and a beer at the Last Kind Words Saloon—a place that recreates the Old West with pictures of min-ers, mounted animals, wooden stools, and a swing-through door.

Fig. 14 | Borax Museum at Furnace Creek, Death Valley. Photo taken by author.

Is DVNP not an example of industrial tourism par excellence? Beyond the basic contradiction of a mining Oasis in the middle of the desert, the place is made for cars because of its open, empty expanse across difficult terrain, which requires reliable vehicular transportation to safely get to one's destination and experience the desert. The extreme climate also allows companies to test how cars hold up under those conditions. No wonder car companies like GM regularly drive through the park to promote its vehicles. To Edward Abbey, industrial tourism, or a process where companies and developers "modernize" national parks for tourists, "is the enemy of wilderness and a threat to human rights": "Industrial tourism is a threat to the national parks. But the chief victims of the system are the motorized tourists. They are being robbed and robbing themselves. So long as they are unwilling to crawl out of their cars they will not discover the treasures of the national parks and will never escape the stress and turmoil of the urban-suburban complexes which they had hoped, presumably, to leave behind for a while."[48] At the same time, how to do that at DVNP, where "crawling out of cars" for more than fifteen minutes can be lethal? Abbey himself, as many have argued, overlooked more than a few privileges of race, class, and gender in what Amy Irvine has rightly called a "desert cabal," and it is not difficult for one to see how those privileges allow one to "crawl" in the desert in the first place.[49]

But maybe tourists should just not be here. Why work so hard to live in an unlivable place if not to flaunt one's Anthropocentric hubris and feel the romance of mining pasts? As Abbey has said elsewhere, "There is no shortage of water in the desert but exactly the right amount, a perfect ratio of water to rock, water to sand, insuring that wide free open, generous spacing among plants and animals, homes and towns and cities, which makes the arid West so different from any other part of the nation. There is no lack of water here unless you try to establish a city where no city should be."[50] As cities, parks, and mines continue to sprawl where they may not belong, DVNP is becoming our artificial lot in the Anthropocene. Hot, dry, lifeless. Industrial tourism in these places will not desist in this age; it will only become more rarefied and reserved for the privileged few. The same goes for human life.

Regardless of industrial tourism, polemics, and cabals, is this Oasis not an uncritical celebration of extractive desires, and ideologies, that have everything to do with the living legacy of settler colonialism? Is Rio Tinto therefore a colonialist that circulates extractive rhetorics of coloniality to manage its presences throughout the American West? Such questions may loom large around this vernal inquiry, but they cannot yet be answered since Rio Tinto's ontology cannot yet be established. We have only just encountered one of three of Rio Tinto's sites of extractivism.

In this chapter we have observed how Rio Tinto extracts from the past to associate its persona with stories of American mining in the Old West. The following chapter takes readers to a presentist example of a Rio Tinto mine in Salt Lake City, Utah. Unlike Boron—a place with only two thousand people in the middle of the desert—Salt Lake City is a clearer example of how Rio Tinto manages its persona to wider publics in the city. With more than one million persons living in the Salt Lake Valley, most of which see the Bingham Canyon Mine on a daily basis, Rio Tinto is forced to ramp up its alchemical rhetorics to pass as a reasonable, and necessitous, member of the community. At the same time, like Borax, Rio Tinto's subsidiary, Rio Tinto Kennecott (RTK), extracts from mining pasts in ways that make it seem that it has always been part of the local cultural memories attached to mineral mining in the Oquirrh Mountains. As we will see, Rio Tinto both associates and appropriates memories of pioneerism shared by Mormon populations to give the impression that it too is a local pioneer with just as much claim on Utah's history. Rather than dwelling on the past, though, such as Borax does with the iconicity of twenty-mule teams, Rio Tinto plays an active role in present-day public affairs. Through material rhetoric at different places and spaces, Rio Tinto culturally educates locals to see the mine as a mundane part of the landscape. More than that, Rio Tinto alchemically becomes a monument to ongoing pioneerism in the Beehive State.

3

Experiencing Copper | Touring Rio Tinto Kennecott and the Bingham Canyon Mine

In 1848 two Mormon pioneers named Thomas and Sanford Bingham stumbled upon rich deposits of copper in the Oquirrh Mountains while they were grazing cattle. Without any mining experience and few tools for extracting the precious mineral-metals, the Bingham brothers were told by their leader, Brigham Young, to focus their attention on more practical matters, such as harvesting timber.[1] "We cannot eat gold and silver," admonished Young in his journal.[2] So the Bingham brothers moved on and focused on more practical activities than mining in what became known as "Bingham Canyon."

As they were helping Young and his followers build what they saw as a Deseret—a sort of "promised land" for Mormons—specters of Rio Tinto swirled around the mouth of the canyon where the tiny bits of red metal lay. The Bingham brothers almost surely did not notice the company's gas-like presence as they assiduously worked for Young, but rest assured, based on Rio Tinto's affinity for historical extractivism, the mining company would come to present itself as not only beside them when they accidentally "discovered" copper but as already drafting plans to extract the mineral metals at an unprecedented scale. While copper, like gold and silver, cannot be ingested for survival, Rio Tinto knew too well they could be consumed in very different, and more lucrative, ways.[3]

As noted in chapter 1, Rio Tinto would not own what became known as the Bingham Canyon Mine until 1989 after it acquired assets from British Petroleum and Kennecott Utah Copper (becoming known as Rio Tinto Kennecott). Nevertheless, Rio Tinto incorporated the Bingham brothers' pioneer pasts in ways that made it seem like it was there all along. Rio Tinto has even come to carry out Young's dreams for creating what was called the Utah Deseret. Taken from the *Book of Mormon* to mean "honeybee," or "land of the working bee," the Deseret was believed to endlessly provide its hive with "milk and honey."[4] Symbolized by a beehive, the idea of the Deseret signified the very kind of "cooperative work" and "industriousness" that Mormon pioneers displayed as they built Salt Lake City as the center of the Church of Latter-Day Saints. Dreams of Deseret faded when Utah was incorporated into the Union (formerly the Utah Territory), but tropes of pioneerism continue to animate this past.

Since 1848, this alpine region has become "the largest [hu]man-made excavation on earth."[5] The mine itself is 2.75 miles across, 0.75 miles deep, and covers approximately twenty-seven thousand acres of land.[6] Named after the Bingham brothers, the BCM has produced more copper than any other mine in the history of the planet (nineteen million tons and historically 25% of US refined copper), which is why it is touted as an icon of industrial progress as "the richest hole on earth." For more than one hundred years the BCM lived large in the imaginations of many, and according to Rio Tinto, "there [is] as much ore in the ground as miners have taken out of [the BCM] since it began production in 1906."[7]

Rather than out of sight and mind in the deserted hinterlands like the Borax Mine, the BCM is part of Salt Lake City's urban-scape. This propinquity between mine and city puts Rio Tinto in a very different rhetorical situation, especially when environmental challenges call the visuality of the mine into question. For instance, Salt Lake City has some of the worst air quality in the nation. SLC's air quality is uniquely problematic because the bowl-shaped topography of the Salt Lake Valley creates an "inversion" effect that traps pollution in the valley until a storm wipes it clean. Whereas some have projected that the costs of maintaining the BCM account for approximately one-third of SLC air pollution, such numbers do not account for the human cost of exposure to fine particulate matter (PM10 and PM2.5) from mineral airborne metals such as arsenic.[8] For the most part, though, these environmental antagonisms remain below the surface of Rio Tinto's extractive politics. Like issues of labor at the Borax Mine, Rio Tinto effectively keeps such matters submerged beneath the public's subconscious. How Rio Tinto accomplishes this in Salt Lake City is the basis of the chapter.

In the previous chapter I argued that Rio Tinto's persona is a somewhat famous actor attached to the cultural narratives of Western extractivism and its links to Hollywood, Death Valley, and homesteading. Here I make the argument that Rio Tinto adopts a pioneer persona adapted to Utah's dominant cultural memories of pioneerism, which lives large in the "popular consciousnesses" of Salt Lake citizens.[9] Similar to how scientists have taken on the persona of pioneers to warrant financial support for their cutting-edge research on the "scientific frontier," Rio Tinto invokes the frontier myth to pass as a fellow pioneer and frontier explorer.[10] Contrasted with the more rugged individualism of borax mining in the Mojave Desert, however, Rio Tinto's frontier narrative in SLC tends to be more cooperative and akin to the memories surrounding Mormons' beehive-like work in the formation of the Deseret. This shows how Rio Tinto creates different iterations of its frontier persona to pass as an insider that knows, and actively contributes to, place-based memories.[11]

Rio Tinto's pioneer persona is consummated by place-based memories of pioneerism that, per Dickinson et al., "is the action invited by the 'mere' existence of the memory place."[12] Rio Tinto becomes part of the very texture of Utah's public memory of pioneerism based on actual events (i.e., Mormon pioneers' one-thousand-mile journey to the Salt Lake Valley in 1847).[13] Every year the Mormon emigration is remembered on the annual holiday known as "Pioneer Day," which commemorates the arrival of Mormon pioneers to the Salt Lake Valley on July 24. Many people, especially during the parade and various festivities, can be seen dressed up in pioneer garb as they recreate the tales of Mormon emigration. Many others take this day to visit historical sites, picnic at Frontier Homestead Park, or hike along the famous Pioneer Trail before the fireworks show.[14]

These cultural reenactments are deeply connected, in both discreet and explicit ways, to the authenticity of Utah's mining pasts and presents.[15] As Samantha Senda-Cook has argued, experiencing certain recreational activities such as hiking as "authentic" requires significant amounts of rhetorical-work within cultures that set up the expectations for certain experiences as authentic (and not degraded).[16] In SLC, Rio Tinto is part of the culture that shapes norms about how to augment authentic experiences through tropes of pioneerism and mining. For instance, parents may bring their children to This is the Place State Park—where Mormon emigrants decided that "this is the place" for settlement—so they can visit the Treasure House, which offers kids a "hands-on" experience of mining in Utah. Children can look for gemstones in Prospectors Pit, identify the rocks at the Assay Station, or pan for gold. From the top of this little house of treasure, kids are also encouraged to take a look at the BCM on the other side of the valley.[17]

Another good view of the BCM is the state capitol where pioneer iconography incorporates the meaning of the mine in narratives of emigration. For instance, as visitors walk the capitol grounds they will notice a life-sized monument of a beehive, with the state motto, "Industry," etched into its stone. With the BCM in the background, they may also notice how that same motto is on the state flag, seal, and coat of arms of Utah. This spatial juxtapositioning of mine, flag, and capitol is evidence of the effectiveness of Rio Tinto's historical incorporation and attachments to exceptionalism. Not only has the mine become part of Mormon culture, but it is monumentalized as such. The mine has become so tightly wound in narratives of Mormon pioneerism, that it is somewhat of an indexical for an actual, albeit inversed, beehive, as artists such as Jean Arnold have illustrated in paintings that depict the mine-as-hive.[18] As a sort of contemporary latter-day saint, or "Queen Bee," of the twenty-first century, Rio Tinto carries on the torch of Mormon industriousness through its mining operations at the BCM.

All of this pioneerism no doubt perpetuates a "frontier myth" that ideologically necessitates "the erasure of indigenous peoples and 'nonwhites,'" while celebrating the "triumph" of (white) civilization, community, and democracy.[19] However, like the environmental problems associated with the BCM, these questions remain below public consciousness as Rio Tinto works its steady hand across the valley with cultural rhetorics that articulate the BCM as a hallmark of modern civilization throughout the valley. While these erasures are of critical importance for our eventual argument about Rio Tinto's possible colonial face behind its mask, the main task, for now, is to determine Rio Tinto's rhetorical modes of existence at each of its mines. In SLC, Rio Tinto is made a pioneer that not only rode into town in a covered wagon with Brigham Young in 1847 but also discovered copper in the Bingham Canyon the following year.

How Rio Tinto does this adds an important layer of alchemical rhetoric not yet revealed, since our previous chapter was in a small corporate town in the middle of the desert. Rio Tinto mobilizes its main resource, copper, as a resource for inventing material rhetorics that imbue Rio Tinto's identities in the architecture of place and community. Rather than hiding behind corporate forebears as Rio Tinto does in Boron, Rio Tinto and its principal resource, copper, are made highly visible, and culturally present, actors affectively associated with the experiences of dominant cultural life.

This alchemical rhetoric is most explicit on its "Experiential Tour" of the BCM. As a contemporary example of what I call a "corporate tour," Rio Tinto shuttles intrigued visitors to the top of the mine, where they can see the mine in all of its glory. Akin to how U.S. Borax once brought visitors through DVNP on mining carts or the tourism at *Minas de Riotinto*, Rio Tinto allows visitors to tour the mine *as a park* full of adventure, progress, and awe. Narrating the experience with stories about the mine's pasts and presents—along with a showing of a video entitled "From Ore to More" on the shuttle's public screen— Rio Tinto's spokesperson, or tour guide, turns viewing the mine into a memorable experience. Seeing the BCM for the first time is one thing, but *experiencing* the mine, and its affordances, is quite another.

Through different affects and experiences throughout Salt Lake City, Rio Tinto manufactures its own "culture industry."[20] Once described by cultural theorists Theodore Adorno and Max Horkheimer as an "Enlightened" form of "mass deception" that more or less manipulates publics into accepting false psychological needs (i.e., the consumption of popular culture) that ultimately lead to political passivity, the culture industry here refers to the way Rio Tinto invents and stabilizes an affective-driven cultural apparatus that sustains its own existence.[21] By building cultural relationships with publics, visitors, and tourists, Rio Tinto becomes a good neighbor associated with the enjoyment (*jouissance*) of copper. As a sort of cultural pioneer that wants publics to see and experience the BCM as a monument to civilization, it invents a place-based persona that is circulated through mundane and spectacular cultural experiences. In this way, publics also experience copper. While copper, like borates, is frequently invisible in most commodities, it is also a precious metal, not just a mineral, and an aesthetically pleasing one at that—one that has been used since ancient Mesopotamia for jewelry, pottery, and currency.[22] To this day, copper is frequently used for many of the same objects, including the third-place bronze medals for minor and major athletic events. Is it any surprise that Rio Tinto sponsored the 2012 summer Olympics in London?[23]

Taking its cue (or the chemical Cu) from the beauty of copper, Rio Tinto, unlike U.S. Borax, reveals itself in Salt Lake City to alchemically create and nurture a cultural experience of Rio Tinto's extractivism at the BCM as a living form of pioneerism. Like magic, the BCM goes from sacrifice zone and "toxic sublime" to beehive and monument.

Rio Tinto also performs this cultural alchemy through its claims to renewable energy. Unlike more "dirty" resources such as coal, copper is one of the prized elements that many believe is key to sustainable futures. Because of its high efficiency for conducting electricity, in addition to the fact that it is recyclable, copper is implicitly called upon for environmental technologies such as electric vehicles, battery storage, solar panels, and wind turbines. As companies such as GM, for instance, commit to going 100 percent electric by 2035, copper is only beginning to enjoy its "golden age."[24]

Another implied element during these heightened calls for renewable energy is tellurium. Tellurium is a thin and brittle, metallic mineral that is crucial for solar panels, as it is used for a compound called cadmium telluride that serves as a semiconductor for photovoltaic panels. Coincidentally or not, tellurium is also a byproduct of copper smelting. This is why Rio Tinto has recently decided to expand its operations at the BCM to include a tellurium plant that will extract the mineral element from "waste streams" during the process of refining copper. Investing $2.9 million in operations, the proposed plant is estimated to produce twenty tons of tellurium each year.[25]

Responding to global environmental crises with more extractivism, Rio Tinto positions itself with even more rhetorical authority as an environmental pioneer. Like the ongoing air pollution debate in Salt Lake City, Rio Tinto's extractive practices are made part of the solution rather than the problem causing environmental woes. As one of Rio Tinto's managing directors, Gaby Poirier said, "The minerals and metals we produce are essential to accelerate the transition to renewable energy." To Utah's governor, Spencer Cox, Rio Tinto's "new tellurium plant is another valuable contribution to critical mineral independence and energy security in the U.S."[26]

Tellurium and copper are both part of Rio Tinto's wider objectives to meet twenty-first-century demands for minerals and metals. As environmental arguments continue to demand more renewable energy technologies, companies such as Rio Tinto must ramp up mining operations from the most unlikely places (including, potentially, tailing sites). So essential is Rio Tinto to renewable energy technologies that it has partnered with the US Department of Energy's Critical Materials Institute to determine different ways of recovering critical minerals such as lithium and rhenium, in addition to tellurium as byproducts at its different mines.[27] One of these is the Borax Mine, which is another place that Rio Tinto is planning new facilities for twenty-first-century renewable needs, where the desired elemental material is not more borates but "battery-grade lithium" from "waste rock."[28]

For many of these reasons, Rio Tinto is awarded for its commitments to sustainability. In 2020, Rio Tinto was named the first recipient of what is called the "Copper Mark," which is awarded by the copper industry for "responsible production" of copper, based on thirty criteria, including environment and community.[29] Rio Tinto is also expected to "contribute" to the United Nations Sustainable Development Goal 12 regarding matters of sustainable production and consumption.[30]

All of this environmental rhetoric flies in the face of the mine's legacy of toxic waste, contribution to the valley's air pollution problem, and other ecological disturbances, but at the same time there is a level of truth to Rio Tinto's claims. If we as a society take seriously matters of sustainability, will we not become more dependent on copper, tellurium, and lithium for everything from electric vehicles, solar panels, and geothermal energy? Is this not a Faustian gambit? Recall, though, that alchemical rhetoric is less of a greenwashing technique than a real, and material, consequence of using elemental resources for rhetorical invention. Rio Tinto in this way is not necessarily misleading publics about truer environmental conditions as much as creating new possibilities as a personified pioneer of many different sorts.

One example is Trax. Trax is an award-winning light-rail transportation network that sprawls across the Salt Lake Valley that has been praised for its reduction of air pollution and traffic congestion, in addition to its overall ease of use and affordability. From Trax, passengers can go from the Salt Lake City airport to downtown Temple Square, the University of Utah medical campus, and nearby communities such as West Valley, South Jordan, Murray, and Draper. It also runs on copper to transmit energy to its electrical cables. One of its lines can take passengers to the base of the BCM. As this chapter will show, this end-of-the-line is a community named Daybreak that itself exists on land reclaimed, and formerly owned, by Rio Tinto. From Daybreak, passengers can take a sort of Rio Tinto tour throughout Salt Lake City by visiting the former Rio Tinto Stadium (currently, America First Stadium), the Rio Tinto Kennecott Mechanical Engineering Building, and the Natural History Museum of Utah (also called the Rio Tinto Center).

Does the BCM take away from the significance of Trax to environmental issues or does it merely alter the mode in which environmental relations are experienced? In a cultural situation where these kinds of technologies are valued to meet current environmental needs, passengers appreciate Trax no less than they would without the BCM in the background. If anything, those that do see the connection between Trax and BCM may come to appreciate the BCM more.

Rio Tinto makes people, technologies, and ore "go," which is why these movements and mobilities are perhaps best read in motion.[31] In this vein, the remainder of the chapter follows Trax from mine to city and reads its role in the architecture of community. Because two of the places we will visit, the America First Stadium and Daybreak, are sites formerly associated with Rio Tinto (by name or ownership), they tell us something about the temporality of the corporate persona. As observed in the previous chapter, certain symbols and narratives can be timeless rhetorical resources for corporate personae, but this chapter indicates the corporate persona itself is time-bound. This is an important reminder that mining companies like Rio Tinto are geological visitors that, once all the minerals are extracted, leave. The withdrawal of Rio Tinto from these two places of rhetoric is indicative of this inevitable corporate departure. At the same time, Rio Tinto, like the companies that mined the BCM before it—namely, the Utah Copper Company and Kennecott Utah Copper (KUC)—will never fully disappear from the SLC urban-scape; it will always be part of the architecture of SLC, even if those histories are forgotten with time. What this implies for the future of Rio Tinto at the BCM is something I discuss below.

Starting with the Experiential Tour, I show how Rio Tinto offers visitors a unique experience of the mine that makes copper visible. As opposed to toxic tours, corporate tours culturally educate visitors to experience the affordances their commodities create, which wards off environmental antagonisms of these sites as toxic. I then visit the Daybreak community at the base of the mine. Daybreak is a suburban community that exists on land reclaimed by Rio Tinto in the early 2000s. While Rio Tinto sold the community in 2016, it nevertheless continues to build Rio Tinto's pioneer ethos because of its place-based history and propinquity to the mine. Next, I travel to what was, until recently, called the Rio Tinto Stadium. Home to the Major League Soccer Stadium, Real Salt Lake, this stadium, now named America First Field, was associated with Rio Tinto from 2008 to 2022 through rhetorics of fandom. I then move to our last stop, the Natural History Museum of Utah. Also called the Rio Tinto Center, this museum posits Rio Tinto as a knowing environmental actor pioneering sustainable futures. I conclude with a discussion of Rio Tinto as environmental pioneer.

Experiencing the Largest Mine on Earth: Pasts and Presences of Pioneerism

Ontically, the BCM is an irreducible, wild force. Its awesome magnitude escapes words, meaning, language itself. As a sublime object, the BCM is both terrifying and beautiful. As observed in chapter 1, the BCM is characteristic of what

Fig. 15 | The former Kennecott Visitors Center that was wiped out from a 2013 landslide. Photo taken by author in 2011.

Peeples has aptly called the toxic sublime, which describes "the tensions that arise from recognizing the toxicity of a place, object or situation, while simultaneously appreciating its mystery, magnificence, and ability to inspire awe."[32] No doubt these tensions are present at the BCM, visually, but what does it mean to actually experience the BCM? How do embodied encounters alter, or reinforce, this reading? Moreover, how does experiencing the mine possibly shape Rio Tinto's corporate persona?

These questions are complicated by the fact that experiencing the BCM has changed over time, alongside changes in the materiality of the mine itself. The most significant change was ushered by a massive landslide in 2013 that wiped out what was once the Kennecott Visitor Center.[33] Sitting on the top of the mine, where visitors could gaze into the mine's massive void, this place of corporate memory once stored a surfeit of rhetorical fragments about the history, geology, and cultural significance of the BCM (see fig. 15). From photographs, rock samples, films, historical timelines, soundbites, and commodities made possible by copper, the visitor center was a symbolic storehouse for making sense of the visual absence of the mine.

Fig. 16 | From Ore to More. Photo taken by author.

What is now nothing more than loose rock and debris (and ultimately part of the BCM's absence) was once a storehouse for industrial memories where visitors learned about the historical significance of the BCM through a smorgasbord of objects and paintings of the mine, ore deposits dubbed "nature's gifts," a documentary film about the industriousness of miners at the BCM, and an animated video entitled "From Ore to More: The Story of Copper" (see fig. 16). Even though the visitor center no longer exists, its presence-made-absent has nevertheless shaped the conditions for Rio Tinto to emerge as a knowing actor that writes and performs history as an immaterial place of memory. Like the disappearing memories of the once "full-fledged Western mining town" of Bingham, Utah—which was once described as a "beehive of activity" until it was subsumed by the mine in 1972—not to mention racial histories of Native Americans, and other mining "ghost towns" such as Lark, Utah, the BCM exists through numerous erasures that stabilize Rio Tinto's various presences (chapter 1).[34]

In more ways than some, the forlorn Kennecott Visitor Center performs the rhetorical modus operandi of the BCM as active force: erasure. The most visible erasure, of course, is the mine itself.

The BCM is still without a visitor center; however, in 2019, Rio Tinto introduced a *corporate tour* of the BCM called the "Visitor's Experience." As Phaedra Pezzullo argues, toxic tours can become forms of public participation that can alter perceptions about places in ways that create impetuses for change.[35] She also mentions how "plant tours" can frame experiences "within discourses of safety and containment, industrial progress, and objective science."[36] Given the ways industrial corporations and their "factories" have changed in a "postindustrial" society—not to mention the changes that come along with added corporate agencies in the Anthropocene and the age of corporate "personhood"—what I am calling *corporate tourism* is a more lively, and expansive, form of plant tours that have expanded their agentic operations beyond the factory. Corporate tours such as Rio Tinto's "Visitor's Experience" work in the opposite direction of toxic tours by reinforcing, rather than calling into question, business as usual approaches to the environment. Arguably a form of what Deleuze and Guattari might call capitalistic axiomatization, corporate tours shape the dominant rhetorical landscape about how to feel the world.[37]

At the BCM, Rio Tinto uses various corporate tours (not just the "Visitor's Experience") to lionize the BCM as a monument to modernity through industrialism. In so doing, it erases toxic effects from those mining activities—such as air pollution or toxics noted in the mine's toxic release inventory—from the visitor's consciousness and displaces any possible singular responsibilities. Consider a journey on Rio Tinto's Visitor's Experience Tour taken in the summer of 2019.

The Visitor's Experience Tour starts at the base of the mine outside a gift shop that sells not just tickets for the tour but also other kitsch items such as magnets, posters, keychains.[38] From here, visitors are picked up on a bus that takes them to the top of the mine, about a five-to-seven-minute journey. The driver is also the commentator, and on the way to the mine visitors hear about the history of the mine, the workers, its significance to modern life. These talking points are reinforced by a short film that visitors watch on a public screen located at the front of the bus. Showing the same "From Ore to More" video that visitors once watched at Kennecott's Visitor's Center, Rio Tinto uses cartoon characters to walk visitors through the process of turning what was once a

Fig. 17 | "Mountains." Photo taken by author.

mountain into 99.99 percent copper cathodes. Those who take the tour learn about the massive 2013 landslide that demolished the visitor's center.

As the shuttle climbs mountains of waste rock, visitors encounter Rio Tinto's presences through "sight sacralization" as they learn how Rio Tinto has "moved mountains" to "create" its own "mountain range" (see fig. 17).[39] Visitors know exactly what the guide means as they witness vast heaps of mineral tailings that resemble mountains. "The mine never closes!" the tour guide repeatedly exclaims.

When visitors arrive to the top of the mine at the observation deck, they experience the subliminal force of the BCM's 1,900 square acres of absence (see fig. 18). The sight in many ways is a "traumatic kernel of the Real" until visitors encounter a surfeit of objects, such as machine parts, expositions, and images that explain how to see the mine as a monument to industrial progress through advanced science and technology.[40]

Old and new objects scattered about the platform create a material-semiotic network that posits Rio Tinto as an emergent, knowing subject. These objects include an archaic minecart displayed on tracks leading toward an archaic mining tunnel, a historic steam-powered shovel, a modern bulldozer loader, a dump truck bed used as a tourist platform featuring a timeline of events, and

Fig. 18 | The Bingham Canyon Mine. Photo taken by author.

an eighteen-cylinder Cummins engine for powering the "world's largest class of haul trucks." There is also a larger-than-life tire of one of the dump-trucks, several viewscopes, a giant map of all of Rio Tinto's mines throughout the world etched into the cement, and several expository signs detailing the history of the BCM and the significance of copper to everyday life (see fig. 19).

As visitors exit the shuttle and approach the fenced-in observation platform, they see the bed of a modern dump truck that is transformed into a timeline of historical events at the BCM from 1862 to the present. Offering a sort of genealogy of industrial progress, Rio Tinto shows how it carries out the *tradition of pioneerism* at the BCM passed down from its former company, Kennecott Utah Copper. KUC also appropriated cultural values of pioneerism when it owned the BCM (1903–89). For instance, consider a 1956 advertisement retrieved from the Marriott archives in its "Kennecott Collection." Entitled "Still Pioneering," the ad depicts KUC carrying out the legacy of pioneer families by continuing to "do the impossible!" It says, "By following the pioneer tradition of meeting problems with faith, planning and hard work, Kennecott is still building for the future—for continued copper production that means much to the prosperity of Utah and its people."[41]

Fig. 19 | "We are Pioneers in Mining Metals." Photo taken by author.

This transfer of the corporate persona from KUC to Rio Tinto reinforces what was noted in the previous chapter about how corporate persona can endlessly mine rhetorical resources. In a way, Rio Tinto mines itself for rhetorical resources that can be used in the present. Like the symbols of frontierism Rio Tinto mines in the Mojave Desert, Rio Tinto extracts and transforms symbolic meaning from historical mining operations that have created conditions for Rio Tinto's arrival. While some of these rhetorics of progress and pioneerism already exist as inartistic appeals—considering the historical rhetorical labor that KUC put into its operations—maintaining the corporate persona over time requires tremendous amounts of work in the present. Hence Rio Tinto's alchemical efforts that transform rhetorical meanings of mining pasts for the present needs of renewable energy.

Rio Tinto constructs a corporate genealogy at the BCM that has everything to do with a living legacy of industrial progress. Readers, for instance, learn that the mine's industrial history is attached to the winning sides of World War II, struggles for gender equalities, and environmental sustainability, which are all framed as part of the living legacy of industrial pioneerism.[42] "Before we were pioneering progress," reads the timeline, "we were just pioneers." These place- and

Fig. 20 | Machine part with "mountains" in backdrop. Photo taken by author.

space-based objects connect visitors to Rio Tinto's intensive mining operations through the lens of an industrial pioneer.

After descending to a lower-level platform, experiential visitors encounter more machinic objects, including the bucket of an outmoded steam shovel (see fig. 20). Once used to haul ore from the mine, the bucket has been repurposed as a dingpolitik object that materially and symbolically articulates Rio Tinto as the culmination of years of "human progress, 120 tons at a time." The appended sign states how "for more than 100 years shovels, trains and trucks have operated in the Bingham Canyon area." The sign adds, "24 hours a day" Rio Tinto is "*producing materials essential to modern life.* From satellites to cell phones, without copper modern life wouldn't be possible."

These objects-made-platforms create conditions for Rio Tinto to emerge as a corporate subject with agency and persona. Rio Tinto builds affective relations with visitors' bodies to exert agency as a knowledgeable, scientific actor rooted in time, space, and place. Objects such as dump truck beds and shovels stabilize Rio Tinto's rhetorical presence through affects of industriousness, extractivism, and awe. There is also a spatial politic here that fills the absences of the mine with all these affects and symbols from a God-like position. As an actor with epistemic authority over the environment, Rio Tinto establishes its separation from nature through cultural objects that mediate space- and place-based experiences of the mine by tying its persona to SLC's history of pioneerism.

On the way back to the base of the mine, the tour guide / shuttle driver continues to animate the life of the mine with exuberant narratives of techno-industrial progress that are supplemented with fun, cartoonish videos about the necessity of copper. As a sort of ventriloquist dummy for Rio Tinto, the guide hailed the mine as a monument to civilization that was "built" with scientific ingenuity to supply 15 percent of the world's copper. Passengers are once more repeatedly told, "The mine never closes!" These audible presences of Rio Tinto's fun and energetic personality sharply contrast with the howling silence of the mine itself.

Daybreak: Rio Tinto the Sustainable Pioneer

Rhetorical pilgrims can extend their corporate tour of Rio Tinto by following Trax, our copper-infused public transportation system, toward the city. Our first stop from the BCM is Daybreak. Daybreak, as observed in chapter 1, is a growing suburban community of twenty thousand residential units developed by Rio Tinto's land development company Kennecott Land as a sustainability initiative to reclaim land previously defined by environmental hazard. In 2016, the community was acquired by the Minnesota-based company, Värde Partners, which recently sold the assets to the Larry H. Miller Company.[43] Even though Rio Tinto no longer owns Daybreak, the community still does rhetorical work for Rio Tinto and the BCM as an alchemical reaction.[44] What was a toxic wasteland is now a suburban community. As a sort of mediator of rhetorical possibilities, Rio Tinto has manufactured a community that hybridizes mine, copper, and home to create a vision of environmental harmony.

Daybreak may no longer be owned by Rio Tinto, but it still remains squarely within its territory. The BCM is quite literally in residents' backyards. The community is arguably a contemporary version of a corporate town, even though it has changed corporate hands. At the same time, Daybreak has very different sets of appeals than other corporate towns such as Boron. For one, Daybreak's dominant attractiveness is its visual splendor, community, and accessibility (see fig. 21). Daybreak has the feel of the country without its inaccessibilities. Rather than being in the middle of the desert, it is nestled in the Oquirrh Mountains

Fig. 21 | Daybreak. Photo taken by Dean Derhak. CC A-S 3.0.

yet is still connected to SLC's larger urban-scape. Also on a lake and connected to numerous trails, Daybreak is alchemized as a beautiful place to live, work, and play. Like Death Valley, Daybreak is an example of how Rio Tinto can use its resources to transform the most inhospitable places into something.

With schools, cafes, restaurants, community gardens, parks, and public pools— not to mention soccer programs, family fun nights, and handfuls of clubs— Daybreak manufactures "the good life" through "built topoi" that alchemically transforms *the BCM as home.*[45]

Rio Tinto builds off these topoi to create an environmental ethos. As a pioneer of sustainability initiatives, Rio Tinto expands the "spatial imagination" of Rio Tinto at the BCM by hybridizing the mine, and its history of environmental hazard, with a sustainable suburban home.[46] Daybreak affords Rio Tinto opportunities to forge connections between residents and the BCM. Rio Tinto is made an environmental authority through its material relations with the land, the houses, the residents, and the greater Daybreak community.

Rio Tinto is also part of Daybreak's hip and trendy lifestyle. Residents are drawn to Daybreak precisely because of its intersections with nature and culture, which afford them with a liminal space that services many different personal interests and lifestyles. One family that moved to Daybreak from New York said they "enjoy an outdoor lifestyle, know their neighbors, hike and bike regularly and canoe together on man-made Oquirrh Lake come summer." "I love the community," one family member said.[47]

To Rio Tinto, Daybreak does not just offer "a great place to live" but is part of an attractive "lifestyle" for those "buying their first home or their last home," or their in-between home. Rio Tinto at Daybreak is "a world-class example of what you can do with excess land and post mining land use" that delivers "a vision" of "a sustainably developed community where people have the opportunity to work, live, and play in one location."[48] Residents are cosmopolitan. Some work in Daybreak, others commute to downtown, and many are employed through Rio Tinto.

One of the main effects of this spatial hybridization, for our purposes, is that it builds Rio Tinto's sustainable persona. Environmental sustainability is built into the very design of Daybreak because the community exists on reclaimed land that was once an environmental hazard, due to many years of unsustainable mining practices at the BCM. Rio Tinto inherited the toxic plumes that once contaminated the entire southwest valley, but with effective networking, strategic planning, and cooperation with the EPA, it alchemically transformed the visualities of that environmentally compromised land by planning Daybreak in 2001 as a "sustainable use of post mining land and as a showcase of the progressive thinking that embodies Rio Tinto."[49] To Rio Tinto, Daybreak serves as a living example of how corporations can work with communities to "ensure future generations have the opportunity to enjoy a great neighborhood, beautiful land, abundant water, and clean air."[50]

Daybreak is rhetorically constructed as an idyllic community that hybridizes nature and culture to articulate the BCM as an environmentally sustainable home. Divisions of nature and culture cannot be separated at Daybreak because they are both in beautiful relation with each other at the café, on the hiking trails, and at home. Daybreak's hybridity of nature and culture is important because it puts Rio Tinto in harmony, rather than competition, with the environment. "Daybreak really is that living example of what a post-mining land use can be. . . . It's really given us the opportunity to build some pretty strong relationships with some people who may not necessarily have been interested in building a relationship with us."[51]

Rio Tinto has changed citizens' structures of feeling about the BCM by turning a place once characterized by its toxic plumes into a beautiful community. It is precisely because the BCM is so close to Daybreak that it naturally becomes part of the backdrop of residents' everyday lives. Without it, residents are reminded, there would be no Daybreak, as the mine has become intimately part of the stunning landscape that families call home. Daybreak is thus a prime example of how Rio Tinto alchemically combines different elements—copper, toxic waste, homes, and Trax—to invent new possibilities for living with the BCM.

Like Boron, Daybreak might be another example of a heterotopia because it maintains numerous spatial incompatibilities, contradictions, and strange juxtapositions.[52] As a material-semiotic convergence of many heterogeneous networks, Daybreak is a sort of nowhere place conjured in the image of Rio Tinto's corporate community even though some have recently complained that their houses are "falling apart."[53] The BCM and many other environmental sacrifice zones across the world—including all of Rio Tinto's mines but also oil fields, toxic wastelands, other mines—can also be understood as heterotopias since they rupture metabolic relations so severely, they create entirely new networks of relations and material places "othered" from the rest of society. Daybreak is unique, of course, because it articulates the BCM *as home*. In this regard, Daybreak may also be called a "doubled heterotopia" that nevertheless works to Rio Tinto's rhetorical favor.[54]

Altogether, Daybreak is a place of corporate community that associates Rio Tinto and the BCM with environmental sustainability, corporate community, and a beautiful, country-style living in ways that make Rio Tinto an environmental, and communal, pioneer. Daybreak is a place of corporate community that imbues Rio Tinto's corporate persona into the architecture of community. Rio Tinto mediates corporate relations with the environment by embedding its identity into materialities of community—of which have remained even after Rio Tinto sold Daybreak. The constitutive effect of this is that Rio Tinto is made an indispensable member of SLC's community with epistemic trust, good will, and integrity. In this way, Rio Tinto is positioned as a steward of the environment and integral to the materiality of community itself, even after it leaves. This point about the withdrawal of corporate personae from their sites of rhetoric is something I develop below with the archival example of what was known as The Rio Tinto Stadium.

The (Former) Rio Tinto Soccer Stadium: Rio Tinto the Cultural Pioneer

Rio Tinto has shaped the architecture of SLC by drawing from a surfeit of past and present rhetorical resources to alchemically imbue its corporate persona into the fabric of the city. However, what happens to Rio Tinto's corporate persona when there is no more copper left in the BCM worth extracting and the mining company leaves? Before long, Rio Tinto will join the ranks of other mining companies, Utah Copper and KUC, that after extracting all it can from the BCM, disappears. Through different symbols, discourses, narratives, and objects, though, corporate personae can persist over time through different alchemical reactions with cultures and persons. The rhetorical life of the former Rio Tinto Stadium (currently America First Field) helps us understand the temporality of the corporate persona.[55]

Between 2008 and 2022, Rio Tinto paid between $1.5 and 2 million per year for the naming rights for the Rio Tinto Stadium. In September 2022, however, the America First Credit Union and RSL agreed to a fifteen-year deal worth nearly $100 million.[56] What is now named America First Field (AFF) is an architectural wonder completed in 2008 as the home stadium for the Major League Soccer (MLS) team Real Salt Lake (RSL). It is an open venue with two field-length Teflon-coated fiberglass canopies that protect fans from the harsh sun during the summertime and comfortably seats 20,000 spectators during RSL games and 25,000 for music concerts. With an average attendance of 20,351 for games (100.68 percent capacity), it is the sixth most attended soccer stadium in the country. In a *Salt Lake Tribune* article titled "Real Salt Lake's Fan Base Keeps Growing," MLS President Mark Abbott is quoted: "The stadium is one of the finest soccer venues of its size, and RSL supporters provide an environment that often rivals great soccer crowds throughout the world."[57]

Until apparently 2022, soccer was a rhetorically important dimension of Rio Tinto's local and global citizen subjectivity given the cosmopolitan, "*glocal* culture" of the sport.[58] Consider some of the signs that once promoted Rio Tinto as a cultural pioneer that has traveled through time and space to bring soccer to SLC. With an image of Daybreak and the BCM in the backdrop, the sign said, "In the late 1800s, it was Rio Tinto employees who first introduced soccer to Spain. It created recreational opportunities for people in the communities that we were a part of. More than a hundred years later, we still have a love for soccer, and so we are proud to put our name on the Rio Tinto Stadium. For us, it's a natural fit." Through soccer, Rio Tinto connected its local and global subjectivity in ways that build multicultural levels of community and outreach.

Rio Tinto used fandom rhetorics to build its corporate persona. As Ashley Hinck convincingly argues in her book *Politics for the Love of Fandom*, "fan-based citizenship" is as important a form of citizenship as traditional political acts through political parties.[59] One of her examples is the fandom of football, particularly that of the Nebraska Cornhuskers. Through different rhetorical practices, traditions, and media, Huskers fans stabilize an ethical framework from "the drama of the football field."[60] To Hinck, the Husker community collectively values hard work, respect, and helping your neighbor. These values enable rhetorical actors, such the mentoring nonprofit TeamMates, to use strategies of "connection" that pair the organization's initiatives with that of the ethical framework of Huskers fandom for civic engagement (e.g., "joining the team").[61]

In similar ways, Rio Tinto rhetorically connected RSL fandom, and its shared sets of values, to that of Rio Tinto. To be an RSL fan, in other words, was to become a fan of Rio Tinto. Fandom is thus a rhetorical accomplishment that stylized Rio Tinto's persona through the fans' cultural practices and performances. This also allowed Rio Tinto to shape RSL's values through place-based rhetorics that emphasized industrial pioneerism at the RTS.

While I attended a game in 2015 as a secular pilgrim, what I observed was something closely related to a religious activity, or a form of what Robert Bellah calls civil religion, where fans were akin to nationalists united through religious beliefs and practices.[62] Within MLS soccer culture, the RTS was akin to a place of worship full of different rituals and traditions that define RSL fandom and are connected to Rio Tinto. Consider the sound arguments from the steady beats of synchronous snare drums coming from the south section of the stadium during games.[63] These drums march to the RSL anthem, which powerfully rings throughout the stadium just before the first kickoff and after RSL goals. Fans sang, "If you believe then just stand up on your feet and shout it out 'REAL!' Here at the RioT the battle hymn's begun. We're here for RSL!"

Note that the term "RioT" is short for Rio Tinto. Even though Rio Tinto no longer owns naming rights to the field, fans still commonly refer to the stadium as the RioT through songs, chants, and vernacular talk. This is illustrative of how Rio Tinto's naming strategies have become part of the fans' cultural performances. In a way, Rio Tinto's persona still exists at the AFF through these discursive utterances associated with RSL fandom.

These cultural creations and transformations are themselves alchemical reactions to different place-based rhetorics during games. To RSL player Tony Beltran, the best part of playing at the stadium is the fan culture, which makes being part of RSL nation so meaningful (almost religious): Fans have "developed this culture[,] and they've made Salt Lake City a soccer destination. . . . It's such a high. It's great."[64] Consider also the aesthetic of dozens of streamers unfurling from the upper stands, sometimes landing on the field. Glitter and newspaper graffiti flicker in the sky and glide down to unknown destinations. These audible and visual rhetorics are spectacular corporate performances that create *sensus communis*. All of this contributed to the development of Rio Tinto's cultural persona in palpable ways.

Rio Tinto also cultivated a civically engaged culture reliant on public-corporate partnerships as the basis for citizenship.[65] The company asserted that it was at the helm of economic development, sustainable land practices, and community. In an area of the stadium that was once called Kennecott Plaza—now part of the Ford Zone (sections 13 and 14)—Rio Tinto culturally educated visitors about the significance of copper to the very idea of community. The plaza included several signs that advertise Daybreak as a sustainable community on reclaimed land, which adds to the rhetorical affordances of copper for "spatial imagination" of the suburban "good life" even though Rio Tinto technically no longer owns the homes.[66]

In this area, billboards and signs also promoted Rio Tinto's communal ethos as an economic pioneer. One sign, for instance, said in bold letters, "We're Part of Something Bigger: Community and Partnerships." In the background was a beautiful visual backdrop of the Daybreak suburban community. The sign read, "In addition to stadium naming rights, this investment in the community provides us with the opportunity for Rio Tinto Kennecott to be involved in important education and youth sport programs in the [SLC] area." Rio Tinto supported this claim with a list of its community partnerships: it donated land to build schools in Daybreak; it provided scholarships to students studying sciences and trades; it funded nonprofits and community organizations such as the Kennecott Nature Center, Tracy Aviary, Red Butte Arboretum, the Road Home, and Fallen Officers Memorial; it funded volunteer efforts such as fundraisers and food drives; and was "a proud partner" of the NHMU at Rio Tinto Center, which emphasizes education about "natural and cultural wonders," "careers in the natural environment," and safety. Rio Tinto concluded by stating, "This is our way of building sustainable relationships characterized by mutual respect, trust, active partnership, and long-term commitment." To Rio Tinto, engaging with the community is a moral duty that fulfills its commitment to Corporate Social Responsibility, which is defined as "the long term connections that you're making with people and businesses and . . . the long term benefits you provide to the community."[67]

The Kennecott Corner also had a "copper counter" that mundanely itemized global commodities made possible by copper such as "dehumidifier," "blender," "crock pot," "garbage disposal," "door knobs," "freezer," "paint sprayer," "heat gun," "chain saw," "generator," "table saw," "lawn mower," all textually inscribed in the counter. The copper counter makes the argument that copper is inextricably part of modern civilization. Given its hidden hand in public screens—several of which are noted (e.g., "laptop," "television," "cell phone")—copper is central to what it means to be a consuming subject in the networked public sphere.

The copper counter was mundane, but it evoked fragments of thought through glances and looks, rather than gazes, from fans that may have noticed the counter while reaching for their food or drinks.[68] This way of engaging the world is met-onymic of how twenty-first-century consciousnesses are mediated through public screens, also through glances, which rely on copper.[69] Consistent with Hinck's reading of fan-based citizenship, experiencing RSL fandom is also mediated by public screens, especially the massive 4,200 square foot video board—which, as I write, is the largest stadium screen in the league.[70] Did fans make the connection between the $3 million screen and the BCM? Regardless, they were invited to quite literally take a look at the mine through one of several viewscopes aimed directly at the BCM. "Take a closer look," one of the signs said, and "see a variety of our operations, each with a role in taking ore from the mine to the market." Others asked viewers to see how Rio Tinto was "part of something bigger" through different partnerships and commitments to sustainable development. All of these objects extended Rio Tinto's epistemic and sustainable agencies from other land-scapes of rhetoric to the realm of community by bringing together a sort of corpo-rate "family" that was housed at RTS as a basic unit of society (*oikos*).[71]

Elsewhere, visitors read about the legacy of modern mineral mining at the BCM, which as observed in chapter 1, dates back to 1903 with the formation of the Utah Copper Company under the direction of Daniel Jackling and his por-phyry mining methods. Here, Rio Tinto is associated with Jackling's method-ological "pioneerism" as a progenitor of this legacy of industrial pioneerism with its "cutting edge technology . . . in a global market" and "highest safety standards." Through objects such as signs, viewscopes, the copper counter, and images— and within a cosmopolitan landscape of experience—Rio Tinto became a cul-tural pioneer that is knowledgeable, historical, and sustainable and from its goodwill has decided to use its global agency to create a home for corporate community. "After all," says one sign, "our employees are your friends, neighbors and family members."

While Rio Tinto's persona may exist as a sort of ghostly substance through chants and songs that still refer to the stadium as the RioT, the AFF is currently almost entirely devoid of Rio Tinto's former symbols, narratives, and objects.

No more Kennecott Corner, copper counter, billboards, viewscopes, or logos.[72] Now the America First Credit Union builds new alchemical rhetorics from the many different affects, symbols, and objects that once served Rio Tinto's persona. Looking back, is it ironic that Rio Tinto made so many claims about its long-term commitment to the community, yet it withdrew its name from the stadium? Perhaps. Another reading is that Rio Tinto simply no longer finds it necessary to rhetorically instantiate its persona at this place or that it sufficiently shows its commitment to the community in other ways. Given that Rio Tinto sold Daybreak and no longer owns the naming rights to RSL's stadium, is it possible that Rio Tinto is withdrawing its communal presence as it prepares for the day it leaves the Salt Lake Valley? What will become of the meaning of the BCM without Rio Tinto or any other mining company using it as a wellspring for alchemical rhetorics in SLC?

One way to anticipate this inevitable future is to consider other historical mines such as the Berkeley Pit in Butte, Montana. The Berkeley Pit was once owned by the Anaconda Mining Company and is currently one of the most contaminated sites in America. Filled with nearly 900 feet of highly acidic water, this Superfund Site is a highly toxic soup of many different heavy metals and chemicals and is located at the edge of town. Like the *Rio Tinto* (the river) and the BCM, this pit is also a tourist attraction. For a fee visitors can visit the pit's viewing platform or visit the nearby giftshop. A few miles away, the 585-foot-tall Anaconda Smelter Stack monumentalizes the history of mining that once defined this place. While this stack and pit are remembered as landmarks of mining pasts, what is missing is Anaconda itself and its corporate persona that once defined this part of Montana. Is this the future of the BCM or is it possible that this mine continues to bring meaning to the SLC community as a sort of beehive of pioneerism without an extractive company actively shaping its corporate persona?[73]

Only time will tell what Rio Tinto, its corporate persona, and the BCM may become. The rhetorical transference of the corporate persona at both Daybreak and the AFF indicates that Rio Tinto is already beginning to step away from SLC. Below I take readers back to the present at the Natural History Museum of Utah (aka Rio Tinto Center).

Technological Pioneerism at the Natural History Museum of Utah

Our last stop is the Natural History Museum of Utah (NHMU), which is located on the eastern side of the Salt Lake Valley in the Wasatch Range. Taking

Fig. 22 | Natural History Museum of Utah (Rio Tinto Center). Photo taken by author.

the blue line to Central Point and the red line to Fort Douglas, we are close enough to walk to an architectural wonder that is also named the Rio Tinto Center. The museum is covered with a 42,000-square-foot copper façade mined from the BCM and donated by Rio Tinto, designed to wear over time in ways that blend in with the surrounding mountains.[74] The museum's façade gives Rio Tinto a mundane presence that is imbued in the architecture of the museum itself. Blending nature with culture, this façade matches Rio Tinto to the colors of the desert landscape (see fig. 22). To Rachel Harris of the *New York Times*, "it is so in tune with its environment that it almost blends into the landscape."[75] The museum is "meant to be a metaphor for Utah's geology," one of the museum directors explained during an interview.[76]

There are even "fractures in the copper" that are "offset" like geologic seismic breaks. In this regard, the museum is "really meant to be a geological lesson."[77] As Edward Rothstein of the *New York Times* commented, the architecture produces a "powerful impact" because while most natural history museums are found in "urban centers," the NHMU "is housed in the realm it surveys; it is at home."[78]

As a metaphor, the museum's façade visually represents Utah's natural history. It also materially educates visitors about the geologic composition of Utah.

In addition to the vertical and fractured strata, the copper was intentionally not treated with any chemicals so it would evolve with the surrounding foothills over time. Rio Tinto thus becomes the chemical agent that mixes with this evolutive rhetoric to alchemically transform itself into the geology of the landscape.

All of this creates a living museum that evolves in real time. Like natural history, the museum is built to evolve with time and will never be the same museum twice. To the NHMU director, "the exterior of the building is intentionally not treated in any way, and allowed to patina over 5, 10, 15, 20 years. So as visitors come back to the museum, they will constantly see a façade that is weathering and changing."[79]

Rio Tinto also earned naming rights to the museum because of its sizable $15 million donation to the museum during its development stages; thus, the museum's full title is, The NHMU *at the Rio Tinto Center* (emphasis added). Naming is a powerful rhetorical strategy that shapes human orientations toward the natural world and "influences our interaction with it."[80] Similarly, Tema Milstein suggests the rhetorical ability to point and name is "a foundational act" that creates a "basic entry to socially discerning and categorizing parts of nature."[81] Naming the NHMU *the Rio Tinto Center* not only frames the museum as a corporate domain, but it also allows Rio Tinto to territorialize the museum as part of its corporate network, much like the RTS. All the affects that occur within the NHMU, then, are associated with Rio Tinto, which is rhetorically constructed as an environmental authority that offers citizens education about Utah's natural history and Rio Tinto's place in it.

Like the corporate tours of Daybreak and the BCM, Rio Tinto at the NHMU associates its persona with a wide range of affective relations with visitors at the NHMU. Visitors temporally, spatially, and affectively associate copper with advanced sustainability initiatives through technology. For those visitors who navigate through the museum using the NHMU's digital application on public screens called the "Sustainability Trail" (which was sponsored by Rio Tinto), they also become extensions of Rio Tinto's rhetorical network.

As visitors enter the museum, they encounter a timeline of geological history—and directed by the Sustainability Trail—signified by weathered markers that identify geological periodizations from the Precambrian and Cambrian eras to the Holocene and Anthropocene. Beside the museum entrance lies the indexer to the Anthropocene—which reads "Welcome to the Anthropocene—the age of humans!"—defined as "an era of human impacts on global ecosystems so significant that it constitutes a new geologic era."

Through rhetorics of spatialization and temporalization, Rio Tinto's corporate presences are apparently rooted in geological time. As visitors gallivant through the museum, they gradually ascend from that Precambrian period to the present. At the top of the museum, on the building's outdoor terrace called the "Sky Terrace," they encounter 1,300 solar panels—all powered by copper—that flank the northern and southern ends of the roof. The BCM is visible in the background. Through the Sustainability Trail visitors are informed that solar panels reduce global dependencies on fossil fuels and help combat SLC's air pollution problem. Within a temporal space that can be characterized as the Anthropocene—the pinnacle of Earth's history after billions of years of geologic change—Rio Tinto is made a modern pioneer of sustainability initiatives for an era wrought with environmental problems. Visitors may even conclude that corporations like Rio Tinto are the next stage of geological evolution.

Recall also how Rio Tinto is networked with visitors through public screens on the Sustainability Trail. The Sustainability Trail is one of many "trails" that NHMU visitors can access on their smartphones while visiting the museum as it performs the utility of copper as a conduit for screens' electricity. To Rio Tinto, it also demonstrates how copper is key to the future of renewable energy. As part of the smartphone application "Trailhead to Utah," the Sustainability Trail is designed to educate visitors about some of the environmental dynamics of museum exhibits. To Brian Maffly of the *Salt Lake Tribune*, it allows visitors "to personalize their tour."[82] Visitors can access these digital commonplaces by "entering a stop" from specific exhibits. This "trail" is described as a place where visitors can "explore the strategies nature uses to sustain earth's species . . . and take a deeper look at how *we humans* are tackling the sustainability challenges facing us today."[83]

One digital module titled "Copper and Kennecott Mine" opens with a brief discussion about the museum's copper panels mined from the "nearby" BCM, which can be physically observed through "viewscopes" on the NHMU's outdoor patio. The copper that encloses the museum is described on the module as "not only beautiful" but also "lightweight, strong, and 100% recyclable." Stop 290 informs viewers about the museum's alternative energy project and mentions that it has plans to install over 1,300 solar panels on the roof, which "is a demonstration of a unique public-private partnership that includes support from a wide variety of partners."[84] This information is visually confirmed by the numerous solar panels that flank the roof and help produce energy for the NHMU's electrical grid, and keep it sustainable and LEED (Leadership in Energy and Environmental Design) certified.

Rio Tinto's copper façade, naming rights, and public screens allow Rio Tinto to alchemically create a corporate identity associated with tropes of scientific progress, technological determinism, and sustainability that further instantiate Rio Tinto's pioneerism. Aaron Phillips aptly argues that the NHMU skews geological deep time and commits "anthropocentric hubris" in ways that "elide extraction;" however, this reading suggests that the NHMU also makes extraction visible and transparent to visitors to show its alchemical possibilities for modern life.[85]

Rio Tinto's alliance with the NHMU has helped create a powerful cultural space that is about natural scientific curiosity and exploration. Rio Tinto is framed not only as a credible actor on the topic of science and technology but also as an educator that wants to teach publics about natural history. Rio Tinto is associated with the fun, interactive affects that occur within the NHMU's walls, which creates identifications between visitors, scientific education, and Rio Tinto. Visitors may realize they are already part of Rio Tinto's networks as they use their phones to navigate through the museum. Corporate community is thus a structure of feeling, an affect, centered on sensational forces rather than just logical appeals. This is a rhetorical force that gives Rio Tinto epistemic authority and goodwill toward the environment.

Questions and Provocations About Rio Tinto's Personae

Our corporate tour has shown how Rio Tinto adapts its persona to SLC by crafting different articulations of pioneerism. Taking one of the mobile affordances of copper, Trax, from the BCM to Daybreak, the RTS, and the NHMU, we have experienced different past and present renditions of RTS's pioneer persona that make Rio Tinto, and copper, visible. As a sort of rhetorical stew that takes care of itself, Rio Tinto becomes part of the cultural context of SLC that is constantly creating new affective relations with tourists, residents, fans, and visitors. By effect, Rio Tinto alchemically becomes an environmental steward, a cultural architect (and fan), and technologically knowledgeable. Using copper as its main resource for rhetorical invention, Rio Tinto has transformed different places and spaces into pleasurable experiences that show care for the environment.

Tapping into the "Beehive State's" motto of "industry," and the folklores of Mormon pioneerism since the time of Brigham Young, Rio Tinto embodies a "spirit of capitalism," or as Emma Bloomfield has recently put it, a "neoliberal piety," that is deeply tied to Utah's rhetoricity of place.[86] Rio Tinto, in many ways, becomes the branded image of the Beehive State. No wonder various artists, such as Jean Arnold and Jonas Lie, have pointed out the visual correlations between the mine and a hive in their artwork. As just two of many paintings of the Bingham Canyon displayed at a 2014 special exhibit at Utah Museum of Fine Arts called *Creation and Erasure: Art of the Bingham Canyon Mine*,[87] Arnold and Lie's work entitled *Civilization* and *Bingham Canyon Mine*, 1917 show how "human industrial prowess" has become deeply tied to local cultural iconographies. Like the wasp and the orchid, to Deleuze and Guattari, Rio Tinto and SLC are vital to each other's survival as an assemblage that is as a network constantly in motion and becoming-incorporated.[88]

Rio Tinto's persona is an irreducible image of a multiplicious actor that does things in the world by creating new modes of thinking, acting, and existing. As the image of a rhetor that is otherwise invisible, Rio Tinto is brought to life as an epistemic, environmental, and communal pioneer through material and discursive rhetorics in SLC. While Rio Tinto's character encounters a bundle of relations through a broad range of associations with various objects, affects, and environments, what remains constant is the condensation of Rio Tinto as a single, communal actor that associates Rio Tinto's corporate identity with the affective splendors of "the good corporate life" that come from the BCM and the more metaphoric image of the beehive. Technology is just one example of this, given our increased global dependencies on minerals and metals such as copper, tellurium, and also borax for renewable energy technologies, screens, and batteries. Is Rio Tinto creating a technological, rather than energy, utopia at SLC?

As another example of Rio Tinto's corporate persona—which recall is broadly understood as a single identity from an invisible rhetor that is otherwise multiple—this chapter has read Rio Tinto's image in SLC as an industrial pioneer strategically condenses its subjectivity to fit the needs, and pass, as a necessary citizen-subject in the community. Using copper as a base resource for alchemical rhetoric, Rio Tinto creates a localized identity that not only adapts to its changing environments but also becomes a generator of culture in SLC's "culture industry."

By creating a single image of subjectivity in SLC as a caring member of the community with goodwill, Rio Tinto can carry out rhetorical objectives within the community through a stable identity that is otherwise in constant flux. It also permits the company to remain above controversial environmental matters kept below the surface. In the winter months air pollution becomes so thick that locals struggle to see across the street, let alone the BCM, unless one stands from elevated ground at, for instance, the Utah Capitol building or the artificial "mountains" at the BCM itself. Like the visuality of the BCM, however, air pollution becomes a mundane issue that people are culturally taught to live with as they stay indoors for health concerns.

Air pollution is far from the only environmental concern that has stemmed from over one hundred years of mining at the BCM, as the mine is also responsible for more than a few "metabolic rifts" that disturb ecological systems with toxic releases of lead, arsenic, zinc, cadmium, mercury and other heavy metal contaminants.[89] In February 2004, the EPA and the Utah Department of Environmental Quality proposed listing the BCM's South Zone Site on the National Priorities List (NPL) of Superfund Sites.[90] In fact, the EPA's latest toxic release inventory reveals Utah is the fourth-most-toxic state in the United States with 90 percent of this total waste coming from the BCM. In 2018 alone, Rio Tinto reported a release of 229.2 million pounds of waste from its concentrator and smelter and refinery.[91] This extraordinary amount of waste covers 9,400 acres of land at various tailings sites and contains over two billion tons of total toxic residue.[92]

Rio Tinto exists as cascades of affects and forces that can, and oftentimes do, collide with these environmental realities. But like the labor issues at the Borax Mine, Rio Tinto's persona effectively keeps these issues at bay. In some ways, Rio Tinto's persona is simply more real than air pollution and metabolic rifts.

While it is tempting to conclude that Rio Tinto is a duplicitous agent intentionally trying to greenwash its environmental footprint, such a reading would overlook the complicated networks, relations, and forces that constitute Rio Tinto's pioneer persona, which is a reticulate set of relations that escapes such essentialisms, hence the ontological shift to the study of corporate rhetoric. Rhetorical agency, then, is irreducible to didacticism or "capitalistic agency"; it is a constellation of relations that give material and discursive networks force.[93]

Places and spaces, I have argued, are key artifacts that serve as affective support of Rio Tinto's public image. Like Borax, Rio Tinto materially summons the corporate persona to pass as a pioneer that cares about the environment, science, and culture. Unlike U.S. Borax, however, copper is made a visible part of Rio Tinto's rhetorical alchemy in a relatively large city in close proximity to the mine. While copper is typically invisible—located within circuits, networks, and batteries—Rio Tinto encourages publics of all stripes to "experience" copper at Daybreak, the RTS, and the NHMU, not to mention its corporate tour at the BCM.

At this point in the book, after having read Rio Tinto's personae at the Borax Mine and the BCM, it is becoming clearer how Rio Tinto's persona is far from a symbolic representation of Rio Tinto's "true" identity as a multinational conglomerate. Neither is it a false consciousness. Personae (*prosōpon*) are masked *performances*, or *roles*, irreducible to anything else, so the persona adopted in SLC is just one of numerous personae adapted to local audiences in the attempt to produce a passable image. Personae are multiple, and these agencies eviscerate every vestige of the Cartesian *cogito ergo sum*.

However, there are still questions of Rio Tinto's rhetorical existence in the Southwest. If Rio Tinto is a historical figure at Boron, attached to cultural memories of twenty-mule teams, Ronald Reagan, and Death Valley, does that also mean that it carries that same persona with it to Salt Lake City? Surely such persona would not pass among Salt Lake citizens the same way it does in its corporate town in the Mojave Desert, but if corporate personae *are* tokens of being, then is not Borax also Rio Tinto Kennecott? Is Rio Tinto one or many? What about all the other mines Rio Tinto manages in other parts of the world such as Mongolia, Namibia, and Australia? Are we ever dealing with the same Rio Tinto or are all these mines, and possibly different personae, always distinct? If so, how is it ever possible to hold Rio Tinto accountable as a singular actor?

Moreover, what happens when Rio Tinto's antagonisms are more rhetorically present than its persona? Or when its persona is not yet firmly established enough to keep environmental or labor issues below the surface? Do these issues ever reveal themselves as a Freudian process of cathexis in the public's consciousness? Do they then become the essence of Rio Tinto's being?

The following chapter puts us in a better position to answer some of these questions by considering one such case study where troubling matters about Rio Tinto's existence otherwise submerged have risen to the surface and taken center stage in the nation's consciousness. I take readers to a beautiful hiking and camping area in the Tonto National Forest known as Oak Flat, in Arizona. Beneath Oak Flat lies one of the last largest deposits of copper in North America. For over fifteen years Rio Tinto and BHP Billiton have been trying to extract this deposit to supply over 25 percent of the copper in America. Through its joint venture Resolution Copper, Rio Tinto gained access to the land in 2014 when Arizona politicians John McCain and Jeff Flake added the Southeast Arizona Land Exchange (SAE) to the "must pass" National Defense Authorization Bill. Essentially a land swap, the SAE gave Resolution Oak Flat, and its subterranean deposits, in exchange for 5,344 acres of private property.

Since "time immemorial," however, this place, also referred to as Chi'chil Biłdagoteel, has also been sacred ground for the Western Apache. A site of prayer, burials, petroglyphs, and coming-of-age rituals, Oak Flat on several occasions has been compared to the Apache people's "Mount Sinai." That is why an activist group called Apache Stronghold has taken up numerous initiatives— from protesting in Washington, DC, occupying Oak Flat with teepees and wikiups, and participating in several marches and caravans—to protect this sacred place. Make no mistake, the unfolding case at Oak Flat is a harrowing example of resource colonialism that is part of a living legacy of forced removal, imprisonment, and genocide of American Indian persons for extractivism.[94] We must also understand how Rio Tinto, through Resolution, crafts its rhetorical persona in this fraught circumstance.

Resolution is a case where Rio Tinto's extractive politics have overshadowed, even replaced, its rhetorical being. Unlike our previous two examples, the next chapter illustrates a case where matters otherwise submerged have risen to the surface and rhetorically overcome Rio Tinto's efforts to keep them buried. Resolution has responded to this unwanted spotlight in a myriad of ways, not least of which is by trying to create a persona capable of warding off criticism. In a struggle of life and death between Apache Stronghold and Resolution, both have vied over dominant meanings of corporation, place, and resources. In other words, this case offers a unique window through which to view Rio Tinto's persona still in formation. It also posits numerous questions about Rio Tinto's being that relate to the series of provocations noted above. If Rio Tinto is a colonial actor at Oak Flat, does that also mean it is a colonial actor at the BCM and the Borax Mine? Does Resolution's rhetorics of colonialism, or colonialities, speak to its true essence as the face behind the mask that we have been searching for all along? If so, how can we decolonize from Rio Tinto?

These questions will be answered throughout the last few remaining chapters as we encounter Rio Tinto's possible futures at Oak Flat and discuss their implications to environmental justice, rhetoric, and social change. In what follows I introduce this rhetorical exigency and make the argument that Rio Tinto's persona, while under scrutiny, attempts to stabilize its identity through "rhetorical colonialisms" that reinforce the living legacy of extractivism in this part of Arizona known as the "copper triangle."[95] Appropriating historical and presentist significations of mining in this area, Resolution materially inscribes its identity into the architecture of place with its mining apparatuses, folksy ethos, and securitized presences. Time will tell if it is enough to overcome the powerful decolonial rhetorics from groups like Apache Stronghold. As enumerated in chapter 5, these kinds of counterrhetorics for our purposes are process-oriented forms of direct action. They also use extractivism against itself by reducing Rio Tinto's essence to a subterranean politic extracted, and appropriated, by countermovements. Before determining how this kind of protest rhetoric, aka "monkey wrenching," might dismantle or jam Rio Tinto's networks of coloniality, we must foremost understand how those networks work as another, and more hotly contested, persona. For that I take readers to Superior, Arizona.

4

Extractive Coloniality at Oak Flat

Superior, Arizona is a striking mining town nestled in the Pinal Mountains at the edge of Tonto National Forest. As I drove from Phoenix on Highway 60, I approached peaks that jutted out across the Sonoran Desert with medleys of cacti below: saguaro, prickly pear, organ pipe. I arrived at dusk when the mountains just began turning to silhouettes. The aromata was intoxicating. As the desert began to breathe once more, it released euphoric scents unique to this part of Arizona. At the nexus of the Arizona-Sonoran, Central Arizonan plateaus, and the Pinal Mountains, Superior is a multilayered place with competing historicities, rhetorics, and possible futures.

One knows they have arrived in Superior when they encounter the towering five-thousand-foot cliff named Apache Leap that looms over the town (see fig. 23). As legend has it, around 1877 the US Cavalry raided an Apache tribe to advance mining interests at nearby Camp Pinal. The Apaches fought back until they found themselves at the edge of the mountain's cliff. Rather than surrender to the cavalry, scores of them leapt to their fates.[1] Hence the name. Left behind, according to myth, are shards of "translucent obsidian" named "Apache Tears" found at the base of Apache Leap and throughout Pinal County.[2]

These names are symptomatic of this region's legacy of extractive coloniality, which has coded this land, and its Indigenous persons, as extractable and exploitable.[3] As examples of rhetorical colonialism—where the Euro-centric "power of naming" has transformed and "naturalized the process of colonization"— Apache Leap and Tears conceptually "reflect and reinforce" the "colonial power[s]" that have defined this region as an "extractive zone" for white settlers and miners since colonization.[4]

As one keeps on driving east of Superior, this rhetorical situation become clearer. Here one encounters the Reymert Mine, the Carlota Copper Mine, the Pinto Valley Mine, and one of several Freeport-Mcmoran mines. These are just a few of the 380 active mines and development projects in Arizona, not counting

Fig. 23 | Apache Leap from Superior Welcome Center. Photo taken by author.

the more than 100,000 abandoned mines scattered throughout this state. No wonder Arizona's state seal features an iconic miner holding a pick and shovel beside a quartz mill. This is not to mention its state motto, *Ditat Deus* (God Enriches).[5]

Along the way, just outside of Superior, drivers pass a sign for a place in the Tonto National Forest called Oak Flat. As readers are aware by now, this is the proposed site of Rio Tinto's and BHP's future Resolution Mine. Through its joint company, Resolution Copper, Rio Tinto intends to extract one of the last of the largest deposits of copper in North America. Using a "new mining method" known as "block cave" mining methods—which undermines ore deposits allowing them to fall by their own weight—the mine would create a massive crater, or subsidence, at least one thousand feet deep. This would cause irreparable damage to soil, vegetation, wildlife, and groundwater, not to mention rocks that many boulderers consider "world class." More than that, the mine would destroy burial sites, petroglyphs, and countless other sacred sites that are central to Indigenous identities.[6]

The effects of this kind of mining are uniquely consequential for Western Apache. To the former chairman of the San Carlos Reservation—and also leader

of the social advocacy group Apache Stronghold—Wendsler Nosie Jr., the Resolution Mine is "just like Mount Sinai. . . . It's part of our identity as a people."[7] In a
2019 Environmental Impact Statement (EIS), he asked how the lost "spirituality
of our people" will "affect the future generation? How is that going to be replaced?"[8]
Because of the sanctity of this site, and the place-based identities and performances attached to it, more than a few have also argued the proposed mine is part
of the legacy of colonialism that "perpetuates the genocidal history of America."[9]

While this site currently exists under the National Forest Service's juris-
diction, the right to mine Oak Flat was transferred to Resolution Copper as a
"midnight rider" to the 2014 National Defense Act (a military spending bill) by
Arizona senators John McCain and Jeff Flake—both of whom previously
received various campaign contributions and kickbacks from both Rio Tinto
and BHP.[10] The transfer was made despite the fact that Oak Flat is protected
under the National Register of Historic Places and a bill signed by President
Eisenhower (Public Land Order 1229) banning federal mining in this area.[11]
However the Southeast Arizona Exchange (SAE), essentially a "land swap,"
exploited a loophole that since the Nixon administration allowed for the land to
be "traded to private holders" that would be exempt from such restrictions.[12]

Like the geological formations that have created these massive deposits of
copper over billions of years, this rhetorical situation is in a constant state of
change.[13] Since Congress passed the SAE there have been numerous develop-
ments, and holdups, in the extractive process, both legislatively and legally, that
can be credited to the tremendous rhetorical force of Apache Stronghold, which
has helped make protecting Oak Flat a national priority.

As I write, Resolution is barred from extracting copper from this site because
of President Biden's recent rescission of the Final Environmental Impact Statement—which is a necessary part of the land transfer under the National Environmental Policy Act (NEPA). After President Trump tried to expedite the
process in his final days of office, Biden's position came as a relief to many. There
is, however, room for doubt. For instance, in a lawsuit filed by Apache Stronghold that recently went to the US Court of Appeals for the Ninth Circuit,
Biden's Department of Justice held that a lower court was right to deny the
injunction because the group could not "establish that they will suffer irreparable harm absent preliminary relief."[14] The court also suggested only Congress
can provide the Indigenous community environmental relief through its ple-
nary powers. This is why so much weight is currently being placed on the fourth
version of the Save Oak Flat Act introduced by Raúl Grijalva, which would

entirely reverse the SAE. Currently being considered as a possible amend-
ment to Biden's Infrastructure Bill, the Save Oak Flat Act, like Oak Flat itself,
has an uncertain future, considering the living legacy of extractive colonialism
in this region.[15]

This exigency shows how Rio Tinto manages its persona when that very
identity is the object of intense debate, derision, and protest. Recall how Rio
Tinto has recently come under fire for its destruction of sacred Aboriginal sites
in Western Australia's Juukan Gorge that date back forty-six thousand years.[16]
Since firing its CEO, Rio Tinto has been working on repairing its image to prevent conflict with Indigenous communities, which has everything to do with
(mis)managing its corporate persona.

While Apache Stronghold members and supporters call out and name
Resolution as colonial and even genocidal—which is something I analyze in
the following chapter—Resolution doubles down its economic and communal
rhetorics in its efforts to neutralize the situation. Producing an image of a job-
producing actor vital to many different environmental, economic, and civic
futures, Rio Tinto taps into legacies of industrial mining in the Pioneer District
to which many, at least in Superior, already adhere.

Like both Borax and RTK, much of this historical work is already part of the
composition of cities in which they dwell. Let us take a closer look at Superior,
which plays a significant role in Rio Tinto's politicking as the site of its second
persona, or "implied auditors."[17] This is also the location of Rio Tinto's regional
headquarters and main offices.

In the wake of many different kinds of "conquest," Superior stands as a
modern-day mining colony celebrated for its extractive pasts, presents, and possible futures.[18] In fact, the town and its mining communities have historically
moved with its mines. For example, when prospectors discovered massive
amounts of pure silver in 1875 at what became known as the Silver King Mine—
hailed as "the richest silver mine in Arizona history"—the site was several miles
northeast of present-day Superior in Picket Post, or Pinal City.[19] By 1890,
though, all the silver was depleted and the community was forced to migrate
toward the Silver King's companion mine, the Silver Queen, located on the out-
skirts of what is now Superior.[20] Not long after silver was extracted from this
new site, prospectors discovered substantial deposits of another precious metal
at what became known as the Magma Mine: copper.[21]

Over the Magma Mine's eighty-six-year lifespan, it has produced 27.6 million short tons of copper, making it one of the most productive copper mines

in Arizona's history, and it is remembered as such.[22] Because of Superior's many different "booms and busts" that have directly impacted the livelihoods of miners, many locals see themselves as a "resilient and proud community."[23]

Even though the Magma Mine is no longer in operation, its legacy has an indelible imprint on this community, which is affectively felt at places such as the Miners on Main Café, the Silver King Smokehouse and Saloon, and the Copper Mountain Motel. This is not to mention all the trails and mining artifacts that offer locals and visitors recreation with a bit of minerology. For example, from the Legends of Superior Trail, hikers can walk the trail that miners, and their community, moved over the years since its early Pinal days. Starting at the "Picketpost Trailhead," hikers walk through the "Pinal Townsite," where miners lived during the heyday of the Silver King Mine before following the trail through town—where the Magma Mine led to prosperous lives in Superior—and continue onward toward the Historic Claypool Tunnel, which made it possible for nearby copper mines from Globe and Miami to transfer ore to milling facilities in Superior while en route to Phoenix.[24] Along the way hikers encounter all sorts of residuals from mining pasts. In addition to old mining carts and their tracks, hikers, for instance, can marvel at the imprints from wagons and mules that were so heavy from hauling ore their tracks are visibly etched into stone to this day.[25]

Linking this beautiful scenery with mining once more shows the many connections between mining pasts and lived experiences with nature. Even though many mining activities have ceased, its legacy lives on through places that have been alchemically transformed by its historical imprint for the betterment of society. To authentically experience and enjoy nature, per Senda-Cook, is in this case to implicitly appreciate mining pasts.[26] Another example, briefly, is the Boyce Thompson Arboretum located just outside of town. Just down the street from a small mining park that welcomes visitors to Superior, this arboretum features more than six thousand plant species from deserts across the world to create a spectacular place for outdoor enthusiasts to walk, learn, or meditate. Importantly, Boyce Thompson was a famous mining engineer who worked at Magma. After moving to Superior in 1923, he purchased the land of the former Pinal City and created the arboretum by 1929 with his mining wealth and created a beautiful environment of nature as pristine.[27]

Resolution attaches itself to the extractive genealogy of Resolution as a parent-like figure that has inherited the legacy of mining and is committed to carrying the colonial torch. In this narrative, Resolution is the historian, memorialist, and archivist of an extractive colonial legacy. Although Resolution did not yet exist during the days of the Magma Copper Company, it nevertheless appropriates memories of Magma in the present to connect its ethos with a legacy of extractivism persuasive to many locals, such as those that visit places such as Miners on Main Café, the Silver King Saloon, and the Copper Mountain Motel.

So revered was the Magma company that its former smelter, the Magma Smelter, was commemorated as a monument to mining pasts when Resolution was forced to take it down in 2008 as part of its land reclamation.[28] Even the mayor of Superior, Mila Besich, spoke of its significance and its homage to the "next mine":

> As we bid farewell to the smelter stack, we are reminded of all that it has represented to generations of our citizens. It is an iconic reminder of every miner, engineer, craftsman and staff who have worked the Magma mine.... We will miss seeing this important and historic structure from our skyline, but we also celebrate the new era that is before us today—a new mine, abundant economic and community development opportunities, and our community working together to create greater opportunities for the benefit of all—not only for today but for future generations. Superior's best days are truly ahead of us, and together we will establish Superior's growth and prosperity in the twenty-first century.[29]

Resolution pays homage to Magma by preserving images, oral histories, and material objects of its past through the hired consultant firm, Westland Resources. This archival project includes a collection of maps, photographs, and company records in addition to aerial photography of existing structures; interviews with fourteen persons who once worked for Magma for a video history of the mine; and the commemoration of the Magma Smelter that was removed in 2008. These practices reinforce a landmarked extractive history of the community.[30] In commemorating historic mining artifacts and using them to construct a prideful and romantic history of mining, beginning with the arrival of white colonial settlers and prospectors, Resolution materially performs the living legacy of extractivism in Arizona's Pioneer Mining District.

Resolution also structurally reinforces its evolutive colonial presence through mining shafts. For instance, Resolution has poured $200 million into "rehabilitating" a mining shaft constructed, and formerly owned, by Magma.[31] To meet

Fig. 24 | Resolution's mining shafts. Photo taken by author.

the extractivist needs of Resolution in the present, Resolution contracted engineering company Hatch to deepen the mining shaft by two thousand feet to bring it to the celebrated depth of seven thousand feet, as told at Resolution's office.[32] Completed in 2021, the two shafts stand as monuments to the continued legacy of copper mining in this region (see fig. 24). It is also worth noting that when the mining project is approved, these mining shafts will tower over Oak Flat's inevitable subsidence from their elevated position as witnesses, or overseers, to annihilation. In fact, they will be all that remains of this site.

These archival efforts facilitate the extractive view of this site through the naming of objects, places, and spaces in the "Copper Triangle."[33] In retrieving and preserving data of this place's mining past, Resolution provides archaeological evidence for its extractive public vocabulary that labels this site part of "Arizona's historic mining district," where "copper mining has been the driving force of Arizona's economy for over a century."[34] This historicity implies that *copper itself hailed Resolution*. As such, *responsibility is shifted to the land rather than the company*. As beholder of Arizona's extractive genealogies, Resolution is authorized to advance its mining plans with impunity. Similar to how Rio Tinto becomes an epistemic authority on Utah's geology at the Natural History Museum of Utah, Resolution here is made a historical subject that knows the land, the people, and their extractive needs. Through a careful construction of the past, using selective archival material as testimonial evidence that is linked to its naming practices, Resolution rhetorically calcifies an extractive genealogy contingent upon the erasure of Indigenous persons, cultures, and identities that once thrived in this area prior to their forced removal.

These are some of the ways that Rio Tinto attempts to create a genealogical image of a paternalistic company at the apex of a mining legacy already instantiated in the architecture of place. For all intents and purposes, without Rio Tinto (and its former companies) Superior remains a corporate town without a corporate subject. Rio Tinto thus not only appropriates cultural memories of mining pasts but fills possible needs for the meaning of the town and validates its rhetorical mode of existence. The Resolution Mine, to many, is symbolic for the next generation of mining in this potentially nostalgic community longing for its next "boom" cycle.

While Rio Tinto is working diligently to solidify a passable corporate persona through different alchemical rhetorics, Apache Stronghold attempts to essentialize it as colonial and genocidal. For now, Apache Stronghold is winning the rhetorical battle being waged over the future of Oak Flat, which is illustrative of how subterranean matters noted in the past few chapters (class, race, colonialism) can at times rise to the surface, as a form of cathexis, in ways that pose real rhetorical and environmental challenges for Rio Tinto. The struggle, no doubt, is one that revolves around competing valuations of place.[35] To Rio Tinto, Oak Flat is the last largest deposit of copper necessary for securing viable economic futures. To San Carlos Apache, Oak Flat is home.

From these symbolic and material rhetorics, Rio Tinto and its local and political allies attempt to secure a legacy of extractivism that unfortunately comes with tremendous environmental injustices for affected communities. Below I walk readers through this volatile rhetorical situation in the Copper Triangle. I begin with a tour of Superior and Oak Flat that highlights Resolution's folksy, but securitized, affects that constitute "the people." I then develop this tour showing how Resolution uses these affects to build a paternalistic persona of cultural and environmental significance.

Resolution and "the People" of Superior

Rio Tinto is in a unique rhetorical situation in Superior. Whereas at its other mines, its corporate persona is part of the dominant rhetorical frames that define the meanings of extractivism, it faces higher rhetorical burdens in this part of Arizona. No doubt, Rio Tinto is in a tremendous position of power and privilege; however, the decolonial rhetorics from Apache Stronghold members and supporters also create more constraints for possible action than Boron or Salt Lake City.

As suggested earlier, Resolution appropriates cultural memories of mining pasts to pass as the next mining company to give the town new, transformative meanings. I argue that Resolution does this through a sort of paternalistic folksiness that becomes consubstantial with "the people." To Michael Calvin McGee, "the people" is an ideographic accomplishment that can "short circuit . . . reasoning processes" in ways that constitute persons as part of a larger, fictionalized body politic that has everything to do with a rhetoricized "people's history."[36] McGee writes, "The people . . . are not objectively real in the sense that they exist as a collective entity in nature; rather, they are a fiction dreamed up by an advocate and infused with an artificial, rhetorical reality by the agreement of an audience to participate in a collective fantasy."[37] Such is the nature of "the people" at Superior where Resolution appropriates historical narratives of extractivism with which these people collectively identify.

While Resolution may be part of a global empire that Apache Stronghold names colonial, dominant publics in Superior see the company as the most recent mining company to instantiate town and its persons with "booming" significance. Magma, the most recent and long-lasting company to mine this area, ended operations in 1996 after it was purchased by BHP Billiton for $3.2 billion.[38] The meaning of Superior as a mining town was empty and left with mounds of mining waste on the outskirts of town where Magma once primarily operated. What is a mining town without an active mine or a company to extract its ore?

When Rio Tinto (55 percent) partnered with BHP (45 percent) that same year under the joint venture Resolution—as one of the post-Magma "results of these write-offs"—the company began to fill a rhetorical void by serving Superior, and its people, as a sort of "medicine man" capable of curing these people from their nostalgic ills.[39] Resolution does this by restoring Superior's dreams of prosperous futures through a folksy persona that blends in with historical pasts. Giving the impression that mining builds wealthy mining towns and is forever sustainable, as a sort of treadmill model of rural capitalism, Resolution appropriates a rhetorical "fiction" about the life and legacy of mining.

Resolution's rhetorical presence is mundane but visible enough to securely present itself as the most recent historical mining actor. Taking on the characteristics

Fig. 25 | Miners on Main Café. Photo taken by author.

of a town shaped over one hundred years of mining, inclusive of its range of small shops with historic pictures, wooden benches, and different historic mining arti-facts, Resolution mixes with the architecture to alchemically create a benign, but essential, presence.

I began my search at 7:00 a.m. at the Miners on Main Café (see fig. 25). When I entered the door, I suddenly found myself in the 1950s. Did I somehow enter a time machine? I was surrounded by midcentury portraits, vintage ads, kitchenware, and booths. Back to the future? I took my seat at the counter and was offered coffee.

I talked with the waitress about the café and the meaning of mining in the community. After telling me about the café's claims to fame—which was fea-tured in several movies including *Eight Legged Freaks*, *U Turn*, and *How the West Was Won*—she spoke with enthusiasm about mining pasts and presents, suggesting various places to visit. Regarding the proposed Resolution Mine spe-cifically, she said with downcast eyes that progress had been stalled. Many min-ers and engineers had been waiting for promised jobs for more than ten years, she said, but because the mine had not yet begun operations, many were forced to leave town. She also took somewhat of a fatalistic standpoint about environ-mental futures. Since the planet is already more or less destroyed, she suggested, folks might as well do what they can to make money (from the mine) to work with what is already provided. Why not keep going?

Superior is instantiated with this kind of borderline melancholic, yet spirited, mining culture. Places such as the café preserve memories of Magma and the miners that once called this town their home. Walking around downtown after breakfast, I encountered numerous plaques commemorating past miners, colorful murals depicting different Indigenous and mining communities, and various shops and points of interest with mining paraphernalia, all of which created a friendly, folksy mood of a town, perhaps, struggling to hold on without a mine in town.

A few blocks down on Main Street, adjacent to the Silver King Smokehouse and Saloon—of which was decorated with festive mining décor in its outside patio, including a mining frame and "Silver King" written on a lean-to—I came across a small office with many different mining memorabilia in its windowsills next to two wooden benches with many different carvings, one of which read "Rio Tinto." Hanging above the small office was a handcrafted, stained sign that read "Resolution Copper" (see fig. 26). Behold, as written on the wooden doors, this was Resolution Copper's Mine Information Office. Was this the same colonial subject Apache Stronghold has accused of genocide? The office was so seemingly innocuous.

The office, sadly, had been closed because of COVID-19 restrictions, so I was unable to extend my tour inside and ask questions. Even still, I was able to window shop for clues about its rhetorical presence in Superior. On the sills were many different objects, signs, and photos visible from the outside. The most discernable was a rather large screen that showed different slides about the company and the proposed Resolution mine. Some of these slides showed historical images with small captions about the Silver King Mine in the 1880s, twenty-mule teams that hauled ore from it, and downtown Superior in the early 1900s. Others showed images of two towering mining shafts at Oak Flat, the #9 and #10, with facts about these shaft-made-monuments (especially #10). Apparently, at seven thousand feet deep, Resolution's recently completed #10 shaft is the deepest of its kind in the United States. So deep is the shaft, it takes about fifteen minutes to "ride to the bottom" and the temperatures in these underlands "can reach near 175 degrees," which apparently creates the need for the "autonomous vehicles."

Other slides tell more about the specific project at hand and speak directly to the controversy by pointing out "myths" and "facts."

Fig. 26 | Resolution's information office. Photo taken by author.

MYTH: The local economic benefits of the project will be short lived.
FACT: Once in operation the Resolution Copper mine could supply up to one-quarter of the nation's copper demand.

Another slide with a different image provides the same "myth" with a different "fact": "When the mine is fully operational, Resolution Copper expects to support 3,700 direct and indirect jobs, paying around $270 million per year in total compensation. The project is expected to contribute up to $61 billion in Economic Revenue for Arizona over the project's 60-year estimated life."

More slides demythologize similar apparent falsehoods:

MYTH: The Land Exchange was slipped into legislation in the middle of the night.
FACT: Legislation to facilitate the land exchange between the Tonto National Forest and Resolution Copper passed with bipartisan support in December 2014. It was signed into law by President Obama.

And:

> MYTH: Once the Land Exchange is completed the public will no longer
> have access to areas in Oak Flat, including the campground."
> FACT: We will maintain public access to areas within Oak Flat including
> the campground and recreational trails and climbing, after completion
> of the Land Exchange. We will work with a local small business part-
> owned by members of an Arizona Native Tribe to maintain the camp-
> ground areas infrastructure and access trails.

Debunking what it sees as "myths" Resolution rhetorically "sets the facts straight"
to reestablish itself as not just a contributing member of the community but an
authority capable of sifting through truths and untruths. One of several ironies
about these slides is that these slides are used to affirm Resolution's own "political myth" about its persona. "Short circuiting" processes of reason, or warrant-
ing claims, these corporate mythologies are important indicators of how
Resolution constitutes "the people."[40] A sign is taped on the window: "We're
proud of our efforts at being a good neighbor, but there's always room for
improvement. We welcome your feedback through our Community Complaint
e-mail and phone line."

Surrounding the screen are photos of miners in hard hats in front of the #10
shaft, stacks of (copper) pennies, a bottle of Centrum (which contains copper as
part of its dietary supplement), copper pipes and fittings, and a rock commemorating the "last blast" of the #10 shaft on November 17, 2014. Inside the office I
see many more mining "things," including a posterboard of Resolution employees, awards, and a timeline that borders the walls, enveloping the room. Starting
in the early nineteenth century, the timeline tells the story of how metallic minerals such as copper, silver, and gold have been drivers of prosperity, not least
through mining companies and their industrialization. In 1873, the timeline
says, about the time when "silver miners arrived in Hayden" (another nearby
mining town), "The Rio Tinto Company is formed to mine the ancient copper
workings in Spain." Sixteen years later, Phoenix became the "territorial capital."

Slipping in that Rio Tinto was part of the legacy of mining in Arizona, even
when it was mining copper in Huelva, Spain, is once more suggestive of how the
company alchemically incorporates its history into its presentist identity. As if
Rio Tinto were there all along waiting to benefit the people of Superior with the
Resolution Mine, the timeline sows its spawn, Resolution, in Arizona's linear

Fig. 27 | Resolution's West Plant. Photo taken by author.

narrative when it was created in 2002 by Rio Tinto and BHP. Since then, the company has "transition[ed] to manager of the Resolution Project," witnessed the original introduction of the SAE, and "conducted" a "feasibility study." Then the timeline stops. With an uncertain future, Resolution is hanging on a limb waiting to, potentially, benefit Superior and its people with its proposed copper mine.

Without being able to enter the office building, I continued my walk down Main Street, entered my car, and drove to what is called Resolution's West Plant. Recalling my directions from the waitress at the Miners on Main Café—down Magma Avenue, past Lime, Porphyry, and Copper Street—I took my search to what seemed like the "shiny city on top of the hill" (see fig. 27).

There was a very different mood at the West Plant. Rather than the folksy and friendly vibe from the information office, this was a securitized place closer to a small fortress than a visitor's center. With two main gates regulating the flows of traffic, and a multilayered retaining wall behind what appeared to be a visitor's booth, I grew anxious. The confusion was also due in part because of the numerous official vehicles parked around the site and perhaps the flagpole in front of the building. I was also unsure where to park since there were no discernable parking spaces before the gated entrance. Should I park on a side street and walk up to the visitor's booth or drive up to the gate?

I drove toward the gate hoping to speak to someone. Nobody appeared, but I noticed three parking spaces adjacent to the entrance so slowly moved in that direction. I was confused where, or how to park, though, because of the relatively small spaces to park. The lanes themselves were wide enough but vertically limited, for there were yellow hash marks perpendicular to the parking lines and bumps several feet from the end of the lane. Was I supposed to drive over the bumps?

I parked in the middle lane and exited the car and took two or three steps when I was almost tackled by a security employee. "Stop!" she said. Her voice was harsh, and I felt as if I had done something wrong and was about to be accosted. *Did she think I was a terrorist?*

Then I was told to walk along the "the crosswalk," but all I saw were yellow hazard lines. Crosswalks are usually white. Could these lines be the crosswalk that she was referring? As I contemplated what to do, she again told me to stop. How can I walk on this crosswalk, which I could not see, and stop at the same time?

"What do you want?" she curtly asked as I stood their paralyzed by my confusion. I tried to explain that I was working on a project about Rio Tinto and wondered if I could enter the building and talk with employees. Not sure what lay inside—a visitor's center akin to what I encountered at Borax or the BCM, offices full of computers and assays, or something else (a vault of copper?)—I stated the nature of my research but was cut off with a curt reply: "Call the Media Hotline and leave."

The contrast between Resolution's folksy persona at its information office, and the securitized rhetorics I felt here, were palpable. This did not seem like the Resolution described by my waitress hours prior. How could Resolution be both friendly and personable while also counterterrorist? As I pondered the meaning of this contradiction for Rio Tinto, I took a cue from the security office and immediately left the premises. Next stop Oak Flat.

Visiting Oak Flat

I went to the Oak Flat Campground to see, and feel, its place-based rhetorics for myself.[41] Potentially, this would help me make sense of Resolution's competing

Fig. 28 | Teepee and wikiup at Oak Flat. Photo taken by author.

affects felt in Superior. I had originally intended to camp at Oak Flat for the duration of my stay, but when I arrived in Superior the night before with my camping gear, I quickly realized it was monsoon season. Camping would not be wise. That is also why, I was told later by an employee at the San Carlos Cultural Museum, members of Apache Stronghold were also not there.

Following Highway 60 to "Magma Road," I entered the Oak Flat Campground for my afternoon hike. Here I saw what "stronghold" meant as I encountered a teepee, several wikiups, and a fenced area that resembles a fort (see fig. 28). All of this creates powerful Indigenous presence, or survivance, that defiantly occupies a place articulated by Rio Tinto as nothing more than a sacrifice zone. How does one pay respects to this scared site or mourn its possible future loss?

I meditated for several hours at the Oak Flat Campground. Thinking about the pasts, presents, and possible futures of this site, in situ, I allowed my body and its breaths to become part of the dense ecologies of this place. Stillness was also an important part of my meditative practice, which was knowingly anathema to dominant extractive aesthetics that thrive off dominant tropes of mobility that constantly compel bodies to move, especially through fossil fuels and metals that make them "go."[42] Can meditation also be a decolonial praxis?

I walked along several trails and observed the many different plants and flow-ers along the way. What would happen to all these species, and different insects and animals, postsubsidence? Could they survive a one-thousand-foot plummet below earth? I thought about these questions of life and death as I encountered a burned area that was indicated by signs on the road to the Oak Flat Camp-ground. As signs of regenerative life began to visibly flourish, I wondered if it was possible that Oak Flat could do the same over tens, hundreds, or thou-sands of years.

The prospects of ecological survival weighed heavily on me as I lightly plod-ded along the trail. Do Emory Oaks grow in craters? I think of images of the Meteor Crater Natural Landmark and even the moon as I walk toward several signs of protest.

As I walk toward a colorful wooden sign that says "Protect Oak Flat," out of nowhere, I hear a rather large buzzing sound that seems to be getting nearer and louder. An airplane? A helicopter? Armageddon? After listening so intently to the stillness and quietness of this site that is sacred to so many, this sound was a discernable disturbance to my meditative state. After about two minutes of strong hissing and whirring, the apparatus disappeared as quickly as it arrived. It was a drone. I was being watched.

As I searched for the flying apparatus in the skies, I set my gaze on two min-ing headframes in the distance. These must be the two mining shafts celebrated at Resolution's information office. On an elevated ledge at least two miles away, the #9 and #10 shafts oversaw the entire ecological crisis waiting to unfold. Try-ing not to dwell on the possibility that my every move was being surveilled, I moved onward and encountered the different signs of protest and tokens of Indigeneity, focusing more closely on the heteronomies of space between Oak Flat-as-home and Oak Flat-as-Copper Mine.

This spatial juxtapositioning was made clearer as I walked further toward some ribbons that I noticed in the distance. Here are four multicolored crosses representative of the elements of Apache identity that come from this sacred place: water, animals, oak trees, and other plants (see fig. 29). Apache Strong-hold has created a powerful decolonial space that takes back Oak Flat from extractive visualities. As Resolution's mining shafts gaze at Oak Flat from its colonial nest, Oak Flat "looks back" and challenges its epistemic ordering of this place as mine.[43] "This Destruction Will Not Stop Us: The World & Our Cre-ator Is Watching," says a nearby sign.

Fig. 29 | Four crosses at Oak Flat. Photo taken by author.

As it seems, these different protest signs are not just meaningful to the community that put them there but also potentially for wider media dissemination. This is further evidenced by the various lights placed at the base of the crosses, which were also apparent at the "stronghold" and teepee. Do these lights illuminate these signs of protest at night? Would those lights be visible from Resolution's extractive hill?

Regardless, that is where we must go next at least to possibly get some answers to our lingering questions. From this vantage point Rio Tinto certainly does not create a folksy and inviting mood. If anything, overlord. To be sure, I followed Magma Road to the top of the hill.

There I encountered, unsurprisingly, a gated entrance with security signs warning drivers that the place was private property off-limits to visitors: "NO TRESPASSING. PRIVATE PROPERTY. This property is under video surveillance," and a stop sign that read, "Do not proceed beyond this point until instructed by Security" (see fig. 30).

I parked my rental car on the side of the road and approached the gate. At least with a fence, I thought, I knew the rules and could not potentially get

Fig. 30 | Entrance to Resolution's East Plant at Oak Flat. Photo taken by author.

tackled. Sure enough a hard-hat employee walked toward me and asked about the nature of my business. I asked about the possibility of entering the facility to take pictures. As I was trying to explain the nature of my project, as I had before, I began to hear how ridiculous I must have sounded. Standing before a gated fence with security cameras pointed at me on contested land that had made headlines for more than a decade. I was once more told to call the media contact. At least this time I was given a business card. I called and left a message but never heard back.

Resolution's Paternalistic Persona

What do these tours tell us about Resolution's corporate persona? Foremost we must recognize Resolution's rhetorical persona as an example of extractive coloniality. By extractive coloniality, I mean the rhetorical ways in which Rio Tinto warrants modern/colonial ambitions through extractivism, and this rhetorical technique is made clear in the materiality of Superior itself, which stabilizes a legacy of resource colonialism on Indigenous land.[44] By imbuing a folksy and secure rhetorical identity into the architecture of town, Rio Tinto "seals" Superior as its extractivist "home."[45]

Resolution, however, does not see itself as a colonialist but as a business partner of the people that knows their needs and the needs of Indigenous persons that call Oak Flat home. Through the circulation of folksy, yet secure, affects, Resolution crafts a paternalistic persona that suggests, despite so much tumult, Superior's extractive legacy is in good hands. This corporate persona attempts to create a codependent relationship with Indigenous populations that masks its intrinsic colonialities. This persona has its roots in Western colonial practices that extirpated American Indians in the nineteenth century. As Jason Edward Black has argued, the US government created a masked "paternal persona" that stabilized father-child relations with Native American communities through the rhetorical embodiment of a "republican fatherhood" that was the "agent of civic preparedness."[46] In horribly violent ways, this persona facilitated Native American assimilation, removal, and allotment leading up to the Indian Removal Act.[47]

Similarly, Resolution produces a localized rhetorical presence as the father-like steady hand of Superior's possible futures. Through the folksy façade mixed in with the terrifying security, Resolution is a father-like image that is friendly but frightening, that promises assistance with securing your future but is also ready to mete out punishment if you misstep. These characteristics are consistent with the US government's persona in the nineteenth century that, argues Jason Edward Black, were used to rhetorically warrant American Indian extirpation.[48] Like Rio Tinto's personae in SLC and Boron, Resolution's persona is uniquely adapted to place in ways that ossify extractivist codings of the land.

Resolution becomes a meaning-making teller of history that with paternalistic authority passes on its genealogy to future generations. While the history of mining in this region predates Resolution by many years, Resolution nevertheless creates a unified history of mining in Arizona from a patchwork of archival texts and objects. Resolution positions itself as the most recent incarnation of a genealogy of corporate mining in Arizona that "knows" how to handle emergent cultural and environmental challenges.

As I further discuss below, Resolution's paternalistic corporate persona is made culturally sensitive to local Indigenous concerns even though its proposed mine would destroy a religiously significant site. Through tokenism, Resolution extracts and exploits Indigenous personalities from the San Carlos Tribe, assumes it knows best about tribal concerns, and speaks on behalf of their needs. Additionally, in response to environmental criticisms, Resolution shifts environmental discourse from preservationism to conservationism and emphasizes that its company knows best how to carry it out. Similar to how Rio Tinto responds to environmental challenges in SLC with arguments about the necessity of copper for sustainability, Resolution frames a narrative of environmental futures through an ethic of conservationism that is dependent on, rather than competitive with, extractivism. This rhetorical alchemy is how Rio Tinto adapts its persona to pass as a member of the community that not just shares but carries out the legacy of mining in this part of Arizona. I develop these rhetorical expressions below as different parts of Resolution's paternalistic persona.

Resolution as Culturally Sensitive

Resolution's paternalistic persona attempts to "pass" as culturally sensitive to Indigenous persons and issues. For instance, throughout its website, and in various public releases, Resolution claims to cooperate with Indigenous stakeholders, maintain federal compliance relating to sacred sites, and protect areas of cultural significance. These claims articulate Resolution as a multicultural corporate subject that uses indigeneity itself as an extractable commodity, or token, that enhances Resolution's image.

Tokenism broadly refers to the construction of a persona from a person belonging to a marginalized or oppressed group who is given latitude to speak as "a culture hero" but only insofar as those narratives reinforce dominant cultures, ideologies, and hegemonies.[49] Resolution extracts and appropriates the presumed indigeneity of a tokenized employee as an extractable commodity to communicate cultural sensitivity from the extractive view. In numerous online videos called "On Site with Mike," Resolution uses Indigenous tokenism through its Native Affairs Coordinator, Mike Betom, to convey cultural sensitivity as an expression of its paternalistic persona. In one video entitled "Protecting Cultural Resources," Resolution, through Betom, says, "We rely on local knowledge ideas and culture to find the right balance between economic development and protecting cultural heritage."[50] Elsewhere, Betom suggests miners have always coexisted with Indigenous persons, recreationalists, campers, and ranchers. Resolution thus carries on that tradition as a multicultural subject that is cooperative, flexible, and tolerant of alternative meanings of place.

As an extension of Resolution's persona, tokenism allows Resolution to lay claim to cultural sensitivity by more or less "playing Indian," using American

Indian symbols, iconography, and personalities for anti-Indigenous, extractivist motivations.[51] While Betom enables Resolution to acquire new cultural agencies, we must also consider the sovereign agency of Betom in deciding to work for Resolution even though, as Endres notes, those decisions uphold rather than challenge colonialism through "self-colonization."[52]

In an interview with Laura Redniss, author of the recently published illustrative book *Oak Flat: A Fight for Sacred Land in the American Southwest*, Betom discloses how his decision to work with Resolution, rather than against, is coming from a desire to "better [his] community" by creating new possibilities for partnerships with the company (e.g., economic, educational, social).[53] He knows his "On Site with Mike" videos are met with mixed reactions from fellow members of the San Carlos Tribe, but he sees himself as a solution-oriented individual rather than just focusing on problems. "We have to pick and choose our battles," he notes, speaking of the lack of economic and social opportunities on the reservation. "I want to be an advocate for my community, so San Carlos can actually be at the table."[54]

It is hard to fault Betom for making this decision. At the same time, we must also recognize how that choice allows Resolution to appropriate his voice on behalf of entire tribes and nations to advance its exploitative goals at Oak Flat. This form of rhetorical colonialism expresses cultural sensitivity without acknowledging Indigenous claims to sovereignty. Also a form of epistemological injustice, this view reinforces the idea that corporate settlers are the knowing authorities burdened with civilizing natives, which historically led to horrific acts of cultural, sexual, and physical violence against natives in public schools.[55] As an extension of its paternalistic persona, Resolution extracts cultures and persons to exert rhetorical authority to define place, values, and Indigenous needs.[56]

Resolution as Conservationist

Resolution's persona also portrays care for the environment. Through various videos, images, and press releases, Resolution creates an ethos of an environmental steward that can be trusted to do what is best for the land in the Sonoran Desert. As a protector, manager, and inventor, Resolution is rendered a knowing corporate subject that conserves *through* extraction. For instance, Resolution invokes a paternalistic "wise use" ideology that deflects the need for governmental regulation.[57] As part of its sanctioned land swap, thousands of acres of otherwise private land were given to the forest service, including particular ranches known as 7B Ranch and the Research Ranch, where environmental firms such as the Nature Conservancy exist as caretakers of its biodiversity and resources.[58] These acts enable Resolution to shift environmental discourse from preservationism to conservationism in ways that benefit its extractive practices in the name of the dominant "public interest."[59]

Resolution is not just a steward; it is, alchemically, a creator of land. Through various reclamational projects, Resolution asserts the claim that it adds to, rather than depletes, the environmental landscape. For instance, in a video on Resolution's reclamation projects, the company, through Betom, boasts how the company is reclaiming land affected by tailings from Magma. In "reshaping and revegetating the land," Betom states, Resolution will "leave a positive legacy for the community and surrounding area."[60] Elsewhere, Resolution claims to attend to "long term stability and environmental protection" by thinking carefully about its future tailings site, which will also be reclaimed. These comments suggest that Resolution is a creator of new environments that will be conserved and reclaimed (e.g., tailings). Reclamation after all can only occur after a site has been environmentally compromised. Like the *Río Tinto* (the river), Resolution is capable of alchemically transforming some of the most unlikely base ingredients to golden realities.

Resolution also invokes rhetorics of reclamation by suggesting that the company will conserve billions of gallons of water used at the Magma Mine, which will help thousands of acres of farmland for irrigation. Resolution's reclamation rhetoric, then, suggests that from extraction comes new possibilities for conserving environmental landscapes. To Resolution, landscapes are always changing, and as a creative environmental steward the company is reshaping the meaning of place in inventive and responsible ways. The 3,583 acres of anticipated tailings from the mine and also the 16,000 to 20,000 acre-feet of water that will be used every year are framed as positive alterations to the environmental landscape, because from them will come new vegetative growth, water conservancy, and better land practices.[61]

Resolution is made a paternalistic subject that wants to be trusted to conserve nature and its resources, creating a codependent relationship with not just genealogy or the people and their cultures but also the land. Rather than an environmental destroyer, Resolution is made a steward that through its inheritance of the earth is engaging in "wise use" practices that displace needs for regulation.[62]

The Politics of Resolution's Persona

While Resolution's personalities may be disparate, they are smoothed over through its corporate persona, which gives each personality local presence. These differences, though, are also important in and of themselves because they are reflective of how Rio Tinto maintains many different, and sometimes contradictory, personalities and agencies throughout the world as actors at many different places at once. For instance, while Resolution builds relations in Chi'chil Biłdagoteel as a paternalistic subject, it simultaneously exists in many different parts of the world through Rio Tinto and BHP's vast networks. Rio Tinto, recall, manages 60 other mines in thirty other countries.[63] BHP has at least 43 different mining operations in ten different countries, not to mention 420 global mining subsidiaries.[64] Most of BHP's mines are in Australia, South Africa, and South America, but the company also has plans to take over the San Juan Coal Mine in New Mexico. It may be reasonable to assume that part of the reason BHP is linked with Rio Tinto for Resolution is that Rio Tinto has built the reputation in the West as a pioneer.

Corporate ontologies exist as wild networks, especially in neoliberal economies, that are better understood as assemblages than subjects. Nevertheless, personae as material and discursive rhetorical inventions create rhetorical identities that create feelings of localized presence and care. While Resolution may not entirely smooth its different personalities at Oak Flat, its paternalistic persona nevertheless holds them together in ways that pass as a singular actor with goodwill. With this ethos comes new extractive agencies.

As a father-like figure trying to protect its legacy and securitize its territory, Resolution employs genealogical, cultural, and environmental rhetorics to not just warrant but protect its extractive practices—hence the securitization felt when at both the West and East Plant, not to mention feelings of being surveilled.

As Resolution attempts to create an image of paternalism that is both folksy and secure, neighboring members of San Carlos Apache are forced to bear intersectional injustices from these colonial practices, including but not limited to, exposure to toxic waste (tailings), depletion of water supplies and risks of contamination, and loss of sacred sites and other ecologies attached to Oak Flat.[65] In short, while Resolution extracts from afar, Indigenous communities stay and endure. Through Resolution's paternalism, they are told doing so is in their best interest.

As I discuss further in the following chapter, Resolution's corporate persona is also a possible line of flight. As Indigenous actors and activists such as Winona LaDuke, Tara Houska, Nick Estes, and Dana Powell have argued, struggles against extraction and energy projects—for example, Standing Rock Sioux's fight against the Dakota Access Pipeline (DAPL), Navajo (Diné) Nation's art and activism against the Desert Rock Power Plant, and Ojibwe Tribe's ongoing struggles against Enbridge's proposed Line Number 3—can become generative struggles for sovereignty and survivance.[66] Precisely because personae are rhetorical inventions that both shape, and are shaped by, rhetorics of place, they can also be disciplined, appropriated, or "jammed" in ways that "talk back" and "unmask" corporate personae.[67] Through strategies of unmasking, local affected communities can draw from other parts of extractive companies' vast networks to essentialize personae for political objectives. By tying companies to legacies that have impacted places and spaces, these decolonial rhetorics can seek to hold corporations accountable to the places, and their ecological communities, that they impact.[68]

This strategy is not dissimilar from how Black has described American Indian rhetoric in the nineteenth century that "unmasked" the US government's "paternal benevolence" through collective remembrance.[69] While collective remembrances of displacement, imprisonment and even genocide swirl around Oak Flat, members and supporters of Apache Stronghold take up a number of different decolonial rhetorics that I engage in the following chapter.

The Incommensurabilities of Place

This chapter has introduced a very different case study about Rio Tinto from the previous two chapters. Whereas the previous two chapters have shown that Rio Tinto's persona is a dominant rhetorical force in both Boron and SLC—as both a famous actor and a pioneer—this chapter has revealed some of the more harrowing consequences of Rio Tinto's extractivism in a case where its persona is under scrutiny by advocates making powerful arguments that Rio Tinto is responsible for perpetuating extractive colonialism and even genocide. What does this tell us about the nature of Rio Tinto's rhetorical existence?

Resolution attempts to create a paternalistic persona that through affects of folksiness and securitization is genealogical, culturally sensitive, and environmental. In some ways, Resolution, like Apache Stronghold, is also making arguments about home and belonging. One of the main differences, though, is that

Resolution obviously does not dwell in the places it extracts. Instead, it makes a case for how Superior is a suitable dwelling place for Resolution's rhetorical presence, or persona. It does this by mundanely blending in with the dominant rhetorical culture of the town. Acting as a sort of "medicine man" that is capable of restoring the town to its former mining glories—through a much-overdue mining "boom"—Resolution positions itself as the most contemporary mining company in Superior's historical "movements."

Architecture is a key component of this genealogical argument, as through machine parts, mining artifacts, and even folksy "stuff" (e.g., handcrafted signs, benches, timelines), Resolution is able to instantiate its communal presence among "the people" as the next historical mining company. For instance, by commemorating mining infrastructure such as the former Magma Smelter and the Resolution #10 Mining Shaft, Resolution grafts its rhetorical presences on top of mining pasts to create a linear timeline of communal progress qua mining. These material rhetorics, inclusive of their massive investments, importantly seal its commitments to the community and its "people."

At the same time, Resolution also clearly securitizes its presences in both Superior and Oak Flat. Through gated entrances, security protocols, and surveillance cameras (including possibly drones), Resolution is not leaving its future at Oak Flat to fate. While these rhetorics of securitization may seem at odds, or even contrary to, Resolution's folksiness, they can also be read as natural responses to the felt insecurities, uncertainties, and anxieties about the future of this site. What does it achieve if not to assure the community of its commitment and the certainties of its extractive futures amid so much social and cultural tumult? Hence Resolution presents itself as a paternalistic actor that protects what it sees as its kin: the people (just not all). There is no doubt that these security rhetorics further reinforce Apache Stronghold's claim that Resolution is an extractive colonist that privatizes Indigenous land for exploitation, but securitization is also a powerful rhetoric that can stabilize a mercurial situation, especially in a post 9/11 era where memories of different kinds of terrorism have become commonplace.[70]

Another possible reading of Resolution's securitized rhetorics is that it is a policing that controls a dominant aesthetic of place. Through cameras, gates, fences, and possibly drones, Resolution becomes the knowing overseer, or a police actor that regulates the consensus of Oak Flat as copper mine and not home. Think also about how Resolution at both its West and East Plants are elevated on hills, allowing it to form a visual cultural standpoint, see without being seen as a sort of archipelago of power or panopticon.[71] This no doubt is amplified by the fact that Rio Tinto, ontologically, is an invisible actor made present only through its rhetorical personae, and personae, unlike bodies and their organs, cannot be the object of "talking back." How, after all, to decolonize a mining shaft? A screen? Or even a café? Unlike actual images, such as the billboards targeted by the Situationists in 1968, all of these things cannot be easily appropriated, let alone dismantled.[72]

As will be discussed further in the following chapter, these material rhetorics create real challenges for resisting Rio Tinto, but groups such as Apache Stronghold also reveal possibilities of jamming processes of becoming-incorporated.

All this is to say that the rhetorical situation at Oak Flat is illustrative of some of the incommensurabilities of place that are harbingers of what is to come in the Anthropocene with dwindling natural resources and increased demands for precious metallic minerals for "sustainable futures." To Rio Tinto, Oak Flat is a sacrifice zone. To Apache Stronghold, it is home. As Danielle Endres has argued in her case study of Yucca Mountain, the incommensurabilities of place between Indigenous actors that see land as sacred dwelling places and governments or corporations that see them as sacrifice zones involve a mutually exclusive competition of values that does not necessarily work itself out. In our case, such incommensurabilities are at a stasis that is representative of larger environmental climates as society becomes willing to plunge deeper and deeper for extractive futures (seven thousand feet to be exact).

While companies such as Resolution attempt to extract from afar without dwelling in their affected areas, groups such as Apache Stronghold show the radicality of place-as-home. Place is of increased importance in an age defined by constant movements of persons, communities, and ideas where subjectivity itself is defined through mobilities across time and space via transportation, digital networks, and communication technologies—all of which are generated by copper. In our current century, the trope of mobility is supreme. It also happens to reinforce dominant carbon-based economies that depend on fossil fuels—and for our purposes all the elements such as copper, borax, palladium, and tellurium—to make them move faster and faster toward oblivion. Standing one's ground by making place a "stronghold" resists this ethic of mobility, as it is suggestive of this place here and now mattering more. Then again, when I visited the site, nobody was there, physically. While I may assume that this was because it was monsoon season, and the weather made it inhospitable for this kind of place-based rhetoric, the site also looked abandoned. Is it possible this was more of a staged act of protest than an actual place-based protest where bodies dwelled?

Rio Tinto simultaneously occupies multiple subjective roles at Superior as it does at SLC and Boron, considering its range of alchemical rhetorics, affects, and many issues that remain below the surface. For our purposes here, our case has shown how some of those issues otherwise in the underlands burrowed with the copper have risen as a Freudian cathexis and settled in the national consciousness where they are still being debated. While Resolution attempts to push these issues back below the consciousness, Apache Stronghold members and supporters continue to keep them alive. The following chapter continues our investigation of these kinds of counterrhetorics by taking cues from this group to determine various ways Rio Tinto's persona can be jammed.

5

Essentializing Rio Tinto's Corporate Persona

In November 2013, one year before the passage of the fatal SAE, fourteen-year-old Naelyn Pike traveled to Washington, DC, to speak against the mining of Oak Flat to legislators who would decide the fate of this sacred site. In an interview with Lauren Redniss, author of *Oak Flat: A Fight for Sacred Land in the American West*, Pike was wearing "her buckskin" dress with "tin jingles" and was nervous about going through the metal detector. Previously, she had also been nervous about flying for the first time. "Everything was new," she recalled.[1]

When she approached the security guards, just as she had anticipated, the metal detector went off. "The security guards were like, 'Oh my gosh,' but I couldn't take my dress off," she recalled, "so they kind of patted me and said, 'just go.'" When she entered the Capitol, she noticed that "people were staring" and "everyone was like, 'what are you?'" "Like, 'I'm Apache,'" she told Redniss in an interview.[2]

Pike went to DC with the chairman of the San Carlos Apache, Terry Rambler, to give testimony about the proposed Resolution Mine before the Senate Subcommittee on Public Lands, Forests, and Mining. Arizona senator John McCain could not attend, but the cosponsor of his proposed Southeast Arizona Exchange, Jeff Flake, spoke on behalf of the legislation, saying there were "bound to be disagreements."[3] Rambler spoke about the intersectional impacts of the mine to the Native community and submitted various written arguments into public record.

Oak Flat is "a place filled with power" and dwelling place of *Gaan*, or the "mountain spirits," read his statement. Should the Resolution Mine pass political muster, "our spiritual existence will be threatened." "Just as Mount Sinai is a holy place to Christians, Oak Flat is the equivalent for us. . . . There are no human actions or steps that could make this place whole again or restore it once lost," he said.[4]

Naelyn Pike spoke about her personal attachments to Oak Flat. Just one year prior she had participated in her Sunrise Dance at Oak Flat—a multiday, coming-of-age dance for Apache girls who "reenact the Apache creation myth" when they begin menstruating. As Rambler distributed pictures of Naelyn in the same "beaded buckskin dress" she was wearing in the meeting, Naelyn spoke:

> My younger sister, Nizhoni, will be having her Sunrise Ceremony at Oak Flat in October. Oak Flat was brought to her in a dream. Now I am preparing for her ceremony. We pray that this holy place will not be destroyed by this time, so my great-grandmother can see her great-granddaughter be blessed into womanhood where our ancestors once called home. . . . Why would you want to mine and destroy Oak Flat and Apache Leap? Will there really be that many jobs? For a long period of time? Can you not see the life it gives? Are you blinded by your greed? Please make me understand why you could do such horrid things to these holy precious lands.[5]

A year later, Senator McCain and Senator Flake's SAE passed as a last-minute "rider" of the "must pass" National Defense Act, and since then, oppositional rhetorics such as this have only become more amplified through the group Apache Stronghold.

Apache Stronghold is led by Naelyn's grandfather, Wendsler Nosie. The protest group has launched a spiritual movement against the proposed Resolution Mine to protect their holy ground and place-based cultural practices. For instance, the group facilitates an annual forty-mile "March to Oak Flat" from the San Carlos Reservation and has led several "convoys" to Washington and elsewhere to participate in anti-SAE protests, including a recent "Moral March" with the Poor People's Campaign. During the COVID-19 pandemic, the group hosted a "letter writing workshop" for those wanting to learn how to convincingly address political representatives, in addition to various virtual marches and rallies—one of which included Indigenous guest speakers from Mongolia who are also fighting "monster mining company Rio Tinto."[6]

As cofounder of Apache Stronghold, Naelyn Pike has played no small part in oppositionally resisting Resolution. Pike has spoken about the importance of preserving Oak Flat for future generations. While standing in front of the Capitol in another Washington, DC, trip, she said, "The Resolution Copper Mining Proposal [is] like taking away a church. But the thing about Oak Flat is it's worse, because you can rebuild a church. Oak Flat will be completely destroyed and it could never come back."[7]

Apache Stronghold has raised national awareness about the religious, cultural, and environmental costs of the proposed Resolution Copper Mine. To Terry Rambler, his people are obligated to fight for "humans and religious rights" that are at stake with Resolution Copper. "If we do not," he admonished, "our beliefs, our spiritual lives, the very foundation of our language, our culture and our belief will no longer be in balance, and we will become undone."[8]

Apache Stronghold names Resolution a colonial, even genocidal, actor perpetuating a legacy of extractive colonialism. Through various protest rhetorics, the group argues for the central importance of place-as-home rather than the center of a future copper mine. While Apache Stronghold may not stop Resolution from mining copper at Oak Flat, it is nevertheless winning the narrative and raising national consciousness about the stakes of this mine that, like labor issues in Boron and environmental issues in SLC, Rio Tinto probably hoped would go unnoticed. This case shows that not all of Rio Tinto's stakeholders acquiesce with its dominant extractive logics as more than a few are speaking back to Rio Tinto's corporate persona. Direct action of this kind can be seen as a form of strategic essentialism that essentializes the Rio Tinto assemblage— in other words, Rio Tinto as colonial, racist, environmentally destructive—to achieve particular rhetorical motivations.

This chapter shows how social actors can rhetorically interrupt corporate assemblages and the process-oriented formations of their rhetorical identities. As we will see, political actors at Boron and SLC, in addition to Oak Flat, have, through different kinds of direct action, attempted to disrupt Rio Tinto's alchemical rhetorics and alter its corporate persona.[9] These cases are revelatory of how corporate personae are sites of political negotiation between different stakeholders that may vie over their rhetorical meaning or interventionally disturb their affective flows. Rio Tinto's persona politics are processes, and processes can be stopped, reversed, or appropriated. In other words, Rio Tinto is not immune to different forms of direct action against the formation of its personae. For instance, in *OurSpace: Resisting the Corporate Control of Culture*, Christine Harold discusses how corporate consumer culture can be "jammed" through parodies, hoaxes, and pranks that creatively challenge the grips of capitalism on cultural space.[10] As forms of "sabotage" akin to Guy Dubord's concept of *detournement*, "culture jamming" reveals some of the possibilities of targeting corporate images and their personae.

Related to this process of jamming is the notion of monkey wrenching from Edward Abbey's novel, *The Monkey Wrench Gang*, which tells an epic tale of civil disobedience against the systemic destruction of the American West.[11] The book involves four central characters—a polygamist river guide named "Seldom Seen" Smith; an anarchist surgeon, Doc Sarvis; his feminist assistant Bonnie Abbzug, and Vietnam veteran George Hayduke—that band together to defend wilderness through direct action against "planetary industrialism."[12] Mining companies, including Rio Tinto's historically incorporated company at the Bingham Canyon Mine (Kennecott), are at the top of the list. To Hayduke, Kennecott was part of the "megalomaniacal megamachine" that was "changing things" with such force that he compared the American West to the horrors of Vietnam.[13]

This "quartet of Quixotes," says Robert Macfarlane, "monkey wrenches" the "techno-industry" in the American Southwest by "using the tools of industry to demolish the infrastructure of industry in the name of the biosphere."[14] They dump sand in the fuel tanks of "earth movers" (bulldozers), drive hauling trucks off cliffs, and cause havoc at strip mines. These acts of "sabotage" are waged against not humans but industrial property. The holy "grail" of Seldom, Doc, Bonnie, and Hayduke is to destroy the Glen Canyon Dam for its "damnation of a canyon" at the Colorado River.[15] "Sentiment without action is the ruin of the soul," said Abbey.[16]

Abbey's work has inspired many, including David Foreman, who created the radical environmentalist group Earth First! In 1981 for instance, Earth First! unfurled a giant three-hundred-foot plastic "crack" across the face of the Glen Canyon Dam visible from afar. In fact, Ed Abbey attended the event and gave a talk about direct action before the stunt.[17] Writing the foreword to Foreman's book *Ecodefense: A Field Guide to Monkeywrenching*, Abbey wrote, "I think that we're morally justified to resort to whatever means are necessary in order to defend our land from destruction and invasion, and I see this as an invasion." He later clarified he "would advocate sabotage, subversion, as a last resort when political means fails"[18]

Earth First! also participated in other "stunts" and "microperformances" dubbed more "violent."[19] For instance, among other acts of "sabotage," Earth First! spiked trees to prevent "industrial juggernauts" from slaying them and waged various "wars in the woods" with bodies buried neck-deep in the middle of logging roads, in addition to roadblocks, forts, and other guerrilla-like acts of protest and sabotage.[20] While these monkey wrenchers, and the radical environmental groups they spawned, are frequently labeled "eco-terrorists," in Abbey's view, the

mining companies, clear-cutters, and developers are the true terrorists that
through their "technological juggernauts" and "mindless machine[s]" inflict asym-
metrical violence upon the earth.[21]

In similar, albeit uniquely different ways, political actors at Oak Flat, SLC,
and Boron show how Rio Tinto's personae can be subverted or sabotaged during discursive processes of becoming. Rio Tinto, after all, is a process-oriented
subject. In ways similar to how Alfred North Whitehead describes his immanent philosophy in *Process and Reality*, Rio Tinto is made a subject through
constant movements and processes that seek to harden its rhetorical identities
in the places that it dwells. Processes of feelings, discourses, forms, events, and
subjects shape reality. Affects and its "pulses of emotion" are emplaced "processes
of experience" that "precede cognition."[22] While this means that Rio Tinto does
not have a transcendental essence, social actors can nevertheless directly involve
themselves in Rio Tinto's processes of identity formation via appropriation. If
Rio Tinto *is* its persona, and its persona is reverse engineered with counteres-
sential rhetoric, then does not Rio Tinto also become a colonist, an exploiter, air
polluter, and genocidal actor?

To highlight the voices of those speaking back to Rio Tinto's personae, I take
up the submerged (and rising) political matters at Rio Tinto's Resolution, Bingham Canyon, and Borax Mines. These examples neither illustrate, nor advocate
for, actual "eco-tage" against Rio Tinto's machinic parts; instead, they show how
various social actors have, in different ways, essentialized Rio Tinto's corporate
personae during certain processes of corporate subjectification. These rhetorical
maneuvers if anything reveal the violence of Rio Tinto inflicted upon the earth,
and its interconnected ecosystems, cultures, and human/nonhuman life, in the
American Southwest.

I begin by continuing an analysis of Apache Stronghold's decolonial rhetorical performances by specifically focusing on comments made during public
hearings on Resolution's Environmental Impact Statement that talk back to
Resolution's paternalistic persona. As decolonial rhetorics, these comments
illustrate the importance of essentializing corporate persona during decisional
processes that affect future becomings. Apache Stronghold comments show
how this persona politic can work by linking Rio Tinto to the legacies of mod-
ernism/colonialism that Rio Tinto otherwise tries to forget.

In my second example, I return to Salt Lake City and show how locals have
also participated in decision-making processes at public hearings using what
Kathleen Hunt et al. have called "indecorous voice."[23] Local actors have also

attempted to "jam" Rio Tinto Kennecott's conjunctural futures through clean air protests, legal processes, and even shareholder meetings.

I then go back to the Mojave and engage labor rhetorics from the International Longshore and Warehouse Union (ILWU) that "jammed" Rio Tinto's persona at the Borax Mine during a 2010 lockout. I discuss labor as a process-oriented *topos* that temporary halted Rio Tinto's processes of becoming during the 107-day lockout and the importance of the medium of this message through the documentary film, *Locked Out* (2010), which disseminated union messages to wider audiences in ways that appropriated Rio Tinto's persona politic as a Hollywood star.

Apache Stronghold's Strategic Essentialism at Public Hearings

In addition to protests, marches, and caravans, Apache Stronghold has also taken its decolonial rhetorics to public hearings on Resolution's Environmental Impact Statement (Draft). As Kathleen Hunt et al. observe, public hearings can become radical sites of protest through "indecorous voices" that dissent from dominant worldviews about what counts as proper.[24] They can also be sites of direct action. Through EIS comments made in Superior, Globe, Miami, Queen Valley, San Tan Valley, Kearney, and Tempe, Apache Stronghold dissented from the extractive paradigm in calling out and naming Rio Tinto as colonial. Doing so appropriates Rio Tinto's persona in ways that work against its benevolent image as a folksy, and protected, member of the community. Here, members and supporters of Apache Stronghold claim, with historical basis, that Rio Tinto is the most recent extractive colonialist of this part of Arizona.

Pointing to and naming Resolution a colonial actor that has taken on the mantle of colonial pasts stops, or "jams," Rio Tinto's alchemical processes and reduces it instead to a form of colonialism. This strategy involves extracting troublesome parts of Resolution's networks and using them to push its corporate persona opposite of its intended direction.[25] In doing so, these comments tie Resolution to particular places, spaces, and histories to hold it accountable as a singular actor. These arguments have added force with Apache Stronghold's place-based rhetorics through their occupation of Oak Flat.

Consider how commenters have traced Rio Tinto to many different parts of the world to show how the company is intrinsically colonial. For instance, several commenters have pointed out that Rio Tinto's origins, in Spain, show its essential colonial roots.[26] For instance, at several different public hearings, one commenter, Don Zobel, who apparently traveled to Spain and visited Rio Tinto's first mine in the Huelva province, made a point to connect his visit to Resolution. At the first of six public hearings in Superior, Zobel said, "I ran across this thing that said Rio Tinto ... and so I said, Well, we'll go take a look at that, you know. And you go there, and it's this mining area that—where they got their name, as it turned out, and it's this bombed-out moonscape that they've, you know, been mining there probably for millennia."[27] Zobel's point is that Rio Tinto's extractive genealogy matters. Even though Resolution presents itself as a fresh face of progress in Arizona, that is also tied to genealogies of mining in the "copper triangle," Zobel reminds audiences that the company is linked to a dark legacy of plunder. What better way to show the essence of this company than by pointing to its origins as evidence of what may come? Resolution, by extension, exists to pilfer communities for short-term gains, and when the resources are depleted, they leave behind legacies of toxic waste. These "big companies come in and just destroy the place," Zobel said. "Then they went off. They just left. And then they gave them a few shekels for a museum, and that's it."[28] Zobel concludes by suggesting corporate histories should be considered as criteria for evaluating the EIS, since those histories are suggestive of possible futures.[29]

Other commenters raised issues with Rio Tinto's mine in Mongolia (Oyu Tolgoi Mine). Commenters used Oyu Tolgoi as an exploitative analogy to point out how Rio Tinto's technical reports are unreliable and representative of broader tendencies to overlook technical details to advance the profit motive. San Tan Valley commenter Roger Featherstone said the Mongolia mine is rife with problems. "Rio Tinto is building a very similar operation in Mongolia," the commenter said, "and that facility started leaking after three years. Rio Tinto is currently building a block cave operation at that mine. It's shallow, or it's 4,500 feet rather than 7,000 feet, but they're having a heck of a time doing it. The rock just isn't cooperating building that infrastructure."[30]

By drawing from select instances to represent Resolution's whole, these arguments also reappropriate, or "jam," Resolution's paternalistic persona. For instance, consider how commenters drew from regional mines, such as the BCM, to show Resolution is tied to toxic legacies. At the Tempe hearing, Duke Romero said, "The largest open pit mine right now is under their care, their mine in Salt Lake City. And look at the air quality of Salt Lake City. They tried to sue them, you know, and they don't even have the climate that we have. It's going to dry up all that toxic even more and bring it to all of these folks here, you know. And I'm not even talking about the spirituality of it, just the poison you're going to allow. You're part of that. You are part of that."[31] Referring to an attempt by environmental advocates to sue Rio Tinto for going over the federally allocated limits of allowable pollution, this comment uses Salt Lake City as an example of how Rio Tinto pollutes with impunity.[32] Further, the statement, "you are part of that," suggests that decision-makers themselves are culpable and have an ethical obligation to stand up against future toxic onslaughts.

These arguments map Rio Tinto's subjective network to pin the company to its extractive history, flawed mining methods, and toxic waste impacts. They create various scenarios of risk that challenge not just the reliability of the EIS but also ultimately Resolution's character. When grafted upon local histories of extractive coloniality, particularly against Apache and Navajo Nations, these arguments become evidence of a living legacy of environmental injustice that "goes beyond copper."[33] As several commenters noted, Resolution's proposal cannot be separated from other related histories of nuclearism and coal mining on Navajo land. "We have been fighting an 80-year legacy of the uranium mining ever since the 1940s when the ore from the Navajo Nation and up in the northwest territories of Canada was used to make weapons of mass destruction that were used at Hiroshima and Nagasaki," said Manuel Pino in Tempe.[34]

This comment calls out Resolution's project as one rooted in legacies of extractive coloniality that target Indigenous land and communities as sacrifice zones that are left with lethal environmental conditions akin to a nuclear blast. "I don't know how you put a dollar value on human life," said Dwight Metzger at the same hearing, "but that's what we're afforded as compensation for all our ancestors, three of my uncles included, who have died of cancer."[35] These comments show how legacies of extractive coloniality persistently target Indigenous lands, cultures, and bodies. They also support claims made by the previous commenter about Rio Tinto's tendency to create "bombed-out moonscape[s]."[36]

Coal, too, is part of the same legacy of extractive coloniality against Indigenous persons in the Southwest, and many commenters have pointed out its harrowing intersectional violences on environments, cultures, and livelihoods. Consider the following comment made at the Queen Valley hearing regarding the dark history of Peabody Coal at Black Mesa that has, and continues to, affect Navajo (Diné) and Hopi nations: "Now the other thing [that] is a very important consideration is Peabody Coal on Dine, Navajo land, they moved people. They dug up bodies. They dug up artifacts. They said they would take care of them. They sent them to a university somewhere and they just didn't do anything appropriate with them. And here it is 40 years later and the Dine are trying to get their property back."[37] Comments like this are not remote. Many others have noted how Resolution's extractive colonialism is tied to mass deaths and even genocide committed against Indigenous persons. Laura Medina, another self-identified Indigenous actor forewarned, "If this project goes through, you all are committing and allowing the continued genocide to take place, continued genocide, meaning that it is never gone, has never stopped."[38]

In making these connections between different Indigenous histories of extractive coloniality, commenters forge pan-Indian alliances through shared histories of environmental injustice through coloniality.[39] As Manuel Pino said in the earlier hearing in Superior, "We have over [a] thousand abandoned uranium mines on the Navajo Nation that have not been reclaimed. So how can we believe that this is safe mining in Southern Arizona?"[40] By "raising questions," here and elsewhere, commenters not only cast doubt on Rio Tinto's trustworthiness but also unearth systemic and intersectional injustices that stem from extractive coloniality.[41]

Historical extraction of uranium, coal, and copper point to larger, systemic forms of place-based racializations that reduce Indigenous territories to sacrifice zones to churn extractive capitalism in other parts of the country and world. Invoking rhetorics of place, and its historical ties to culture and language, consummates Indigenous identities through shared experiences of extractive coloniality and its genocidal legacy.[42] Through these agencies, commenters essentialize Rio Tinto as a colonial actor that not only exploits, misleads, and silences but also kills. As Sandra Rambler stated, also in Queen Valley, "We have names for the whole area, for all of these mountains that you guys don't know because we are the original inhabitants of this country and we are from here. We were not imported. We were not—we didn't come here by anything. We are from here. And you are murdering us. Rio Tinto is nothing but a murderer. And I will be standing right by Wendsler at Oak Flat where my ancestors are buried. And I'll be in my traditional attire when the bulldozer comes."[43] This comment affronts Resolution's paternalistic claims to genealogy, cultural sensitivity, and conservationism by essentializing the company, through Rio Tinto, as a place-less colonial power that reduces Indigenous communities to graveyards. While Indigenous communities suffer and die, Resolution profits. The decisional process is no less culpable, as Rambler noted in a separate comment: "They're coming out, all these backroom deals that have been made, the millions and millions of money Resolution Copper has spent lobbying, paying people out, even some of our own Native people, which is just not right. They have no soul. They have no morals. They don't understand. All they want is just money, money, money. That's it, all for greed, power and lust."[44] Identifying Resolution as a collusive and soulless force debases its paternal persona and consummates Indigenous identities through spiritual renewal.[45] It is also backed with force that is evident through the "stronghold" at Oak Flat. Noteworthy too is the way some commenters have specifically pointed out Resolution's Indigenous tokenism, as discussed in the previous chapter, as matters of cultural coloniality, which marks felt betrayal at not necessarily the individual(s) but the colonial system that treats Indigenous cultures, voices, and histories as extractable and exchangeable.

Wendsler Nosie called out Resolution's tokenism as particularly cunning. "The Indian monitors that they hired from different tribes," they said, "didn't even know they were being used as a token to list six places and identify one that would be appropriate to put this tailing. Yet, they didn't even know that they're going to be in the mix of this discussion that's going on today about Native people being used to say this is where it should go. So that it eliminates them from the argument, which is really, really, again, divide and conquer."[46] Naming Resolution's cultural technique and pointing out how it works rhetorically pins Resolution's rhetorical performances to show the emptiness of its claims to cultural sensitivity.

By locating, naming, and essentializing Resolution's practices as colonial, commenters disrupt decision processes that otherwise facilitate business-as-usual extractive coloniality. By looking to Spain, Mongolia, Salt Lake City, and Navajo Nation, Resolution is rendered genealogically, culturally, and environmentally colonial, untrustworthy, and toxic. As Venessa Nosie put it at Tempe, "We as Indigenous people have been fighting for over 500 years and it hasn't stopped. When are we going to get a win? When are we going to matter?"[47]

Apache Stronghold thus attempts to essentialize Resolution's identity as a historic colonial actor that threatens the sanctity of home, and at least for now, through their decolonial rhetorics are winning the narrative. Using their place-based identities as grounded examples of embodied witnesses of past and present environmental injustices, commenters argue Resolution is essentially part of a place-less corporate colonist. Rather than allowing their land, culture, bodies, and religion to be extracted by Rio Tinto, Apache Stronghold takes direct action in rebranding Rio Tinto's persona as a modern-day colonist. Time will tell if these comments, and other appropriative techniques, effectively prevent their home from becoming another copper mine in the Pioneer Mining District.

Below I consider another set of public hearings during 2011 comment periods regarding Rio Tinto Kennecott's plans to expand Utah's Bingham Canyon Mine.

"Indecorous Voices" in Salt Lake City

Recall how SLC has some of the worst air pollution in the country. In part this is due to the bowl-shaped nature of the Salt Lake Valley (the "inversion" effect), but Rio Tinto also plays no small part in releasing fine particulate matter, namely, PM2.5 and PM10, from its mining operations. With an estimated two thousand to three thousand premature deaths each year in Utah from air pollution and smog often so thick many cannot see across the streets—especially during the winter months when the inversion is worse—air pollution is perennially a hot-button issue in SLC that captured national attention in 2013 when *New York Times* Dan Frosch wrote about the issue an article entitled "Seen as Nature Lover's Paradise, Utah Struggles with Clean Air."[48]

Several grassroots organizations such as Utah Moms for Clean Air and Utah Physicians for a Healthy Environment have helped organize massive protests in front of the state capitol—one in 2014 was dubbed "the largest clean air protest in US history" with more than four thousand protesters.[49] I attended that protest and, stepping in solidarity with these protesters, held signs of protest, listened to and applauded for speakers, and chanted. As their own persona politic, many protesters wore different kinds of masks (gas masks, surgical masks, and fleece masks) to perform their difficulties breathing dirty air. Others brought their children, using them as resources for protest, and held signs such as "Governor, We Can't Breathe."

When Rio Tinto attempted to expand the life of the Bingham Canyon Mine in 2011, many were outraged. Through what was called the Cornerstone Project, Rio Tinto advocated for expanding the reach of the BCM to increase its overall production levels by 30 percent. Doing so, however, would require state authorities to increase permissible levels of pollution, which is why Rio Tinto submitted various permits and proposals to modify the State Implementation

Plan (SIP) through the Utah Department of Environmental and Air Quality (UDEQ/UDAQ). Like the public hearings concerning Oak Flat, however, many publics took their ire over heightened extractivism and pollution to this comment period and "jammed" Rio Tinto's pioneer persona.

As Hunt et al. have argued, participants used "indecorous voice" to turn public hearings into places for public protest.[50] This style of rhetorical argument deviates from dominant decorum that expects commenters to politely and sequentially follow the rules for commenting by delivering a reasonable comment for political decision-making. When publics feel alienated from that process, though, why should they comply with what many see as a "done deal" between state and corporate alliances that only go through the motions of deciding, announcing, and defending (DAD) public participation?[51]

While the comments, as Hunt et al. observe, were primarily indecorous—in that they used the hearing as an opportunity for protest—they also show how social actors can jam Rio Tinto's identity by pointing to other extractive relations in other parts of the world. In doing so they jammed Rio Tinto's process of becoming Cornerstone, which at least in part explains why this proposal ultimately failed.

As noted in Hunt et al., and based on rhetorical observations by two of the authors (myself and Kathleen Hunt), protesters and commenters alike energetically poured into the room. Many of them were carrying signs of protest, such as "Another Dirty Error from DAQ," "Protect Our Right to Breathe," and "Got Lungs?" Another asked, "Is Utah Zion or Mordor?" On top of this a massive banner, at least twelve feet long, read "Rio Tinto: Change We Don't Believe In." As noted by Hunt et al., "These actions open spaces for thinking differently about how public participation processes ought to occur. By bridging public participation and social protest, Salt Lake City activists alienated RTK from the very process typically structured to serve industry interests."[52]

When the comment period began, publics displayed anger over perceived collusion between the DEQ and RTK. Commenters openly contested the seemingly unfair limitations of institutional decorum and dissented from its instrumentalist form of social and environmental change by performing some of the possibilities of "indecorous voice." Throughout the process, many people, for instance, were hooting and hollering during and between comments to show identification with Cornerstone opponents and disidentification from comments supporting the mine (many if not all of which were from Rio Tinto employees who attended the hearing).

Challenging UDEQ definitions of appropriateness, participants performatively negotiated how politics should be done. Participants vied over interpretations of democratic voice. While publics attempted to transcend institutional approaches to democratic change that conceive social change as a bureaucratic process of instrumental change, UDEQ still enforced rules of decorum that dictated basic features of speech such as the time and location of deliveries. Actions like clapping and cheering are not necessarily radical by themselves, yet they also broke from the taken-for-granted distributions of extractivist sense that privileged Rio Tinto. In this way they were part and parcel of a "dissensus" that aesthetically redistributed what counted as sensible.

These cheers (and "boos" for Rio Tinto comments) performatively negotiated the dominant logic undergirding this particular public forum. Drawing attention to the unfair constructions of decorum, participants attempted to transform the seemingly skewed model of dialogue that was privileging industrial voices over the public interests of clean air.

Commenters also attacked UDEQ decision-makers for organizing a flawed system and treating Utah as a sacrifice zone that was compared to the explosion of nuclear bombs insofar as locals are treated "like targets in a nuclear war."[53] One gentleman said, "It appears that DAQ has already decided that this issue will be approved, and has produced the completed permit stating just that. Imagine our surprise[.] [T]his increase requested by Rio Tinto appears to be a done deal already. This situation then makes a mockery of this particular public comment event. . . . Obviously these Utah voices . . . are not being considered as the permit is already written. Besides being disingenuous to members of the public like us, I am also wondering if this is legal."[54] This particular comment was received with obstreperous cheers from the crowd. People leaped from their chairs and held signs of protest in the air, clenched fists, and hollered.

Advancing the argument that the UDEQ is administering a rigged public participation process was used as a catalyst for transforming the narrow, instrumental public forum into a space for activism and social change. Using their indecorous voices to challenge the nature of the process itself united varied audiences to create a shared community of sense that politicized taken-for-granted assumptions about industry and environmental health. "You are the public servants that have been given the responsibility of protecting our public interest," noted one participant.[55] Another said, "If this proposal is approved, it would make a mockery of the mission statement and of the statement of the value of integrity for the DEQ," said somebody else.[56] Others said, "A job isn't much use if we can't breath[e]," "We need jobs that are not going to kill people," and "International corporations are not citizens."[57]

These comments highlight the outrage and feelings of disenfranchisement over a process of public participation believed to essentially support the financial interests of industrial actors over citizens' health. "What good does it do to provide jobs to a community if you poison its air, its water, its land, and its people?" asked one individual from Utah Valley Earth Firm.[58] One member of Utah Physicians for a Healthy Environment put the matter simply when he said, "DAQ now has a choice, protect public health and say no to Kennecott expansion or to continue to bow down to industry."[59]

All of these comments were powerful in that they verbally lampooned the UDEQ for failing to represent its citizens. Derisive comments against decision-makers and industrial actors were acts of indecorum that departed from the logical consistency of industrial reasons and the expectation that participants must remain polite and civilized. The true rhetorical effects of these comments, though, were observed by their ability to unite disparate citizens, groups, and social movements against what they saw as an unfair model of public participation and in so doing to open spaces for radical democratic potential. Consider the following statement:

> The outcome of this meeting today is already a forgone conclusion with results that have been determined in advance, no matter the nature of public comment. DAQ has already taken the next step in preparing the requisite permit Rio Tinto will need to move forward with their mine expansion. Given that we can no longer trust the process which appears to be fixed in advance, or that we can trust the agency tasked to oversee this process, we would like to go on record voicing our strong disapproval of the proposed modification to Salt Lake County PM_{10} state implementation plan.[60]

This comment elicited immediate boisterous applause that was louder and more sustained than any prior response. It was a unified voice of protest that used its clamor to resist and transgress institutional decorum. Everybody but a small handful of attendants was on their feet hooting and hollering, waving signs, and applauding at the speaker, and themselves, for resisting the instrumentalism of UDEQ. In the meanwhile, RTK supporters sat silently at the front of the room.

There were also other indecorous moments of protest that jammed, or monkey wrenched, the process. One person, for instance, brought his daughter with him to the podium to visually support the force of his argument. After introducing his daughter and stating that they recently moved to the area, he expressed concern over her higher risk of getting sick from poor air quality by just living in Salt Lake City. "I don't think anyone here speaking for this proposal would volunteer their children for [asthma, bronchitis, or RSV], yet if this passes, we will have more kids that get asthma and RSV."[61] The crowd erupted with applause.

As Hunt et al. observe, there was also an important moment of silence that disrupted the decorous expectation that commenters must always talk during their time. One person in particular did not speak for several minutes during his time to perform the silence of many Cornerstone opponents. Before the silent period he said, "For the remainder of my time I invite everyone to consider in silence, what does it mean, to have our children's recess cancelled because of poor air quality . . . what is it you love most in this world, and how can you live in integrity with that thing that you love most, and not use your full creative potential to find other jobs, and to find other ways to grow."[62] These comments, per Hunt et al.'s analysis, used indecorous speech during these hearings, and I argue here that they also attempted to jam Rio Tinto's processes of becoming by targeting its corporate persona. Rather than a communal citizen-subject that pioneers many progressive initiatives, Rio Tinto is associated with an instrumentalist process of governance that alienates public voices. Putting the profit motive before deliberative concerns, and public health, makes Rio Tinto nothing short of a foreign national plutocrat.

Like the comments concerning the future of Oak Flat, these comments were driven by larger efforts of direct action that were happening outside UDEQ walls. For many years, grassroots organizations such as Utah Moms for Clean Air (UMCA) and Utah Physicians for a Healthy Environment (UPHE) have targeted Rio Tinto as a major contributor of Utah's air pollution problem, and both deploy unique rhetorical strategies. Utah Moms, a multichaptered organization throughout Utah, uses dominant tropes of motherhood to melodramatically advocate for better air quality conditions. And Utah Physicians for a Healthy Environment use their rhetorical authority as medical experts to scientifically show the medical risks associated with chronic air pollution inhalation.[63]

These organizations and others such as WildEarth Guardians and the Sierra Club have teamed up on several occasions, not just in organizing clean air protests as noted earlier but also in legal pursuits. For instance, per an earlier noted comment by Duke Romero at the Tempe hearing on Resolution's EIS Draft, these actors have attempted to file a lawsuit against Rio Tinto for violating federal standards of acceptable air pollution outlined in the Clean Air Act (1970). "We filed this lawsuit to protect the health of 2 million people. All air pollution is not created equal and Kennecott's is some of the most toxic there is," said the plaintiffs. "Utah is not going to solve our pollution problems if we let our largest industrial polluters increase their emissions at will, and in this case illegally," said Tim Wagner of the Sierra Club. To Cherise Udell, leader of UMCA, "We can no longer allow Kennecott to pass their costs of doing business on to this community and sacrifice our health and quality of life in the process."[64]

The lawsuit was eventually dismissed but the docs and the moms have not stopped advocating for clean air. They have even picked up international attention through the London Mining Network (LMN)—an organization entirely oriented around mining issues at the center of many of the world's most major mining headquarters and markets (London). In several cases the group has circulated these Utah efforts to different audiences to garner awareness about some of the global effects of Rio Tinto's practices. For many years this group, and its ally, the People Against Rio Tinto Zinc (Partizans), have also used shareholder opportunities to protest Rio Tinto's global business practices and raise awareness among those that benefit the most (shareholders).[65]

Cherise Udell attended at least one of these meetings and stood in solidarity with the LMN. Speaking about her plans to attend the meeting in 2011, when decision-makers were still considering the Cornerstone Project, she said she intended to speak directly to Rio Tinto CEO Tom Albanese and say, "If this expansion is such a great idea for Utahns, come to Salt Lake City and debate your opponents. Come and tell us face to face just how the future health and economic well-being of Utah families are to you just the 'curse' of resource nationalism."[66] Udell here is referring to a statement Albanese made earlier when he complained to shareholders about how Rio Tinto must do "a better job at managing the curse of resource nationalism . . . and the activism of stakeholder engagement."[67] Udell translated this as follows: "Local people throughout the world are tired of being exploited for profit; they're starting to stand up for themselves, and Rio Tinto doesn't like it."[68]

Potentially, these rhetorics are working more effectively than people think. After all, recall how Rio Tinto is scaling back its corporate persona in the Salt Lake community given its selling of Daybreak and failure to renew naming rights for the Rio Tinto Stadium. Perhaps the effectivity of these movements is illustrative of what happens when the persona-developing alchemy fails to achieve its goals for golden futures. This may also indicate that without a strong corporate persona or successful alchemical rhetorics, Rio Tinto may simply care less about its image and more willing to take off its mask and take what it wants via realpolitik force.

Through public hearings, protests, litigation, and even shareholder meetings, these advocates for clean air show how Rio Tinto's persona can be "jammed" through indecorous voice and direct action. Rio Tinto is still a "pioneer" of different sorts in the community, but perhaps these efforts also contribute to the shaping of socially acceptable levels of corporate social responsibility. In other places, both in the United States and abroad, Rio Tinto takes on a much darker role as colonist, war lord, and slave master. Below, I go back to the Mojave Desert to show how organized laborers effectively disrupted Rio Tinto's historical, and famous, persona through more traditional forms of direct action.

Generational Labor Struggles in the Mojave

Rio Tinto's processes of becoming-Reagan, -Death Valley, -Spock, are contingent upon exploitative labor practices that keep the cogs of this "megamachine" running. Without it, the Rio Tinto assemblage slows or stops, forcing the company to make certain compromises, that is, so long as those laborers out of work can sustain themselves. Hence the importance of organized labor.

Back in the Mojave Desert, where Rio Tinto owns and operates the second-largest Borax Mine in the world, workers have had generational struggles with Rio Tinto over its labor practices. In 1974 for instance, just six years after Rio Tinto bought U.S. Borax, massive violence broke out between the police-backed mining company and union members that went on strike for better pay. Splitting the town between "majority pro-union and minority pro-company factions," the strike, to former miner Terry Dill, "was like a civil war" that "turned father against son, salaried workers versus those with hourly pay." After a "famous riot" at the mine's "front gate," workers' homes lit with dynamite, explosions of the mine's power line, and "episodic exchanges of gunfire."[69] For almost a year, Kern County sheriffs, and other hired union busters, implemented "martial law" in Boron that some compared to "a controlled Vietnam." To *The Dispatcher* in 1974, a publication by the International Longshore and Warehouse Union Local 30 (ILWU)—which was on the scene—"ILWU members and their families 'have been forced to live in a police state atmosphere' since the strike began."[70]

During the time these events were unfolding, 110 union members were arrested and "many were shot at and severely beaten." To the president of Local 30, Kenneth Gordon, "Union members have been beaten with clubs.... Loaded shotguns have been pointed at our members. We have been cursed at and arrested for walking on picket duty."[71] This includes six-months-pregnant Kay Barlow, who was "beaten with a billy club causing her to lose her baby."[72]

One of the consequences of this violent and divisive exchange was a massive "exodus" from Boron. "I bet 50% of people moved out of town after 1974," said Dill. "It really hurt us." Since then, Boron's population has been on the steady decline. "One of the teachers at the Boron High School commented on this lingering population problem that he noticed in the classrooms: "Five years ago we had 290 students, and now it is 127."[73]

This diminishing population has only put Rio Tinto in a stronger position to make demands in a town that it more or less brought into existence. Boron's *Mad Max*–like environment also adds to this positioning since being distantly removed from what most call civilization, its residents are almost entirely dependent on the mine.

Today, one quarter of all of Boron's two thousand residents work at the Borax Mine, the same ratio as in the past. "Virtually everyone in the town has some intimate link to the mine and its turbulent history." To David Liebengood—president of the ILWU—"The whole town is tied to that mine. Most of the people who live here now work at the plant . . . it has passed through generations."[74]

While memories of the strike lingered, work at the Borax Mine kept humming along while Rio Tinto amassed capital from afar as workers were met with added pressures from a diminished workforce. Laborers were at a mere 40 percent of its 1980 capacity and were still producing "record outputs" even in spite of a "rapidly aging plant; an ornery, dipping ore body; and an increasingly remote and hostile management."[75]

All of this was fodder for the lockdown that came in 2010 when Rio Tinto tried to squash the union's "generational job security" by drafting a "draconian" revision of worker contracts. Citing global losses in its shares of borax (25 percent over the previous twenty years) and a downed economy, Rio Tinto sought to "modernize its work practices" and increase competition by replacing the company's "seniority system" based on "years of service" with one based instead on "skill and performance," which would allow the company to replace union members with temporary employees.[76] Many workers saw the contract as an attempt to "break the union in order to slash wages and cut benefits" and something that would inevitably lead to "nepotism."[77] To the union's spokesperson Craig Merrilees, the "the contract would allow the right to discriminate and practice cronyism when it comes to deciding who gets a raise, who gets overtime and who gets training opportunities."[78]

In what Mike Davis of *The Nation* called an attempt by Rio Tinto to "rule by divine whim," the company sought "to capriciously promote or demote," "outsource union jobs," "convert full-time to part-time positions with little or no benefits," "reorganize shift schedules without warning," "eliminate existing work rules," "cut holidays, sick leave and pension payments," "impose involuntary overtime," and "penalize the union if workers file[d] grievances."[79] To one employee, Larry Roberts, the contract was a betrayal of trust. "I'm 55 and have been here for 32 years, and suddenly I feel like I have no security," said Roberts. "If I knew this would happen, I wouldn't have come here in the first place."[80]

After five months of intense negotiating between Rio Tinto and the ILWU, Rio Tinto landed on its "final offer" and give the union three days to agree to it. While Rio Tinto offered workers a one-time $5,000 bonus and a 2.5 percent pay raise, many saw this as a "smoke screen for drastic concessions in a region already hit hard by high unemployment." To Craig Merrilees of the ILWU, "the company says 'We'll give you a wage increase, but we'll send your job to a temp agency.'"[81]

If union members rejected, they were told they would be locked out of the mine and without work. As featured in the film *Locked Out*, a 2010 documentary about the labor dispute, the union intensely debated the issue before the clock stuck midnight. To Peter Olney of the *New Labor Forum*, the union deliberated thoughtfully; each worker was asked the question, "What would happen if you stopped working?" While most at first thought about the repercussions of being out of work in a small corporate town, they eventually realized their pivotal "role in the production process" and "grasped that the company relied on their skills and job-specific knowledge to keep the operation humming."[82] In other words, workers came to the realization that Rio Tinto, and its extractivism, is a constant *process* that utterly depends on labor.[83]

The ILWU's deliberation room erupted with applause when all five hundred workers opposed the offer. When these workers, whose lives depended on the mine, arrived to work on February 1 chanting, "We want to work!" and holding American flags, they were "met [with] a battalion of armed guards who kept them out."[84] Rio Tinto was following through with its promise to lock out workers. As the company brought in temporary replacements to replace the union workers, they were escorted by military-like personnel (scabs) hired by Rio Tinto.

The lockout ensued for 107 days. For all intents and purposes, Rio Tinto attempted to "starve out the families in Boron." During this difficult time, workers had to go on unemployment, depend on spouses for insurance, and needed "extensions on auto loans and mortgages."[85] As Rio Tinto launched a "massive propaganda campaign" that framed its proposal as a "'reasonable' economic offer" and "portrayed union leaders as villains," locked out workers "staged a continuous protest at the mine's entrance."[86] Meanwhile, Rio Tinto kept on ushering in new additional workers to keep the mine operational.

The union, however, persisted in their own media campaigns that swayed the community's public opinion by drawing connections to Rio Tinto's larger, and unknown, networks and framing the issue as a classic "David vs. Goliath battle." This was a crucial part of the messaging that allowed the union to frame the matter as a blue-collar issue that affected the entire community. For instance, workers emphasized that they were being *deprived* from work from a *foreign national* company that had too much control over their well-being. As Olney put it, "these were good family-supporting, working class jobs that Rio Tinto was trying to destroy. The miners *wanted* to work, but they could not because they were locked out by a giant company that didn't care about the local community. Children of the Boron miners wore T-shirts that said: 'Give my Dad his job back.'"[87] The union thus created its own persona—that of a small working town, that was "aligned against a marauding, multi-billion-dollar, foreign-owned corporation." One way they did this was by avoiding any talk about the "seniority" issue and instead focusing on the importance of protecting workers' generational commitments to Boron and the Borax Mine. Stressing that worker were "LOCKED OUT" and not "on STRIKE!" resonated more strongly with those who remembered the violent events that unfolded in 1974. Rather than deliberately *not* working for better pay, these workers were prevented from work by a company located many thousands of miles away. "We've got to feed our families— we want to work!" they would shout.

As a sort of blowback of living and working in Rio Tinto's corporate town, this "scrappy group of heroes" not only thwarted Rio Tinto's efforts to show that its efforts were reasonable but also acquired communal agency by showing that they, not Rio Tinto, were the fabric of Boron, which was rearticulated as working, rather than corporate, town. After all, if the Borax Mine and Boron are mutually constitutive, then the workers, not some foreign-national company, are the ones with the most process-oriented power. Workers are the ones that live in Boron, which is why the matter came down to "loyalty and commitment" over profits.[88] In doing so, they found their agency through the widespread support of the community

The Boron community became just as crucial for ILWU as the union members themselves. More than twenty businesses provided the workers with food, discounts, and ultimately their rhetorical support. Realizing how the mine, and its workers, affects the entire town, this solidarity of struggle shaped a powerful communal persona that severely disrupted Rio Tinto's rhetorical presences as word about these struggles began to spread beyond Boron. To Merrilees, "People here are tough and willing to see this through to the end.... It's not just about Rio Tinto but all the companies doing this to people across the country. In this little town people are drawing the line."[89] Boron became a symbol of larger small-town struggles against international companies trying to push them out.

The Los Angeles chapter of the ILWU played no small part in spreading awareness about this epic battle unfolding in the Mojave Desert by "casting Rio [Tinto] as a rapacious, foreign-based company taking advantage of tough economic times to extract harsh demands from hundreds of workers in a hard-scrabble town of 2,000 people."[90] At one such rally, one of the "locked-out-miners" Michael Davenport shouted, "We're American workers. We won't be treated like a Third World county."[91] While this no doubt comes with its own set of problems in terms of Rio Tinto's global racialized biopolitical labor practices, it nevertheless helps illustrate some of the nationalistic rhetoric spread from Boron to Los Angeles and beyond. In a heartfelt display of solidarity, "hundreds of labor activists" from handfuls of different labor unions mobilized a caravan, including several semi-trucks, from the Los Angeles Baseball Stadium to Boron that brought the workers food, supplies, and American flags.

The movement even gained international support from workers from the mine's primary competitor: the Turkish owned Eti Mine. Scheduling the International Maritime Conference in Southern California "to coincide with negotiations," these workers marched side-by-side with the Boron workers and community in a public display of international solidarity with borax labor.[92]

All these events attracted significant media attention and many videos, in addition to the *Locked Out* documentary, show interviews with workers that many identified with as the events unfolded. "I blame Rio Tinto but I also blame the government of the United States," said one worker in an interview. "These multinational companies can come in and pretty much do what they want because they know that there will be very little opposition."[93]

In a separate video an employee said, "They [multinational corporations] are like a virus" in that "their ultimate goal is to enlarge. They say that there is no class system in the United States but the ones on the top keep getting richer, the ones in the middle and the bottom keep getting driven down lower. . . . There is a class system."[94]

After 107 days of protest, Rio Tinto finally compromised with higher wages in a new six-year contract.[95] In a reversal, union members were able to build identifications through the town in ways that worked against Rio Tino's processes of "modernizing its work practices." The lockout became not just a Boron issue but an American one that was pitted against a giant foreign national company—and no less a British one—that tried to put these families out of work and even starve them. Is this what the CEO meant when he complained about "resource nationalism"? Like Cherice Udell, one ILWU employee, Dave Irish, went to a Rio Tinto shareholder meeting in London to find out. After explaining how the contract hampers worker families, he asked the chairman of Rio Tinto, Jan du Plessis, why he "disrespects the employees," some of which have "40 years of experience," by "blaming the union" when Rio Tinto wants to destroy "full-time jobs to turn them into part-time employment" and "take away health care from the family."[96]

This scene, and acts of solidarity noted above, is illustrated in *Locked Out*, which powerfully puts the lockout into global perspective. Viewers not only see Boron, its mine, and the community that holds them together, but they also hear the voices of those affected as they learn about Rio Tinto's more troubling past and present mining practices throughout the world. For instance, workers talk about how Rio Tinto's European roots are tied to the Spanish Civil War when the company praised dictator Francisco Franco for cracking down on unions, and where the company used slave laborers in mines and decapitated members of local unions. They also learned about Rio Tinto's involvement in the deadly civil war, and genocide, in Bougainville, Papua New Guinea, where Indigenous persons were camped out for many years to protest toxic waste. At the time, Rio Tinto was also trying to mine precious mineral metals in Michigan's Upper Peninsula, which, through sulfide mining, would release copious amounts of sulfuric acid along the pristine Yellow Dog River, with additional waste dumping into Lake Superior. There, too, locals were joining forces to protect their land.[97] In other words, workers realized that they were part of a global struggle against Rio Tinto's international "economic terrorism."[98]

Was this Reagan's dream as he promoted Boraxo in Boron for U.S. Borax? Reagan, after all, is remembered for his strong antiunion stance when he was governor of California. Is it any wonder that he sided with U.S. Borax during the 1974 strike and "instructed the sheriffs to step up their actions against the strikers?" To Olney, these generational struggles at the Borax mine are illustrative" of "the massive right-wing drumbeat" that "scapegoat[ed] public sector employees" over the years.[99] As one employee put it in Locked Out, "This is a microcosm of what is happening throughout the country."[100]

These examples show how Rio Tinto's personae can be disrupted by counter-protesters that call into question Rio Tinto's taken-for-granted rhetorical presences and reverse its alchemical process of transformation. They also speak to many of Abbey's points about the importance of direct action for protecting the West from everything from "industrial tourism" to the "megalomaniacal megamachine" that reduces wilderness areas to war zones akin to Hayduke's experience in Vietnam. In these scenarios between Rio Tinto and Apache Stronghold, Utahans for clean air, and the ILWU, who is the terrorist? Readers can answer for themselves.

What Is Called Rio Tinto?

What can we gather from Rio Tinto's rhetorical presences in the American Southwest? Is Rio Tinto a particular kind of subject that can be grouped and categorized? Does it have an essence? Consider where we have been on this secular pilgrimage. Once we determined the nature of the corporate persona, we began our journey in the middle of the Mojave Desert at the Borax Mine. At the corporate town of Boron, we observed how Rio Tino adopts a historical persona that appropriates memories of twenty-mule teams, Death Valley, and Ronald Reagan to establish itself as a famous actor at the Borax Mine.

We then traveled to Utah. On a corporate tour across the Salt Lake Valley, from mine to museum, we saw how Rio Tinto takes on a pioneer persona deeply tied to Mormon cultural memories of emigration, the fleeting dreams of the Deseret, and discovery to pass as a reasonable citizen-subject before publics. By imbuing its identity in different places and spaces throughout the city, Rio Tinto encourages locals to experience the possibilities of copper vis-à-vis Rio Tinto. As such Rio Tinto alchemically invents nature, culture, and even natural history.

The previous chapter revealed how Rio Tinto, through its artificial creation, Resolution, creates a paternalistic identity in Superior, Arizona, amid elevated scrutiny. In defining the needs of "the people," and claiming to provide them, Rio Tinto circulates folksy, yet securitized, affects throughout this small mining town that give form to a corporate identity that is genealogical, culturally sensitive, and environmental. At the same time, decolonial rhetorics from Apache Stronghold challenge this persona by jamming various processes and linking Rio Tinto to its legacy of extractive coloniality.[101] While Rio Tinto may attempt to separate itself from its past and present violent colonialisms, groups like Apache Stronghold rhetorically forge these connections by linking negatively valanced legacies of extractive colonialism to modern/colonial epistemes.

This chapter has encountered other sides of Rio Tinto at each of these mines. Listening to counterrhetorics from those who are otherwise submerged below Rio Tinto's consciousness, and beneath the unexcavated earth, we have seen how Rio Tinto is also an extractive colonist, a toxic polluter, and an exploiter. Through various acts of protest, including "indecorous voice," at public hearings, shareholder meetings, and a stronghold, they show how Rio Tinto's corporate personae are processes that that can be rhetorically jammed for strategic political purposes.

What is Rio Tinto? Asked another way, what is it that we name when we call upon Rio Tinto? Is it a Hollywood actor, pioneer, or father? Alternatively, considering the rhetorics of decoloniality from Apache Stronghold, or the rumblings of other "submerged" environmental and labor rhetorics, is Rio Tinto a colonialist, polluter, mob boss?

Yes. Rio Tinto is all these things and more.[102] Recall, Rio Tinto *is* its personae. From an alchemical standpoint, Rio Tinto rhetorically uses its extracted resources to inventively create affects, cultures, and objects that stabilize particular place-based identities. These different personae, which oftentimes speak directly to its "implied auditors" and perhaps implicitly to investors, allow Rio Tinto to "pass" as a localized actor with goodwill while also displacing other relations and identities that may silence or negate identity claims from other audiences. When Rio Tinto's localized personae are fully formed and stabilized, they become mundane and taken-for-granted while others forgotten; however, when contested, Rio Tinto's persona is made a site of political negotiation and struggle.

From a rhetorical point of view that emphasizes effects, this subjective multiplicity presents problems for accountabilities otherwise attached to singular actors. How, after all, can one hold Rio Tinto accountable as a singular rational actor when it exists at so many different places and spaces, and with so many different personae, at once? Can a clean air advocate in Salt Lake City or laborers at Boron hold RTK and Borax accountable for their genocidal and colonial actions at Oak Flat, or are these always different corporate persons? While Resolution, Rio Tinto Kennecott, and Borax are owned by the same company, Rio Tinto, they are also all discrete with somewhat different rhetorical presences at each of their extractive sites.

As Stuart Kirsch has argued in his book *Mining Capitalism*, companies such as Rio Tinto and BHP are in a constant sort of "tug of war" with "critics" who attempt to hold them accountable for their actions.[103] Based on years of anthropological fieldwork with Indigenous communities affected by the notorious Ok Tedi and Bougainville mines in Papua New Guinea (PNG), Kirsch cautiously argues that the law can become a recourse for environmental justice when mining companies destroy ecologies that communities depend on for survival (e.g., Ok Tedi). While downriver Indigenous landowners in Papua New Guinea were able to settle with BHP for $40 million for catastrophic environmental damages, BHP and its corporate-influenced PNG government also passed legislation that would criminally penalize those who participated in the lawsuit. BHP was found in contempt of court for helping write the legislation, but the still corporate-sponsored PNG government also reenacted laws that rewarded damages only to those who did not participate in the lawsuit and reestablished the penalization of legal participation.[104]

There are also cases such as *Sarei v. Rio Tinto* where Indigenous actors sought to bring Rio Tinto to justice for inciting a deadly civil war (even genocide) under the somewhat contentious US's Alien Tort and Seditions Act at PNG's nearby Bougainville Mine.[105] In the case, the court limited its involvement in foreign national cases in its ruling against the plaintiffs. This troubling case at Bougainville shows how international mining companies, not least of which Rio Tinto, can build collusive networks with state governments and perpetuate what Kristian Lasslett has named "state crimes on the margins of empire" and engage in what Marx describes as "'ruthless terrorism,' 'conquest and plunder,' 'undisguised looting,' 'forcible expropriation' 'stock-exchange gambling.'"[106]

As Marx argued at the end of *Capital*, volume I, capitalists in their search for raw materials for systems of production have led to global colonies that service these processes while also allowing, if not necessitating, the expropriation of both labor and "nature."[107] To John Bellamy Foster and Brett Clark, a crucial, and oftentimes underrecognized, component of these processes are the global metabolic rifts that disrupt ecological systems. This is defined by Marx as an "irrevocable rift in the interdependent process of social metabolism, a metabolism prescribed by the natural laws of life itself." Elsewhere, Marx has said, "As long as human beings exist, the history of nature and the history of human beings mutually condition each other."[108] To Foster and Clark in *The Robbery of Nature*, these rifts have created indelible ruptures between humanity and nature that many have dubbed the Anthropocene. Our current ecological crisis can thus be viewed almost entirely through the prism of Rio Tinto.

From a world-systems perspective, Immanuel Wallerstein also helps us understand how global, and what he names postcolonial, actors such as Rio Tinto perpetuate these global expropriations.[109] To Wallerstein, modern empires have divided the world into divisions of core, semiperiphery, and periphery statuses that determine flows of resources, labor, and capital. The core tends to have sophisticated technological apparatuses for developing and manufacturing commodities, but such production is only made possible from the periphery where the core extracts resources, raw materials, and labor. While the United States is typically considered a core country because of its overall concentration of wealth and its technologies for production, from a postcolonial perspective, all of Rio Tinto's mines in the American Southwest are extractive colonies of England. The Borax and Bingham Canyon Mine, in this regard, are just as much colonies of Rio Tinto as the proposed Resolution Mine.

Consider the transfers of wealth that flow back to the "metropole." During just the first half of 2021, amid the COVID-19 pandemic, Rio Tinto earned a record $12.3 billion, which is more than $3.3 billion higher than the year before.[110] As one Boron resident put it, "The money the company makes is unbelievable. They know they could fill those jobs in a minute if there was a strike," he said. "At the end of the day, I don't think they care."[111] To stay-at-home-mom Kayla

Martz, whose husband earns $55,000/year at the Borax Mine said that Rio Tinto wants "to take from him and give the money to the top executives and shareholders who make millions. . . . We are not just cogs in a machine. We are families, and we have names," she said before a public audience.[112]

In other parts of the world, labor practices are much worse. During apartheid in South Africa, for instance, workers at Rio Tinto's Palabora Copper Mine paid black workers beneath the minimum wage and replicated apartheid-like conditions. In Namibia black laborers lived in conditions that were "akin to slavery."[113]

If Rio Tinto is a contemporary colonialist, or postcolonial actor, it operates very differently than historical imperialists. For instance, if Boron, SLC, and Superior and Oak Flat are "colonies" of Rio Tinto, they are not occupied via corporate settlement. Treadmill expansion may be the goal of "mining capitalism," but it is not through imperial rule that Rio Tinto seeks empire. Rio Tinto does not settle in at these places of extraction. As such, extractive colonialism is beyond settler colonialism and is quite possibly a purer form of colonialism tailored to twenty-first century limits and demands.

While many have named this resource colonialism, have we also equally considered how the corporate persona works as a form of coloniality that stabilizes corporate, and namely colonial, presences where otherwise there is absence? Rather than sending settlers or employees to work and settle at these mines, or even creating a "colonial eye" that oversees social order, Rio Tinto alchemically transmutes what it extracts from the local community into a golden persona that becomes part of the local community and environment. In this way, Rio Tinto can also colonize many different places at once with minimal resources of its own. While local workers and residents endure the lasting environmental and health effects of mining (e.g., those in Bougainville), Rio Tinto prospers from afar without bearing any of its embodied costs.[114]

Rio Tinto is an assemblage. Understood by Deleuze and Guattari as a territorializing set of heterogenous parts, an assemblage is a network that "changes in nature as it expands its connections." An assemblage, to J. Macgregor Wise, "is a whole of some sort that expresses some identity and claims territory." Like how the term is used in archaeology, Rio Tinto is akin to "a group of fossils, that, appearing together, characterize a particular stratum" that "constitute[s] a group and . . . express[es] a particular character."[115] For our purposes, those characteristics have been named the corporate persona, and this persona allows

Rio Tinto to maintain numerous diverse, and sometimes competing, rhetorical presences in places that it dwells.

At the same time, Rio Tinto is a transcendent, rather than purely immanent, assemblage. Obviously, the company has a telos: extract at any cost to serve the profit motive. Therefore, the Rio Tinto assemblage is more akin to a fascistic actor than street performer. Yet at these different mines, Rio Tinto is still in different processes of becoming that may serve (or thwart) its interests but remain out of its control. Rio Tinto may be transcendent via its extractivist motives, but it still is not a Cartesian being with singular, rational, human essence, and this, again, presents problems with dialectical frameworks that attempt to interpret Rio Tinto (and other objects) within larger modern structures and systems of thought.

We saw how this works in each of our case studies. Rio Tinto takes on many different roles as a corporate performer, not a singular, reasonable, speaking subject, let alone a critical-rational, switch-sides debater. Rio Tinto is constantly becoming-Hollywood, -nature, -pioneer, -paternalistic through the relations it builds with people, places, objects. Are we too not constantly becoming–Rio Tinto as we read, write, text, or enjoy any other privileges afforded by earth minerals and metals?

Rio Tinto may be an elusive assemblage that escapes modernistic responsibilities and accountabilities, but it remains agentic. If we cannot determine Rio Tinto's transcendental essence—something perhaps better left for philosophers—that does not at all mean that we cannot take seriously extractive colonialities, air pollution, and exploitative labor. We just need to listen to the "rumblings of the avalanche" among stakeholders that have, potentially, already learned how to essentialize Rio Tinto.[116] In the following chapter, I elaborate this form of "strategic essentialism" and also discuss implications of this monograph to the idea of the "public screen."

Conclusion | Reflections on Becoming-Incorporated, Public Screens, and Strategic Essentialism

We can see now that Reagan's speech at Guildhall was much more complex than auditors may have believed. While Reagan may have tried to use technology as a realpolitik "matter of fact" to spread "the spirit of democracy," he also set in motion relations that were far from apolitical and neutral.[1] Foretelling how "the David of the microchip" would defeat "the Goliath of totalitarian control," he implicitly made the clarion call for mining companies such as Rio Tinto to defeat state control and censorship via extractivism. Rio Tinto was Reagan's secret chemical weapon. Like, if not as, "the oxygen of the modern age" (information), Rio Tinto "seeps through the walls topped with barbed wire and wafts across the electrified, booby-trapped borders."[2] As they both prepared for war, Reagan became–Rio Tinto (again).

Reagan fought China and the USSR with many different invisible weapons—Rio Tinto, information technology, other corporations—to "plant the seeds of democracy" and spread his idea of democracy. Speaking of the Tiananmen Square incident, which had happened just days before his speech, Reagan said, "You can't massacre an idea. You cannot run tanks over hope. You cannot riddle a people's yearning with bullets."[3] As a corporate subject, Reagan presciently said, "The biggest of Big Brothers is increasingly helpless against communications technology. . . . More than armies, more than diplomacy, more than the best intensions of democratic nations, the communications revolution will be the greatest force for the advancement of human freedom the world has seen."[4] Reagan and Rio Tinto won that war, and while Reagan passed away in 2004, he continues to live on through Rio Tinto at, among other places, Death Valley National Park and Boron, California. Today, Rio Tinto has been called upon once more to service global needs. Rather than a warrior advancing the "unstoppable march of technology," Rio Tinto is rhetorically needed as a sort of environmental peacekeeper for, as many have it, saving the planet with resources for renewable technologies. Even though these political actors, including President Biden, seem to treat renewable technology as seemingly neutral realpolitik "matters of fact," as Reagan did with communication technology, this book has shown that the processes of extracting their resources are anything but apolitical and inconsequential.

What does it mean to destroy entire mountains, ecologies, and places of dwelling, worship, and identity for precious mineral metals and the "renewable" technologies they build? How do the Oquirrh Mountains feel about this? Aldo Leopold once discussed how to think like a mountain by understanding its changing ecological systems from a nonhuman point of view. When the young Leopold kills a wolf in the mountains, thinking that it will lead to a "hunters' paradise," he looks into its "dying green eyes" and realizes he is wrong. Overpopulated deer ravage mountains. "Just as a deer herd lives in mortal fear of wolves, so does a mountain live in mortal fear of its deer." He adds, "And perhaps with better cause, for while a buck pulled down by wolves can be replaced in two or three years, a range pulled down by too many deer may fail of replacement in as many as many decades."[5] Thinking like a mountain then is to think ecologically.

How to think like a mountain when it has been turned into "the world's largest" copper mine? As impossible as this may sound, this is what is called upon us as we plunge deeper into the Anthropocene. How to think ecologically when neither mountain nor wolf can speak to the larger ecological networks that have disappeared? Without witnesses of extractive pasts, we are left instead with many different kinds of absences that define life in this epoch. The lost town of Bingham, which was swallowed by the Bingham Canyon Mine in 1972, is but one example. So too are other abandoned mining towns (e.g., Lark, Mercur), the Mormon lilies that Muir once admired, and the pine trees that Young and his followers used for timber. From these absences Rio Tinto comes to life. As the sort of elixir for alchemical rhetoric, the Bingham Canyon Mine is demonstrative of how mining companies have turned mountains into standing reserves for countless taken-for-granted technologies that we are coupled with.[6]

Was Reagan right? Has communication technology allowed global citizens to "sit in the shade of democracy" from the seeds planted since the Cold War? Over the past thirty years, technology has no doubt facilitated massive transformations as we have transitioned "from the public sphere to the public screen" and has led to many different democratic possibilities for social change.[7] At the same time, some would suggest that Reagan's neoliberal ideology set in motion the emergence of new totalitarian regimes, including in the United States, through misinformation, cyberwars, and demagoguery, not to mention the planned obsolescences and failures perpetuated by the unholy alliance of Wall Street and Silicon Valley.[8]

In rhetorical communication, public screens are perhaps the most illustrative of Reagan's dream for democracy vis-à-vis technology. They are also threaded with copper and borax, among many other minerals and metals extracted by Rio Tinto. Rio Tinto is just as much part of public screens as the screens and digital content itself, so if we take networks and assemblages seriously, this extractive company, among others, cannot be separated from the privileged forms of protest screens make possible. This also points to limitations of public screens as "wild" argumentative resources, as we must also consider the greater networks of relations that screens themselves are bound to, namely, natural resources and corporate subjects.[9]

Image events have no doubt enabled new forms of protest by those who otherwise do not have many resources for protest, but I am also suggesting that the very idea of "resources" of protest needs further problematization. Protest resources have always been a crucial component of rhetorics of social protest. From screens, signs of protest, T-shirts, music, metaphors, and, of course, money, resources of different sorts set the range of available means of persuasion—in other words, their affordances and constraints—for social change and advocacy. It is no wonder that private institutions such as think tanks and also fossil fuel companies, conservative networks, and political action campaigns have so effectively stalled climate policy by manufacturing so much doubt and skepticism about its technical basis, as they have direct access to tremendous financial resources for money/speech, advertisements, and campaigns.[10] What, though, about the natural resources, such as copper, borax, palladium, and lithium, that make protest, and not least of which "image events," possible? As "mind bombs" disseminated on public screens, image events have indeed created new worlds of shared struggle irreducible to speech, meaning, and language, but they are also *world-ending* practices that are controlled, terroristic, and incorporated. One look at the Bingham Canyon Mine, for instance, tells critics and media users everything they need to know about the fuller costs of digital media networks. This makes image events no less forceful, but it necessarily accounts for their greater ecological conditions and effects.

Visual rhetoric itself is largely extractive, particularly image events, because of the ways they distil from the world to advance certain political motives across panmediated networks such as Facebook, Instagram, Snapchat, and TikTok. While DeLuca and Peeples discuss "violent" image events disseminated by WTO protesters during the 1999 "Battle for Seattle," we must also bear in mind the violences inflicted upon mountains to build those screens and networks. Not only that but corporations, too, use image events (and all the time) for certain objectives, not least of which is Rio Tinto. Potentially, image events are extractive all the way down, but does it matter? Image events are no less forceful as extractive practices—if anything Rio Tinto accounts for the greater forces that they are tethered to—but we should also bear in mind the full range of costs of these resources for protest as just one of many examples of how our visual culture, is rooted in extractive sensibilities in the digital age.

From a Deleuzian or Latourian standpoint, visual networks, habits, and practices cannot be excluded from their extractive roots that sprawl from the Bingham Canyon Mines of the world to data mining, image events, and rhetorical criticism itself. Of course, this project too is not exempt from this critique given the range of photos—not least of which the image events of the Borax Mine and the Bingham Canyon Mine—that have supplemented the text (or vice versa). Image events and public screens remain crucially important for the study and practice of rhetorics of social protest (and also for plainly understanding how the world works). The broader point I am trying to make is that extractivism is a dominant sensibility that ought to be taken into account during the critical act. As Ronald Greene argued at the 2021 NCA Conference in Seattle, Washington, communication is an "extractive industry."[11]

Below I discuss strategic essentialism as one way of recognizing the role extractivism plays in rhetorical communication, especially during times of social protest, and using it in appropriative ways. If rhetorical communication is intrinsically extractive, then should that not be additional incentive for studying corporate rhetorics, not least of which by mining companies such as Rio Tinto? Said otherwise, why not extract from extraction industries? Radical environmental groups such as Earth First! and Greenpeace are good examples of how this works through image events and public screens, since many of their targets are outright extractive companies (timber, mining, oil). The Situationalists also strategically extracted from the (extracted) resources of corporate culture.[12] If extraction is an inevitable part of visual rhetoric, how to do so in strategic or ethical ways?

More generally, this book shows that these natural resources plainly matter when it comes to public screens, environmental debates, and social change. As political leaders and companies make pledges to decrease carbon emissions and transition to green technologies, we must also come to terms with how those technologies rely on the extraction of precious rare earth minerals and metals such as copper, borax, palladium, cadmium, tellurium, and lithium. Mineral and metal extraction is not a mere taking from some limitless honey pot, as if minerals and metals exist *terra nullius*. It is a world-ending process tied to tremendous violences against the earth, on which we all depend for survival. Extractivism as both an ideology and a practice also disproportionately affects the bodies, religions, and livelihoods of persons of color, women, and Indigenous people.[13]

Another conclusion pertains to the idea of the subject. While poststructuralists have rightly contended over the years that the subject is erased, or "dead," we also see here that Rio Tinto is subjectivized in a myriad of ways as a nonhuman, abstract actor. In Boron, California, Rio Tinto is a Hollywood star that appropriates the ethos of those such as Reagan himself to instantiate this small desert town as a somewhat famous global place that is necessary for global flows of mineral metals. In Salt Lake City, Rio Tinto is a member of the community that generates culture, fandom, and knowledge. And in Superior, Rio Tinto crafts a folksy, yet securitized, personality that creates a paternalistic presence. Clearly these subjectivities are called into question, to say the least, by social actors that see Rio Tinto differently, but for our purposes it shows subjectivity remains a negotiated term without the full presences of singular human actors. To Whitehead, subjects abound in our process-oriented world.[14] At the very least, subjectivity is a useful term for determining how discursive and extradiscursive rhetorics subjectivize actors with personae in our age of networks and assemblages.

To the contrary, Rio Tinto is an assemblage. After all, Rio Tinto exists in a constant state of transformation and change that is "not a content, but a performance, a happening born, existing, and transformed in social discourses" and material practices.[15] What then about accountability and prospects of environmental justice during a time when more and more societies are becoming increasingly dependent on rare earth metals for renewable energy technologies, communication networks, and so much more?

Rio Tinto is also somewhat disciplined and predictable. The very fact that Rio Tinto feels the need to craft particular personae in the Southwest indicates that it does not extract with total impunity like it has historically in other parts of the world (e.g., Papua New Guinea, Namibia, South Africa). Rhetorical communities can still shape corporate personae to meet certain social standards of corporate social responsibility. Certain social structures and institutions can obviously aid these endeavors (e.g., the law, policy). My point is that Rio Tinto is linked to many violences throughout the world, but many more extraction companies have a much worse track record. Rio Tinto, in fact, is not just one of the largest extractive companies of its kind, but it is also plainly one of the most environmental.

We have also seen that Rio Tinto is a colonial assemblage that strategically crafts personae that allow it to pass as a reasonable member of the local community so that it may extract from afar without enduring environmental costs. This suggests, again, that Rio Tinto is a transcendent, and far from purely immanent, actor that strategically crafts images to achieve goals (even if the effects of those efforts are totally out of its hands). This is one of the rhetorical affordances of the corporate personae: companies, extractive or otherwise, can create localized presences and advance objectives yet avoid certain responsibilities or accountabilities as singular actors. When it wants Rio Tinto can distance itself from those relations that could damage its image. At other times, it can build strong ties with the relations more beneficial to its persona. For instance, while Rio Tinto frequently distances itself from air pollution concerns in Salt Lake City, and toxic effects from mining pasts, it is eager to attach itself to possible sustainable futures through renewable technologies. This can also happen across different territories. Does Rio Tinto ever use positive relations at other mines to boost its localized ethos?

From a rhetorical standpoint, maintaining different personae allows Rio Tinto to shift its subjective positioning in ways that elude singular accountabilities. We might call this rhetorical strategy a *networked red herring*. In argumentation studies, red herrings or *ignoratio elenchi* involve a "misconception of refutation" that generally "refers to failure of relevance of argument."[16] Red herrings often involve inventively misleading arguments that may divert attention away from larger argumentative concerns. A networked red herring thus might be an ontological example of this pattern of reasoning wherein Rio Tinto can use its networked identity with many different personae to continuously "pass the buck" or detract from larger questions about its existence that would assume singular accountabilities. This also works to corporations' advantage when it comes to the law and its assumption that all actors are singular, rational human actors with intentionality. Potentially, other arguers also invoke this strategy to likewise escape legal responsibilities to other arguers, especially in an age of digital networks.

Then again, what good is the practice of naming argument fallacies in a post-dialectical world and when dealing with an assemblage that by definition is multiple, nonhuman, yet agentic?[17] When was the last time human publics even had a dialogue with Rio Tinto? Again, how to even have this exchange with an abstract corporate actor that primarily works through affects? Recall how mining shafts do not speak back. But also recall the importance of different forms of direct action. This networked red herring, then, is an ontological strategy wherein networks play into the reticulate nature of their existence to strategically avoid singular accountabilities.

Humans, too, can embrace the networked red herring. One such example might be Donald Trump, who is living proof of the *doxa* that corporations are people. Branded in his own self-image, Trump is, quite literally, the human manifestation of his mogul real estate company, The Trump Organization, which existed as a network on Twitter (at least before his ban). As a form of misdirection, or what Gordon Mitchell has called "strategic deception," Trump's networked arguments not only surpass dialectical standards of debate, but they use them to rhetorical advantage by luring counterarguments to interpret them in the dialectical sense while the network has already moved on to another topic, issue, or tweet.[18] While contradictions and what Monika Bauerlein and others call "partial truths" abound, critiquing such discourse from an outmoded critical-rational paradigm just increases the force of the Trumpian assemblage as it continues to succeed by moving horizontally as a network.[19] Studying Trump's tweets, for instance, from a dialectical standpoint that assumes quality rhetorical argument adheres to normative standards for substance, decorum, and dialogue misses the point that networked arguments need not be substantive to be effective; they operate by networks and force.[20]

Herein lies the strategy of misdirection: by disseminating torrents of fragmented arguments, or sound bites, Trump baits engaged criticism from networks of opposition (e.g., news reporters, editors, talk show hosts) while the Trumpian network moves elsewhere and grows in force by increased attention. Trump is a corporate actor that plays into his networked ontology.[21] Potentially, corporations, and no less extractive ones, are simply better models for subjectivity than the human speaking, rational subject.

Like Trump, Rio Tinto is also illustrative of how social change works. For instance, in each of our case studies, we saw how Rio Tinto builds an image of its authorless self through affects, objects, and forces to stabilize its place-based identities. In Boron, it has built an entire town in its own self-image while exploiting its workers. In Salt Lake, Rio Tinto generates a culture industry that associates its identity with cultural life, entertainment, and knowledge despite contributing to some of the worst air pollution in the United States. At Resolution, it paints itself as a folksy, father-like figure, as it carries out a legacy of extractive coloniality. These rhetorical strategies are hugely problematic for class consciousness, climate justice, and human rights, but they nevertheless show how social change works through persona, affects, and objects.

Strategically Essentializing Rio Tinto

Rio Tinto may be a multiple subject that plays into its ontology to avoid certain responsibilities or accountabilities, but it can also be strategically essentialized as a singular actor to achieve particular political objectives. To Gayatri Chakravorty Spivak, strategic essentialism conceptually refers to the political practice in which subaltern groups represent themselves in strategically essentialistic ways to achieve certain goals.[22] While strategic essentialism has been studied, and practiced, in many ways over the years, the case before us is suggestive of how it can also be used to temporarily essentialize Rio Tinto. Rio Tinto may not have an essence, but it can be rhetorically essentialized, as colonial or otherwise, to achieve certain political motivations by temporarily stopping, or even reversing, the personae used to reach its transcendent goals.[23]

Considering the role of counterprotesters, or publics, advocating for clean air, better labor practices, and self-determination and religious freedoms at all these different locations, strategic essentialism can account for the ways that these actors—and other movements—reduce corporations to essentialistic actors as intrinsically colonial, capitalistic, or racist. For instance, as San Carlos Apache fight for their sacred land and invoke memories of genocide to contest the Resolution Mine at public hearings, they are also strategically essentializing Rio Tinto as colonialist or even genocidal.

Alternatively, while Spivak suggests that strategic essentialism is unique to those who are marginalized or oppressed, have corporations such as Rio Tinto appropriated this strategy for their own advocacies and movements? Rio Tinto's personae are also strategic essentialisms of larger identities synthesized for strategic monetary transcendences. Strategic essentialism thus potentially cuts both ways. In an era of movements defined by networks (social, corporate, and ecological), strategic essentialism takes on new significance for corporations and their critics as it could be a tactic used, and appropriated, by those in tremendous positions of power, not just the subaltern.

That said, are counterarguers not selectively mining fragments of its past, present, or possible future to monkey wrench its personae? For instance, at several 2019 public hearings about Resolution's EIS Draft analyzed in previous chapters, more than a few commenters drew from Rio Tinto's current and historical mining sites to make claims that the company is a colonial and genocidal actor. Drawing from Rio Tinto's different sites of extraction around the globe (e.g., Mongolia or Papua New Guinea) and linking these events to histories of resource colonization strategically essentializes the company's persona as violent, terroristic, and colonial.

Apache Stronghold also does this using place-based and embodied rhetorics at Oak Flat. When Apache Stronghold occupies Oak Flat with its wikiups, teepee, and signs of protest, for instance, they interrupt Rio Tinto's plans to seamlessly extract this site because no longer is it an "extractive zone" but a home worth defending.[24] It is also not by accident that signs and displays of protest at Oak Flat have display lights around them, which are presumably used at night to spotlight the significance of these sites and draw attention to the ensuing violence of Rio Tinto. In other words, they are designed for, and as, image events on public screens, which can be considered appropriative form of extractivism that extracts scenes in real time for exploitative purposes.

Utah Moms for Clean Air and Utah Physicians for a Healthy Environment also essentialize Rio Tinto as a polluter that outsources the costs of business. Consider also the "citizens lawsuit" against Rio Tinto's violation of federal State Implementation Plan limits on pollution. The suit failed to pass legal muster but nevertheless disseminated the larger message about Rio Tinto's business practices. News about the lawsuit also traveled to Arizona and was used as a resource for protest by at least one public commenter in the 2019 EIS Draft (Don Zoebel). The lawsuit may have never had much ground in a state that runs off the motto "Industry," but it nevertheless succeeded rhetorically. An example of what Marek Muller has named a "litigious event," the case raised awareness about larger issues about Rio Tinto's arguably illegal practices that keep the skies full of pollution.[25] By effect, Rio Tinto's persona as pioneer of different sorts, including environmental, is not just called into question but reappropriated as Rio Tinto is characterized as a possible crime boss.

Those in Boron on the 107-day lockout also essentialized Rio Tinto by looking to past and present injustices of Rio Tinto's global network. This is most explicit in the film *Locked Out*, which itself includes many image events on public screens, when laborers look to Rio Tinto's historical ties with Franco's oppressive government and link its operations to the crimes against humanity committed in Bougainville.

Thomas Rickert, as noted in the introduction, has suggested a more worldly and ambient view of rhetorical communication, as opposed to "the extraction model," but is it ever possible to study and produce rhetoric without extracting from the world in some way or another while conducting criticism in the digital age? This is even more profound when addressing environmental effects from extractive Titans such as Rio Tinto. Can we ever replenish or nurture while also disseminating to wider audiences? If not, strategic essentialism may be one way to appropriate extractivism, and exploitation, against those who benefit from this practice the most (e.g., Rio Tinto).

This book at the very least might enable critics to name, and critique, extractive industries in our everyday lives. Rio Tinto is not only a metonymy for how corporate personhood works in the Anthropocene, but it is also exemplary of how extraction companies structure our lives, play politics, and shape work, ideology, and desire. Ronald Reagan is just one of many examples. We must also bear in mind all the Rio Tintos that run the world (Facebook, X, Donald Trump, not to mention journals, departments, conferences) and also the ones we ourselves are coupled with: Microsoft, Apple, Sony. In the age of big data and data mining, rhetorical communication, and the study of it, is an extractive practice. Are we not all becoming–Rio Tinto? Rio Tinto is the story of us.

Notes

Introduction

1. The "corporate persona" is a term that will be unpacked in the following chapter. For now, it can be understood as a singular rhetorical identity from an invisible rhetor/author that is otherwise multiple. The philosophical subject is an important part of this concept. Subjectivity is a term that will be troubled throughout this book, but for the purposes here it is used to suggest the networked agencies tied to corporations, specifically Rio Tinto. Rio Tinto, I will suggest, is an assemblage with many different relations, agencies, and subjectivities. As part of Rio Tinto's assemblage, Reagan was thus "not quite himself."
2. Associated Press, "Reagan Urges 'Risk.'"
3. Ibid.
4. Bellamy Foster et al., *Ecological Rift*.
5. Rio Tinto, "About."
6. Statista, "Revenue of Rio Tinto"; Murray, "Profiling the Top Five."
7. Hardt and Negri, *Empire*, 13.
8. Greene, "Rhetoric and Capitalism"; Latour, "From Realpolitik to Dingpolitik."
9. DeLuca and Peeples, "Public Sphere to Public Screen."
10. Gómez-Barris, *Extractive Zone*. See Paliewicz, "Arguments of Green Colonialism."
11. Greene, "Rhetorical Capital."
12. Bloomfield, "Energy Darwinism."
13. "New Frontiers."
14. Rushing, "Mythic Evolution," 265. As many others have argued in rhetorical criticism, this myth has been used as a rhetorical device in many different contexts. See Dorsey, "Frontier Myth"; Stuckey, "Donner Party"; Rowland, "Mythic Criticism."
15. Ceccarelli, *Frontier of Science*.
16. This point about the links between industrialism and the social construction of nature is in conversation with DeLuca, "Trains in the Wilderness."
17. Bhandar, *Lives of Property*.
18. Ibid.; McGee, "'People.'"
19. Schneider et al., *Under Pressure*. For more on Reagan's rhetorical agency, see Drury, "Beyond 'Rhetorical Agency.'"
20. Schneider et al., *Under Pressure*, 3.
21. Ibid., 145.
22. Ibid., 4.
23. Ibid, 146.
24. Ibid.
25. Brown, *Undoing the Demos*, 31; Asen, "Neoliberalism."
26. For example, see Bricker and Justice, "Greenwashing Through Conciliatio;" Budinsky and Bryant, "Greenwashing of Environmental Discourses"; Plec and Pettenger, "Greenwashing Consumption."
27. Macfarlane, *Underland*.

28. Ibid., 14.

29. BBC, "Rio Tinto Ordered."

30. Wahlquist, "Rio Tinto Blasts."

31. Ibid, paragraph 21.

32. BBC, "Rio Tinto."

33. Copper is also the focus of two of my three case studies (chapters 3 and 4).

34. Basov, "Copper Production Declines."

35. Ibid.

36. Taylor, "'Age of Copper.'"

37. Copper Alliance, "Future Copper Demand"; McKibben, "Terrifying New Math."

38. DeLuca and Peeples, "From Public Sphere."

39. Nogrady, "Materials in Every Phone."

40. Sweney, "Shortage in Computer Chips."

41. Diamond, *Collapse*.

42. Ibid., 467.

43. Ibid.

44. Heffernan, "New Bronze Age," paragraph 1.

45. Burke, *Permanence and Change*, 59.

46. Ibid., 42; Biggs, "Idea of Magic," 363.

47. Burke, *Rhetoric of Motives*, 42, italics added for emphasis.

48. Covino, "*National Enquirer*," 25–26.

49. Johnson, "Magic of *The Eminem Show*," 270.

50. Ibid.

51. Jensen, "Chemical Rhetoric."

52. Ibid. For more on the uses of chemical rhetoric see Jensen, "Improving Upon Nature"; Jensen, *Infertility*.

53. A neologistic blend of haven, heaven, and hell, "Helhaven," to Burke, is a sort of "Mighty Paradisal Culture-Bubble on the moon" to which Earth refugees travel to escape the "waste imperative" of our planetary "hypertechnologism." The irony of course is that these travelers would still have to return to "the placenta of Mother Earth" to replenish their natural resources. Burke, "Towards Helhaven." See also McLemee, "Towards Helhaven."

54. For example, see Jung, *Psychology and Alchemy*; Jackson, "Alchemy of Jim Wallis"; Rojecki, "Rhetorical Alchemy."

55. Gunn and Frentz, "Da Vinci Code."

56. Baudrillard, *Simulacra and Simulation*.

57. West, *River of Tears*, 14.

58. Ibid., 16.

59. For more examples of cases that bring together rhetoric, place, and memory, see Dickinson et al., *Places of Public Memory*.

60. See Nash, *Rio Tinto Mine*. The idea of corporate remembrances is conversant with what Greg Dickinson et al., have called places of public memory, which emphasizes the importance of place for "rhetorical (both symbolic and material) character and function." This is a term I come back to in chapter 2.

61. Phillips, "Eliding Extraction."

62. Burke, *Permanence*.

63. Ahmed, "Affective Economies," 114.

64. Massumi, *Capitalism and Schizophrenia*, 100; Massumi, "Translator's Forward," xvi. See Abel, *Violent Affect*.

65. See Law, "Actor Network Theory."

66. For more on political and economic rhetorics surrounding corporate personhood, see Musgrave, *Persons of the Market*. The history of corporate personhood and empire and expansion has roots in the Dutch East India Company. See Harman, *Immaterialism*; Stern, *Company-State*.

67. Pezzullo, "Resisting 'National Breast Cancer,'" 346.

68. See Jensen, "Chemical Rhetoric."

69. Klein, *No Logo*; see Harold, *Things Worth Keeping*.

70. Bennett, *Vibrant Matter*.

71. For more on historical geological assemblages see DeLanda, *Thousand Years*.

72. Abbey, *Down the River*, 31.

73. Johnson, *Rhetoric, Inc.*, 6.

74. Ibid., 7.

75. Greene, "Another Materialist Rhetoric"; Greene, "More Materialist Rhetoric"; Greene, "Y Movies."

76. See Harold, *OurSpace*.

77. Kennedy, "Hoot in the Dark"; Light, "Visualizing Homeland," 536; Middleton et al., *Participatory Critical Rhetoric*.

78. Kennedy, "Hoot in the Dark."

79. Hasian, "Remembering and Forgetting," 66.

80. Said, *World*.

81. Haraway, "Situated Knowledges," 581.

82. Quoted in Asad, "Historical Notes."

83. See Gourgouris, *Lessons in Secular Criticism*.

84. Middleton et al., *Participatory Critical Rhetoric*; McHendry et al., "Rhetorical Critic(ism)'s Body."

85. Middleton et al., "Articulating Rhetorical Field Methods."

86. See Wanzer, "Delinking Rhetoric"; Hess et al., "Critical Rhetoric," 15.

87. McHendry et al., "Rhetorical Critic(ism)'s Body," 298. See Hartnett, "Communication, Social Justice."

88. Ibid., 294.

89. Regarding the fascistic line of inquiry, readers, for instance, may wish to bear in mind that Benito Mussolini once said, "Fascism should more appropriately be called Corporatism because it is a merger of state and corporate power." In Casey, "Quote of the Day," paragraph 1. See also Lasslett, *State Crime*; Stern, *Company-State*.

90. Deleuze and Guattari, *Thousand Plateaus*.

91. Ibid.

92. Berry, *Another Turn*.

93. Senda-Cook, "Long Memories."

94. Harold, *Things Worth Keeping*.

95. Rickert, *Ambient Rhetoric*, 160.

96. Ono and Sloop, "Commitment to Telos"; Wolff, "Strategic Essentialism."

97. See de Onís, *Energy Islands*; Pezzullo and de Onís, "Rethinking Rhetorical Field Methods."

98. Harold, *Things Worth Keeping*.

99. This is a reference to Haraway, *Staying with the Trouble*; Milstein and Castro-Sotomayor, *Routledge Handbook*.

100. LeCain, *Mass Destruction*.

101. Harold, "Pranking Rhetoric"; see Rancière, *Dissensus*.

102. For more on this kind of dialogue see Bakhtin, *Dialogic Imagination*.

Chapter 1

1. Rio Tinto Kennecott, "Operation."

2. Žižek, *Interrogating the Real*; Heidegger, "Question Concerning Technology."

3. Barnett, *Mourning in the Anthropocene*; Barnett and Gore, "Dwelling in the Anthropocene"; Barnett, "Naming, Mourning." This chapter adapted from previous work on ethos at the Bingham Canyon Mine. Paliewicz, "Copper Mine."

4. Davis, *Inessential Solidarity*.

5. Ibid.; Hawhee, *Tooth and Claw*; Rickert, *Ambient Rhetoric*; Seegert, "Play of Sniffication."

6. See chapters 1 and 2 in Johnson, *Rhetoric, Inc.*

7. Cheney, "Corporate Person"; Cheney, "Rhetoric of Identification"; Cheney and McMillan, "Organizational Rhetoric"; McMillan, "Organizational Persona."

8. Robichaud, *Plato's Persona*, 35.

9. Peters, *Speaking into the Air*; Ong, *Orality and Literacy*.

10. Robichaud, *Plato's Persona*, 35.

11. Ibid.

12. Ibid., 28.

13. Foucault, *Order of Things*; Barthes, "Death of the Author."

14. Lowe, *Bourgeois Perception*; also Ong, *Orality and Literacy*.

15. Ibid.

16. Massumi, *Politics of Affect*, 3, 17.

17. See McKibben, *End of Nature*.

18. For more on the problems of Nature and its assumed subject, see Evernden, *Creation of Nature*.

19. Morton, "Ecology Without the Present," 232.

20. Ibid.

21. Paliewicz and McHendry, "Fascistic Argumentation."

22. Casati and Varzi, *Holes*, 5.

23. Ibid., 6.

24. Derrida, *Of Grammatology*.

25. Morton, "Ecology Without Present," 232.

26. Peeples, "Toxic Sublime."

27. Heidegger, "Question Concerning Technology," 322.

28. Muir, *Steep Trails*, 91.

29. Ibid., 91.

30. Heidegger, "Question Concerning Technology," 322.

31. Dark, "Mining Memories."

32. Wentling, "Ute Brave."

33. Heidegger, "Question Concerning Technology," 322.

34. LeCain, *Mass Destruction*.

35. Ibid.

36. Ibid.

37. Ibid., 7.

38. Ibid., 8.

39. Quoted in LeCain, *Mass Destruction*, 8; Cronon, *Nature's Metropolis*.

40. Rio Tinto Kennecott, "Operation."

41. Lee, "Most Toxic States."

42. Environmental Protection Agency, "Superfund," last modified May 26, 2021, https://www
.epa.gov/superfund.

43. Ibid.

44. Kolbert, *Sixth Extinction*.

45. See Mitchell, *Fourfold*.

46. DeLuca, "Articulation Theory."

47. Black, "Second Persona," 111.

48. Black, *Rhetorical Criticism*, 5.

49. Ibid.

50. Black, "Second Persona"; Wander, "Third Persona"; Cloud, "Null Persona"; Morris,
"Pink Herring."

51. Black, "Second Persona," 110. It will be advanced that corporations' personae are derived
from discursive and extradiscursive networks. Though this relates to Cloud's powerful notion
of the null persona because of the importance of extradiscursive material, it is also important
to bear in mind that corporations come from tremendous positions of power and privilege
rather than disenfranchisement. The effect, therefore, is the opposite of silence. Cloud, "Null
Persona."

52. Black, *Rhetorical Criticism*, 5.

53. Cheney, "Rhetoric of Identification"; McMillan, "Organizational Persona."

54. Hawhee, *Tooth and Claw*; McGreavy et al., *Tracing Rhetoric*; Rickert, *Ambient Rhetoric*;
Seegert, "Play of Sniffication."

55. Black, "Second Persona," 111. Italics added for emphasis.

56. Ibid.

57. Ibid.

58. Morris, "Pink Herring."

59. Ibid., 230.

60. Ibid., 230.

61. Ibid., 228.

62. Sanchez, "Trump, the KKK."

63. Gibbons, "Persona 4.0."

64. There is also the question of intentionality. While communication and marketing teams
certainly craft particular messages, and architectural designs, for maximum effect, the collective
force of Rio Tinto's alchemy can also be an accidental effect of dissemination.

65. Cloud, "Null Persona," 177.

66. Ibid., 178.

67. See Hill, "Conventional Wisdom"; Campbell, "Responses to Wander."

68. Barthes, "Death of the Author."

69. See Rickert, *Ambient Rhetoric*; Rickert, "Toward the Chōra."

70. The corporate persona does not necessarily have to be about for-profit corporations
(forests, mountains, wolf packs, airports, and cities would also count), but it is just the most
convenient for studying Rio Tinto. Nevertheless, it is important to bear in mind that the fifth
persona is not necessarily unique to incorporated for-profit companies in the abstract, as
humans are also incorporated subjects.

71. Ceccarelli, *On the Frontier of Science*.

72. Wander, "Third Persona"; McKerrow, "Critical Rhetoric."

73. Black, "Second Persona."

74. Morton, "Ecology Without the Present."

Chapter 2

1. Bhandar, *Lives of Property*.
2. Quoted in Jaffe, "What You'll Find," paragraph 2.
3. Hasian, "Remembering and Forgetting."
4. Cram. *Violent Inheritance*, 6–7.
5. Ceccarelli, *On the Frontier of Science*; Rushing, "Mythic Evolution"; see Dickinson et al., "Memory and Myth"; Ott et al., "Seeing Guns."
6. Dickinson et al., *Places of Public Memory*.
7. Ibid., 6. For an excellent example of how place manages anxieties in the present, especially through material things within cultures of consumerism, see Sturken, *Tourists of History* and also her new book *Terrorism in American Memory*, which aptly details how our post-9/11 era has transformed memory into a battleground for competing national identities that help explain our current political moment of division.
8. Environmental Protection Agency, "Toxic Release Inventory."
9. Rio Tinto, "Borates."
10. Britannica, "Borate Mineral."
11. National Park Service, "Death Valley."
12. See Jeansonne and Luhrssen, "Reagan and the West."
13. Fox, "'Death Valley Days.'"
14. Hotel Online, "Ties to Furnace Creek."
15. Myfootage.com, "Ronald Reagan Boraxo Commercial" (:58).
16. Evans, "GE Years."
17. 20 Mule Team Borax, "U.S. Borax."
18. Gregg, "Ego-Function."
19. Abbey, *Desert Solitaire*, 39–59.
20. Foucault, Michel. "Of Other Spaces," 22–27.
21. Orr, "History of Muroc."
22. Desert Way, "Boron Federal Prison."
23. 20 Mule Team Borax, "U.S. Borax."
24. Strong, "Ghost Towns."
25. See Sturken, *Tourists of History*.
26. Wachowski, *The Matrix*; Baudrillard, *Simulacra and Simulation*.
27. Encyclopedia, "U.S. Borax." On average these employees make $59,240. "U.S. Borax Salary," SalaryList.
28. Retrieved from poster outside Twenty Mule Team Museum. No source.
29. Schneider et al., *Under Pressure*, 4.
30. Foucault, "Of Other Spaces."
31. This is a pseudonym to protect the identity of the employee.
32. Hudson Institute of Mineralogy, "Rio Tinto Borax Mine."
33. Newspaper clipping; Donna Fairchild, source unknown.
34. Orr, "History of Boron California."
35. Thoreau, "Walking."
36. 20 Mule Team Borax, "Boron 20 Mule Team Days."
37. Racinez, "Twenty Mule Team Museum."
38. Cronon, *Nature's Metropolis*.
39. Evernden, *Creation of Nature*.
40. This is taken from the posterboard in the "Processing" section.
41. Nye, *American Technological Sublime*.

42. Schneider et al., *Under Pressure*, 4.

43. It is worthwhile mentioning that the Spanish roots of this name, Rio Tinto, also helps the company adapt to the cultural landscape of the West, which has its own cultural and linguistic imprints of Spanish colonization. It would potentially be a very different rhetorical situation if Rio Tinto were instead named after a current or past CEO.

44. Milstein and Castro-Sotomayor, *Routledge Handbook*.

45. King, "It Cuts Both Ways."

46. Sekler, *Locked Out*.

47. This is the title of a sign at Zabriskie Point; see National Park Service, "Zabriskie Point."

48. Abbey, *Desert Solitaire*, 51.

49. Irvine, *Desert Cabal*.

50. Abbey, *Desert Solitaire*, 126.

Chapter 3

1. Boutwell, *Economic Geology*.

2. Hammond, "History of Mining," 121.

3. Actually there are traces of these mineral metals in our bodies. Most adult bodies have 50 to 120 mg copper and 0.229 mg of gold. We also consume on average 70 to 88 micrograms of silver every day; National Institute of Health, "Copper"; Petri Dish, "How Much Gold?"; Dartmouth, "Facts on Silver."

4. Malouf, "Behind the Beehive."

5. Heffernan, "Copper Giant."

6. Earthworks, "Problems with Bingham Canyon Mine."

7. Jamasmie, Cecilia, "Kennecott Wins Lawsuit."

8. Klaus and Mayhew, "Kennecott Causes One-Third."

9. Furniss, "Myth of the Frontier."

10. Ceccarelli, *Frontier of Science*.

11. Ibid.

12. Dickinson et al., *Places of Public Memory*, 26.

13. See Young, *Texture of Memory*.

14. Ockey, "20 Things to Do."

15. For more on the significance of cultural reenactments at places (particularly memorials and museums), see Sturken, *Tourists of History*.

16. Senda-Cook, "Rugged Practices."

17. This Is the Place Heritage Park, "About Us."

18. Maxfield, "Creation and Erasure."

19. Stuckey, "Donner Party"; Dorsey, "Frontier Myth."

20. Adorno and Horkheimer, *Dialectic of Enlightenment*; Adorno, *Culture Industry*.

21. Ibid.

22. Dartmouth, "Copper."

23. Gibson, "Protests Groups." For more on greenwashing during the Olympics, see Glasson, "Environmental Myth-Work."

24. Kemp et al., "Clean Energy?"

25. Rio Tinto Kennecott, "New Tellurium Plant."

26. O'Donoghue, "Rarer Than Gold," paragraph 9.

27. Rio Tinto, "Public Comment."

28. Rio Tinto, "Lithium Production."

29. The Copper Mark, "Kennecott the First."

30. Ibid. See United Nations Sustainable Development Goals, "Goal 12."

31. See Light, "Visualizing Homeland."

32. Peeples, "Toxic Sublime," 375. See Barnett, "Toxic Portraits."

33. Adams, "Massive Landslide."

34. Hammond, *History of the Mining*, 123.

35. Pezzullo, *Toxic Tourism*.

36. Ibid., 4.

37. Axiomatization broadly refers to how capitalism controls, and commodifies, desires. As George McHendry points out, the axiomatization of image events on public screens can reproduce capitalistic ideology in ways counter to environmental social movements. McHendry, "Whale War"; Deleuze and Guattari, *Thousand Plateaus*.

38. See Sturken, *Tourists of History*.

39. Pezzullo, *Toxic Tourism*, 2009, 79.

40. Žižek, *Interrogating the Real*, 31; see Peeples, "Toxic Sublime."

41. Marriott Utah Library, Special Collection, Utah Copper Division, 1956, Box 1, Folder 6.

42. This argument is also made in Paliewicz, "Industrial Pioneerism."

43. Larry H. Miller Group, "Estate Acquires Daybreak."

44. Gorrell, "Kennecott Sells Daybreak."

45. Dickinson, *Suburban Dreams*.

46. Dickinson, "Pleasantville Effect," 213.

47. Semerad, "Daybreak's Mission," paragraph 6.

48. Personal correspondence, February 2015.

49. Rio Tinto Kennecott, "Daybreak's History," paragraph 2.

50. Ibid., paragraph 1.

51. Personal correspondence, February 2015.

52. Schneider et al., *Under Pressure*; Foucault, "Other Spaces."

53. See Vaifanua, "Daybreak Homeowners File Lawsuit," paragraph 10.

54. See Saindon, "Doubled Heterotopia."

55. For an archival account of this stadium and other "places of corporate community" in SLC, see Paliewicz, "Country."

56. Byers, "Real Salt Lake."

57. Renzhofer, "Real Salt Lake's," paragraph 12.

58. Waalkes, "Does Soccer Explain."

59. Hinck, *Love of Fandom*.

60. Ibid., 51.

61. Ibid.

62. Bellah, "Civil Religion."

63. See Eckstein, "Sound Arguments."

64. Gaschk, "RSL's Fans."

65. Asen, "Neoliberalism, the Public Sphere."

66. Dickinson, "Pleasantville Effect." This is also a possible dimension of what Schneider et al. have called "energy utopia," which suggests a particular energy source, or for our purposes, metals are key to the "good life" and "transcends the conflicts of environment, justice, and politics." Schneider et al., *Under Pressure*, 4.

67. Personal correspondence, February 2015.

68. Casey, *World at a Glance*.

69. See DeLuca and Peeples, "Public Sphere to Public Screen."

70. Real Salt Lake Communications, "Rio Tinto Stadium."

71. See Engels, "Origin of the Family."

72. Devout RSL fans have reported, via personal correspondence, that the only part of the stadium where one can potentially find traces of Rio Tinto is in the bathrooms.

73. LeCain, *Mass Destruction.*

74. Natural History Museum of Utah, "Our Building."

75. Harris, "Home for Natural History," paragraph 1.

76. Personal correspondence, March 2015.

77. Ibid.

78. Harris, paragraph 2.

79. Personal correspondence.

80. Oravec and Clark, "Naming, Interpretation," 3.

81. Milstein, "Nature Identification," 4.

82. Maffly, "Museum Galleries," paragraph 3.

83. Sustainability Trail, 2015, paragraph 1, emphasis added.

84. Ibid.

85. Phillips, "Eliding Extraction."

86. Weber, *Protestant Ethic*; Bloomfield, "Energy Darwinism."

87. Maxfield, "Creation and Erasure."

88. Deleuze and Guattari, *Thousand Plateaus.*

89. Emel and Huber, "Richest Hole."

90. Environmental Protection Agency, "Abandoned Mine Lands."

91. Environmental Protection Agency, "Toxic Release Inventory Explorer."

92. Shatz, "Tall Tailings."

93. Smerecnik and Renegar, "Capitalistic Agency."

94. Apache Stronghold. "Ever Growing Story." For more on resource colonialism, see Gedicks, *New Resource Wars*; Endres, "Nuclear Colonialism."

95. Stuckey and Murphy, "Any Other Name."

Chapter 4

1. Solis, "Sparky's Quill."

2. "History of Superior Region," http://zybtarizona.com/suhist.htm.

3. Bhandar, *Lives of Property.*

4. Stuckey and Murphy, "Any Other Name," 76.

5. Conway, "Active Mines."

6. GeoEngineer, "Block Caving."

7. Main, "Sacred Native American."

8. United States Department of Agriculture (USDA), "EIS Public Hearing," 32.

9. United States House of Representatives, "Irreparable Environmental."

10. In fact, Flake was once a lobbyist for Rio Tinto's Rössing Mine in Namibia. Goldmacher, "Flake's Past."

11. Burroughs, "Mine at Oak Flat."

12. Ibid.

13. See Lauren Redniss for a beautiful artistic display of these forces and temporalities. Redniss, *Oak Flat.*

14. Kelety, "Biden Administration."

15. H.R. 1884, Save Oak Flat Act.

16. Wahlquist, "Rio Tinto Blasts."

17. Black, "Second Persona."

18. Smith, *Conquest*.

19. So fecund was this mine that it produced an estimated $42 million between 1875 and 1900 and even attracted the likes of Wyatt Earp, Mattie Blaylock/Earp, and Doc Holiday. Wilsdon, "Brief History."

20. Superior was named by one claimant of the former Silver Queen Mine, George Lobb, after selling his holdings in Michigan-based company Lake Superior and Arizona Mining Company (LS&A). Walker and Chilton, "History of Mining."

21. "History of Superior Region."

22. Briggs, "Magma Mine."

23. Superior, "Our Story."

24. Rookhuzen, "Throwback Thursday."

25. Bold Canyon Outdoors, "Old Mining Wagon Wheel Tracks."

26. See Senda-Cook, "Rugged Practices."

27. "History of Superior Region."

28. Westland Resources, "Remembering the Smelter," 2018.

29. Resolution Copper, "Magma Copper Smelter."

30. Westland Resources, "Remembering the Smelter."

31. Lamberti, "Resolution Copper."

32. Mining Connection, "Resolution Copper Completes."

33. Resolution, "Copper Triangle's Economy"; see Stuckey and Murphy, "By Another Name"

34. Ibid.

35. Endres, "Sacred Land."

36. McGee, "'People,'" 237.

37. Ibid., 240.

38. BHP had big plans to extract copper from San Manual holdings—located about sixty-three miles southeast of Superior—but only a few years later shut it down because of excessive costs for "care and maintenance" ($800 million), making it one of the "most disastrous acquisitions to date." Jamasmie, "Rio Tinto."

39. Ibid.

40. McGee, "People."

41. Endres and Senda-Cook, "Location Matters."

42. See Urry, *Mobilities*; Gehl and Cozen, "Passé Media."

43. Mirzoeff, *Right to Look*.

44. See Mignolo and Walsh, *On Decoloniality*. Coloniality and colonialism are not the same. The former refers to the rhetorics or logics invoked to perpetuate colonialism, and the former has to do with legacies of imperialism and occupation that some suggest culminated in the nineteenth century. At the same time, the end of this chapter presents readers with the very real possibility that Rio Tinto is not just using coloniality to service extractivist objectives, but it quite possibly is, at the essential level, a colonial being.

45. Siegfried, "Making Settler Colonialism."

46. Black, *American Indians*, 85.

47. Ibid.

48. Ibid.

49. Cloud, "Hegemony or Concordance," 116.

50. Resolution Copper, "Protecting Cultural Resources."

51. Deloria, *Playing Indian*.

52. Endres, "American Indian," 649.

53. Redniss, *Oak Flat*.

54. Ibid., 169.

55. See Morris, "Educating Savages."

56. Endres, "Sacred Land."

57. See Peeples, "Aggressive Mimicry."

58. Note that these conservationist responsibilities are delegated to many different organizations. This feeds into Resolution's rhetorical strategy by diffusing its accountabilities and responsibilities, even though it creates a singular persona. We might label this strategy a corporate, or networked, red herring.

59. Oravec, "Conservationism vs. Preservationism."

60. Resolution Copper, "On Site with Mike."

61. Resolution Copper, "Water."

62. See Peeples, "Aggressive Mimicry."

63. Rio Tinto, "About."

64. United States Securities and Exchange Commission, "List of Subsidiaries."

65. Welch, "Earth, Wind, and Fire."

66. LaDuke, *Recovering the Sacred*; Estes, *Our History*; Powell, *Landscapes of Power*; Broere, Edstrom, and Trench, *Dodging Bullets*.

67. See Black, "Remembrances of Removal"; Wanzer-Serrano, *New York Young Lords*; Harold, "Pranking Rhetoric."

68. Black, "Remembrances of Removal." This is an example of a place-based rhetoric that can be particularly effective for disciplining extractive corporations that are otherwise placeless.

69. Ibid.

70. See Sturken, *Terrorism in American Memory*.

71. Onís, *Energy Islands*.

72. See Harold, *OurSpace*.

Chapter 5

1. In Redniss, *Oak Flat*, 17.

2. Ibid.

3. Ibid.

4. Ibid., 21.

5. Ibid., 23.

6. Apache Stronghold, "Defending Holy Sites."

7. NoiseCat, "Apaches Rally."

8. EarthWorks, "Oak Flat," paragraph 7.

9. Deleuze and Guattari, *Thousand Plateaus*.

10. Jason Edward Black also uses this term in his book *American Indians*.

11. Abbey, *Monkeywrench Gang*.

12. Ibid.

13. Ibid., 16.

14. Macfarlane, "On *The Monkey Wrench Gang*."

15. Ibid.

16. Ibid.

17. See Yale University, "Energy History."

18. Foreman and Haywood, Ecodefense, 140, 174.

19. DeLuca, *Image Politics*.

20. Ibid., DeLuca, "Unruly Arguments."
21. Abbey, *Monkey Wrench Gang*, 167. See Curry, *If a Tree Falls*.
22. Shaviro, *Without Criteria*, 60.
23. Hunt et al., "Radical Potential."
24. Ibid.
25. The following chapter talks about this strategy as "strategic essentialism."
26. The famous *Ríotinto* (tainted river) mine was owned by the Spanish government until 1873 when it was purchased by investors that incorporated Rio Tinto, the company. Richard West's book, *River of Tears*, thoroughly traces this history and its various social and ecological effects.
27. USDA, "EIS Public Hearing," Superior, AZ, 11.
28. Ibid.
29. Ibid.
30. USDA, "EIS Public Hearing," San Tan Valley, AZ, 33.
31. USDA, "EIS Public Hearing," Tempe, AZ, 68.
32. See Lee, "Environmentalists Sue."
33. USDA, "EIS Public Hearing," Tempe, 35.
34. Ibid.
35. Ibid., 36.
36. USDA, "EIS Public Hearing," Superior, 11.
37. USDA, "EIS Public Hearing," Queen Valley, 60.
38. USDA, "EIS Public Hearing," Tempe, 37.
39. Black, *American Indians*.
40. USDA, "EIS Public Hearing," Superior, 43.
41. Leighter and Black, "'Raising the Question.'"
42. Lake, "Enacting Red Power."
43. USDA, "EIS Public Hearing," Queen Valley, 36.
44. Ibid., 62.
45. See Lake, "Red Power."
46. USDA, "EIS Public Hearing," Superior, 31.
47. USDA, "EIS Public Hearing," Tempe, 15.
48. Frosch, "Utah Struggles."
49. Napier-Pearce, "Utah Clean Air."
50. Hunt et al., "Radical Potential."
51. Depoe et al., *Communication and Public Participation*.
52. Ibid., 163.
53. Utah Department of Environmental Quality (UDEQ), "Public Hearing Comments," Salt Lake City, 27.
54. Hunt et al., "Radical Potential," 31.
55. UDEQ, "Public Hearing Comments," Salt Lake City, 22.
56. Ibid., 43.
57. Ibid., 21, 22, 38.
58. Ibid., 24.
59. Ibid., 16–17.
60. UDEQ, "Public Hearing Comments," Salt Lake City, 31.
61. UDEQ, "Public Hearing Comments," Salt Lake City, 44.
62. Ibid.
63. Paliewicz, "Taking It to the Streets."
64. London Mining Network, "Groups Sue Rio Tinto's."

65. Moody, *Plunder!*
66. Udell, "Rio Tinto," paragraph 15.
67. Ibid, paragraph 1.
68. Ibid.
69. Davis, "Labor War."
70. *The Dispatcher*, "Borax Strikers Get Aid."
71. Ibid.
72. Brehm and White, "1974 Strike."
73. Davis, "War in the Mojave."
74. Kelly, "Labor Dispute."
75. Davis, "Labor War in the Mojave."
76. Gorman, "Locked-Out."
77. Kelly, "Borax Miners."
78. Ibid., paragraph 14.
79. Davis, "War in the Mojave."
80. Ibid.
81. Gorman, "Locked-Out,"
82. Olney, "Battle in the Mojave."
83. Ibid.
84. Ibid.
85. *Mines and Communities*, "Victory for Locked Out."
86. Olney, "Battle in the Mojave."
87. Ibid.
88. Ibid.
89. Kelly, "Borax Miners."
90. Steve Gorman, "Locked-Out."
91. Ibid.
92. Olney, "Battle in the Mojave."
93. World Socialist Website, "Locked-Out."
94. World Socialist Website, "Boron, California."
95. Mattera, "Rio Tinto."
96. Sekler, *Locked Out.*
97. Lois Gibbs even spoke out about the mine as a contemporary environmental injustice at Northern Michigan University. See Gibbs, "Rio Tinto, Kennecott Sulfide Mine." This author also witnessed many of the signs of protest throughout Marquette at this time and heard many arguments at public events, such as music festivals, against the mine.
98. Sekler, *Locked Out.*
99. Olney, "Battle in the Mojave."
100. Sekler, *Locked Out.*
101. Mignolo and Walsh, *On Decoloniality.*
102. This book only studies Rio Tinto in the American Southwest. As it exists in Boron, Salt Lake City, and Superior, it simultaneously exists on thirty-five different countries at sixty different mines. Even if it were possible to make claims about Rio Tinto's essence, this project would be incomplete due to its small sample.
103. Kirsch, *Mining Capitalism.*
104. Ibid.
105. For more on the argumentative dimensions surrounding the ATS, see Hasian and McFarlane, "Jim Aune's Rhetoric."
106. Quoted in Lasslett, *State Crime*, 2014, 1.

107. Marx, *Capital*, 1:873–940.
108. In Foster and Clark, *Robbery of Nature*.
109. Wallerstein, *Modern World-System I*.
110. A big part of this, especially during pandemic times, is due to the price increase of rare earth commodities such as copper, aluminum, and iron ore.
111. Kelly, "Labor Dispute."
112. Ibid.
113. London Mining Network, "Shameful History."
114. Albeck-Ripka, "Abandoned Rio Tinto Mine."
115. Wise, "Assemblage."
116. Carson, *Silent Spring*.

Conclusion

1. Latour, "Realpolitik to Dingpolitik"; Associated Press, "Reagan Urges 'Risk.'"
2. Associated Press, "Reagan Urges 'Risk.'"
3. Ibid., paragraph 2.
4. Ibid., paragraph 10.
5. Leopold, *Sand County Almanac*.
6. See Paliewicz, "Copper Mine."
7. DeLuca and Peeples, "Public Sphere to Public Screen."
8. Appadurai and Alexander, *Failure*.
9. DeLuca et al., "Weibo, WeChat."
10. Greene, "Rhetorical Capital"; Ceccarelli, "Manufactured Scientific Controversy." See McCright and Dunlap, "Challenging Global Warming"; McCright and Dunlap, "Anti-Reflexivity."
11. Greene, "Towards a New Rhetorical Axiology."
12. Harold, *OurSpace*; DeLuca, *Image Politics*.
13. Mack and Na'Puti, "'Our Bodies.'"
14. Whitehead, *Process and Reality*.
15. DeLuca, "Articulation Theory," 339.
16. Walton, "Ignoratio Elenchi," 3.
17. See Paliewicz and McHendry, "Post-Dialectics."
18. Mitchell, *Strategic Deception*.
19. Baurlein, "Trump Fatigue?," paragraph 12.
20. Trump's corporate persona as a celebrity also amplifies the effects of this strategy. As Jennifer Sclafani says in her recently published book entitled *Talking Donald Trump*, "Trump relies on his already well-known persona from his earlier roles as a combative, no-holds-barred, cutthroat executive on his reality show; this established brand gives him an advantage over the other candidates because he can recruit his pre-political brand for new communicative purposes." Sclafani, *Talking Donald Trump*.
21. See Graham, "Bait-and-Switch President."
22. For instance, we might say that Apache Stronghold strategically essentializes its group identity through certain tropes of Indigeneity to help it achieve its preservationist goals. The very term "Apache" is problematic in and of itself since it refers to at least six different tribes. It is also a colonial name given by the Spanish as a "corruption of the Zuni word for 'enemy.'" Nobody is essentially Apache, but Apache Stronghold embraces it to help it advance its rhetorical telos. d'Errico, "Native American Studies"; Ono and Sloop, "Commitment to Telos."

23. Is this also not how Rio Tinto's own persona politics work when it creates its famous, pioneer, or paternalistic personae? While Rio Tinto may wish to give the impression that those personae are nonstrategically essential, and both permanent and transcendental, is it still not "a strategic use of positivist essentialism in a scrupulously visible political interest?" Both Apache Stronghold and Rio Tinto are playing different roles in this extractive drama, and these roles are nondeterministic. Wolff, "Strategic Essentialism."

24. Gómez-Barris, *Extractive Zone*.

25. Muller, "Monkey Business."

Bibliography

20 Mule Team Borax. "Boron 20 Mule Team Days," Borax. Accessed September 29, 2021. https://www.borax.com/borax-operations/history/20-mule-team-days.
———. "U.S. Borax: Pioneering the Elements of Modern Living." Last modified October 5, 2021. https://www.borax.com.
Abbey, Edward. *Desert Solitaire: A Season in the Wilderness*. New York: Touchstone, 1968.
———. *Down the River*. New York: Plume, 1991.
———. *The Monkey Wrench Gang*. Salt Lake City: Dream Garden Press, 1985.
Abel, Marco. *Violent Affect: Literature, Cinema, and Critique After Representation*. Lincoln: University of Nebraska Press, 2007.
Adams, Andrew. "Massive Landslide Damages Kennecott's Bingham Canyon Mine." KSL, April 11 2013. https://www.ksl.com/article/24748916/massive-landslide-damages-kennecotts-bingham-canyon-mine.
Adorno, Theodor. *The Culture Industry: Selected Essays on Mass Culture*. New York: Routledge, 2001.
Adorno, Theodor W., and Max Horkheimer. *Dialectic of Enlightenment*. New York: Verso, 1997.
Ahmed, Sara. "Affective Economies." *Social Text* 22, no. 2 (2004): 117–39.
Albeck-Ripka, Livia. "Abandoned Rio Tinto Mine Is Blamed for Poisoned Bougainville Rivers." *New York Times*, September 30, 2020. https://www.nytimes.com/2020/09/30/world/australia/rio-tinto-abandoned-mine-poison-rivers.html.
"Apache Activist Wendsler Nosie." *AZ Central*, January 15, 2020. https://www.azcentral.com/picture-gallery/news/local/arizona-environment/2020/01/15/apache-activist-wendsler-nosie/4469968002/.
Apache Stronghold. "Defending Holy Sites Protect Biłdagoteel (Oak Flat)." Accessed July 11, 2023. http://apache-stronghold.com/going-home.html.
———. "An Ever Growing Story, Annual March to Save Oak Flat Each February." Accessed February 10, 2023. http://apache-stronghold.com/march-to-oak-flat.html.
Appadurai, Arjun, and Neta Alexander. *Failure*. Medford, MA: Polity Press, 2020.
Asad, Talal. "Historical Notes on the Idea of Secular Criticism." *The Immanent Frame*, January 25, 2008. https://tif.ssrc.org/2008/01/25/historical-notes-on-the-idea-of-secular-criticism/.
Asen, Robert. "Neoliberalism, the Public Sphere, and a Public Good." *Quarterly Journal of Speech* 103, no. 4 (2017): 329–49.
Associated Press. "Reagan Urges 'Risk' on Gorbachev: Soviet Leader May Be Only Hope for Change, He Says." *Los Angeles Times*, June 13, 1989. https://www.latimes.com/archives/la-xpm-1989-06-13-mn-2300-story.html.
Bakhtin, M. M. *The Dialogic Imagination: Four Essays*. Translated by Caryl Emerson and Michael Holquist. Austin: University of Texas Press, 1981.
Barnett, Joshua Trey. *Mourning in the Anthropocene: Ecological Grief and Earthly Coexistence*. East Lansing: Michigan State University Press, 2022.

———. "Naming, Mourning, and the Work of Earthly Coexistence." *Environmental Communication* 13, no. 3 (2019): 287–99.

———. "Toxic Portraits: Resisting Multiple Invisibilities in the Environmental Justice Movement." *Quarterly Journal of Speech* 101, no. 2 (2015): 405–25.

Barnett, Joshua Trey, and David Charles Gore. "Dwelling in the Anthropocene: Notes from Lake Superior." *Ethics and the Environment* 25, no. 1 (2020): 19–49.

Barthes, Roland. "The Death of the Author." *Contributions in Philosophy* 83 (2001): 3–8.

Basov, Vladimir. "Global Copper Production Declines 2% in 2020." *KITCO*, February 12, 2021. https://www.kitco.com/news/2021-02-12/Global-copper-production-declines-2-in-2020-report.html.

Baudrillard, Jean. *Simulacra and Simulation.* Ann Arbor: University of Michigan Press, 1994.

Baurlein, Monkia. "Are You Dealing with Trump Fatigue?" *Mother Jones.* Last modified October 20, 2017. https://www.motherjones.com/media/2017/10/trump-fatigue/.

BBC. "Rio Tinto Ordered to Rebuild Aboriginal Caves." BBC, December 9, 2020. https://www.bbc.com/news/world-australia-55250137.

Bellah, Robert N. "Civil Religion in America." *Daedalus* 96, no. 1 (1967): 1–21.

Bellamy Foster, John, and Brett Clark. *The Robbery of Nature: Capitalism and the Ecological Rift.* New York: New York University Press, 2020.

Bellamy Foster, John, Brett Clark, and Richard York. *The Ecological Rift: Capitalism's War on the Earth.* New York: New York University Press, 2011.

Bennett, Jane. *Vibrant Matter.* Durham, NC: Duke University Press, 2010.

Berry, Wendell. *Another Turn of the Crank: Essays.* Berkeley, CA: Counterpoint, 1995.

Bhandar, Brenna. *Colonial Lives of Property: Law, Land, and Racial Regimes of Ownership.* Durham, NC: Duke University Press, 2018.

Biggs, J. C. "Peter Elbow, Kenneth Burke, and the Idea of Magic." *Journal of Advanced Composition* 11, no. 2 (1991): 363–75.

Black, Edwin. *Rhetorical Criticism: A Study in Method.* Madison: University of Wisconsin Press, 1978.

———. "The Second Persona." *Quarterly Journal of Speech* 56, no. 2 (1970): 109–19.

Black, Jason Edward. *American Indians and the Rhetoric of Removal and Allotment.* Jackson: University Press of Mississippi, 2015.

———. "Remembrances of Removal: Native Resistance to Allotment and the Unmasking of Paternal Benevolence." *Southern Communication Journal* 72, no. 2 (2007): 185–203.

Bloomfield, Emma Frances. "The Rhetoric of Energy Darwinism: Neoliberal Piety and Market Autonomy in Economic Discourse." *Rhetoric Society Quarterly* 49, no. 4 (2019): 320–41.

Bold Canyon Outdoors. "Old Mining Wagon Wheel Tracks in Arizona." April 28, 2020. https://www.boldcanyonoutdoors.com/2020/04/28/old-mining-wagon-wheel-tracks-in-superior-arizona/.

"Borax, the All Natural Cleaning Agent, Has Strong Ties to Furnace Creek Inn in the California Desert." Hotel Online, May 20, 2008. https://www.hotel-online.com/News/PR2008_2nd/May08_FurnaceCreek.html.

Boutwell, John Mason. *Economic Geology of the Bingham Mining District, Utah* 38. US Government Printing Office, 1905.

Brehm, Sheila, and Jerry White. "The Lessons of the 1974 Strike." *World Socialist Web Site,* February 24, 2010. https://www.wsws.org/en/articles/2010/02/bora-f24.html.

Bricker, Brett, and Jacob Justice. "Identifying and Challenging Greenwashing Through Conciliatio." *Western Journal of Communication* 86, no. 4 (2022): 521–40.

Briggs, David F. "History of the Magma Mine, Superior Arizona." *Arizona Independent News Network.* July 19, 2015. https://arizonadailyindependent.com/2015/07/19/history-of-the-magma-mine-superior-arizona/.

Britannica, "Borate Mineral," *Encyclopedia Britannica*. Accessed September 29, 2021. https://www.britannica.com/science/borate-mineral.

Broere, Kathy, Sarah Edstrom, and Bob Trench, dirs. *Dodging Bullets—Stories from Survivors of Historical Trauma*. Fahrenheit Films, 2020.

Brown, Wendy. *Undoing the Demos: Neoliberalism's Stealth Revolution*. Cambridge, MA: MIT Press, 2015.

Budinsky, Jennifer, and Susan Bryant. "'It's Not Easy Being Green': The Greenwashing of Environmental Discourses in Advertising." *Canadian Journal of Communication* 38, no. 2 (2013): 207–26.

Burke, Kenneth. *Permanence and Change: An Anatomy of Purpose*. Berkeley: University of California Press, 1954.

———. *A Rhetoric of Motives*. Berkeley: University of California Press, 1969.

———. "Towards Helhaven: Three Stages of Vision." *Sewanee Review* 79, no. 1 (1971): 11–25.

Burroughs, Asa. "The Mine at Oak Flat: A Timeline of Government Bad Faith." Moyers, December 29, 2020. https://billmoyers.com/story/the-mine-at-oak-flat-a-timeline-of-a-government-bad-faith/.

Byers, Justin. "Real Salt Lake Inks Major Stadium Naming Rights Deal." *Front Office Sports*, September 12, 2022. https://frontofficesports.com/real-salt-lake-inks-100m-stadium-naming-rights-deal/.

Campbell, Karlyn Korhs. "Responses to Wander: Response to Forbes Hill." *Central States Speech Journal* 34, no. 2 (1983): 126–27.

Carson, Rachel. *Silent Spring*. Boston, MA: Houghton Mifflin, 1962.

Casati, Roberto, and Achille C. Varzi. *Holes and Other Superficialities*. Cambridge, MA: MIT Press, 1994.

Casey, Dan. "Quote of the Day: Benito Mussolini on Corporatism." *Roanoke Times*, August 5, 2009. https://roanoke.com/news/local/quote-of-the-day-benito-mussolini-on-corporatism/article_1142b9c9-4df6-5e3c-92b4-33538011d97a.html.

Casey, Edward. *The World at a Glance*. Bloomington: Indiana University Press, 2007.

Ceccarelli, Leah. "Manufactured Scientific Controversy: Science, Rhetoric, and Public Debate." *Rhetoric and Public Affairs* 14, no. 2 (2011): 195–228.

———. *On the Frontier of Science: An American Rhetoric of Exploration and Exploitation*. East Lansing: Michigan State University Press, 2013.

Cheney, George. "The Corporate Person (Re)Presents Itself." In *Rhetorical and Critical Approaches to Public Relations*, edited by Robert Heath, Elizabeth Toth, and Damion Waymer, 165–83. New York: Routledge, 2009.

———. "The Rhetoric of Identification and the Study of Organizational Communication." *Quarterly Journal of Speech* 69, no. 2 (1983): 143–58.

Cheney, George, and Jill J. McMillan. "Organizational Rhetoric and the Practice of Criticism." *Journal of Applied Communication Research* 18, no. 2 (1990): 93–114.

Cloud, Dana L. "Hegemony or Concordance? The Rhetoric of Tokenism in Oprah's Rags-to-Riches Biography." *Critical Studies in Media Communication* 13, no. 2 (1996): 115–37.

———. "The Null Persona: Race and the Rhetoric of Silence in the Uprising of '34." *Rhetoric and Public Affairs* 2, no. 2 (1999): 177–209.

Conway, Michael. "Active Mines in Arizona—Directory and Map." Arizona Geological Survey, December 3, 2019. https://azgs.arizona.edu/news/2019/12/active-mines-arizona-directory-and-map.

Copper Alliance. "Meeting Future Copper Demand." Sustainable Copper. Accessed February 10, 2023. https://sustainablecopper.org/meeting-future-copper-demand.

The Copper Mark. "Kennecott the First to Receive the Copper Mark for Responsible Production." August 24, 2020. https://coppermark.org/kennecott-the-first-to-receive-the-copper-mark-for-responsible-production/.

Covino, William A. "Magic, Literacy and the *National Enquirer.*" In *Contending with Words: Composition and Rhetoric in a Postmodern Age*, edited by Patricia Harkin and John Schilb, 23–37. New York: Modern Language Association, 1991.

Cram, E. *Violent Inheritance: Sexuality, Land, and Energy in Making the North American West.* Oakland: University of California Press, 2022.

Cronon, William. *Nature's Metropolis: Chicago and the Great West.* New York: W. W. Norton, 1991.

Curry, Marshall. *If a Tree Falls: A Story of the Earth Liberation Front.* Widescreen. New York: Oscilloscope Laboratories, 2011.

Dark, Stephen. "Mining Memories." *City Weekly.* June 29, 2016. https://www.cityweekly.net/utah/mining-memories/Content?oid=3355876.

Dartmouth Toxic Metals Superfund Research Program. "Copper: An Ancient Metal." Accessed July 11, 2023. https://sites.dartmouth.edu/toxmetal/more-metals/copper-an-ancient-metal/.

———. "The Facts on Silver." Accessed February 10, 2023. https://sites.dartmouth.edu/toxmetal/more-metals/silver-metal-of-many-faces/the-facts-on-silver/.

Davis, Diane. *Inessential Solidarity: Rhetoric and Foreigner Relations.* Pittsburgh, PA: University of Pittsburgh Press, 2010.

Davis, Mike. "Labor War in the Mojave." *The Nation*, March 12, 2010. https://www.thenation.com/article/archive/labor-war-mojave/.

DeLanda, Manuel. *A Thousand Years of Non-Linear History.* New York: Zone Books, 1997.

Deleuze, Gilles, and Félix Guattari. *A Thousand Plateaus: Capitalism and Schizophrenia.* Translated by Brian Massui. Minneapolis: University of Minnesota Press, 1988.

Deloria, Philip Joseph. *Playing Indian.* New Haven, CT: Yale University Press, 1998.

DeLuca, Kevin Michael. "Articulation Theory: A Discursive Grounding for Rhetorical Practice." *Philosophy and Rhetoric* 32, no. 4 (1999): 334–48.

———. *Image Politics: The New Rhetoric of Environmental Activism.* New York: Routledge, 2012.

———. "Trains in the Wilderness: The Corporate Roots of Environmentalism." *Rhetoric and Public Affairs* 4, no. 4 (2001): 633–52.

———. "Unruly Arguments: The Body Rhetoric of Earth First!, ACT UP, and Queer Nation." *Argumentation and Advocacy* 36, no. 1 (1999): 9–21.

DeLuca, Kevin Michael, Elizabeth Brunner, and Ye Sun. "Weibo, WeChat, and the Transformative Events of Environmental Activism on China's Wild Public Screens." *International Journal of Communication* 10, no. 1 (2016): 321–39.

DeLuca, Kevin Michael, and Jennifer Peeples. "From Public Sphere to Public Screen: Democracy, Activism, and the 'Violence' of Seattle." *Critical Studies in Media Communication* 19, no. 2 (2002): 125–51.

De Onís, Catalina. *Energy Islands: Metaphors of Power, Extractivism, and Justice in Puerto Rico.* Berkeley: University of California Press, 2021.

Depoe, Stephen P., John W. Delicath, and Marie-France Aepli Elsenbeer, eds. *Communication and Public Participation in Environmental Decision Making.* Albany: State University of New York Press, 2004.

d'Errico, Peter. "Native American Studies." University of Massachusetts. Accessed February 10, 2023. https://www.umass.edu/legal/derrico/name.html.

Derrida, Jacques. *Of Grammatology*. Translated by Gayatri Chakravorty Spivak. Baltimore, MD: Johns Hopkins University Press, 2016. Original publication 1967.

The Desert Way. "Boron Federal Prison: Abandoned Club Fed." Accessed February 10, 2023. https://www.thedesertway.com/boron-fpc-ca/.

Diamond, Jared. *Collapse: How Societies Choose to Fail or Succeed*. New York: Penguin, 2011.

Dickinson, Greg. "The Pleasantville Effect: Nostalgia and the Visual Framing of (White) Suburbia." *Western Journal of Communication* 70, no. 3 (2006), 212–33.

———. *Suburban Dreams: Imagining and Building the Good Life*. Tuscaloosa: University of Alabama Press, 2015.

Dickinson, Greg, Carole Blair, and Brian L. Ott, eds. *Places of Public Memory: The Rhetoric of Museums and Memorials*. Tuscaloosa: University of Alabama Press, 2010.

Dickinson, Greg, Brian L. Ott, and Aoki Eric. "Memory and Myth at the Buffalo Bill Museum." *Western Journal of Communication* 69, no. 2 (2005): 85–108.

The Dispatcher. "Borax Strikers Get Aid." *The Dispatcher: Published by the International Longshoremens and Warehouse Union* 32, no. 14 (July 19, 1974): 1, 6.

Dorsey, Leroy G. "The Frontier Myth in Presidential Rhetoric: Theodore Roosevelt's Campaign for Conservation." *Western Journal of Communication* 59, no. 1 (1995): 1–19.

Drury, Jeffrey P. Mehltretter. "Beyond 'Rhetorical Agency': Skutnik's Story in the 1982 State of the Union Address." *Western Journal of Communication* 82, no. 1 (2018): 40–58.

EarthWorks, "Oak Flat/Apache Leap." January 28, 2015. https://earthworks.org/blog/oak_flat_apache_leap/.

———. "Problems with the Bingham Canyon Mine." *Earthworks Factsheet*, January 5, 2011. https://www.earthworks.org/publications/problems_with_the_bingham_canyon_mine/.

Eckstein, Justin. "Sound Arguments." *Argumentation and Advocacy* 53, no. 3 (2017): 163–80.

Emel, Jody, and Matthew T. Huber. "The Richest Hole on Earth? Nature, Labor and the Politics of Metabolism at the Bingham Canyon Copper Mine." In *Engineering Earth*, edited by Stanley D. Brunn, 353–66. New York: Springer, 2011.

Encyclopedia. "U.S. Borax." Accessed February 10, 2023. https://www.encyclopedia.com/books/politics-and-business-magazines/us-borax-inc.

Endres, Danielle. "American Indian Permission for Mascots: Resistance or Complicity Within Rhetorical Colonialism?" *Rhetoric and Public Affairs* 18, no. 4 (2015): 649.

———. "The Rhetoric of Nuclear Colonialism: Rhetorical Exclusion of American Indian Arguments in the Yucca Mountain Nuclear Waste Siting Decision." *Communication and Critical/Cultural Studies* 6, no. 1 (2009): 39–60.

———. "Sacred Land or National Sacrifice Zone: The Role of Values in the Yucca Mountain Participation Process." *Environmental Communication: A Journal of Nature and Culture* 6, no. 3 (2012): 328–45.

Endres, Danielle, and Samantha Senda-Cook. "Location Matters: The Rhetoric of Place in Protest." *Quarterly Journal of Speech* 97, no. 3 (2011): 257–82.

Engels, Friedrich. *The Origin of the Family, Private Property and the State*. New York: Penguin, [1884] 2010.

Environmental Protection Agency. *Abandoned Mine Lands Case Study: Kennecott Mining Site: Transformation Through Collaboration at a Superfund Alternative Site*. June 2, 2006. http://www.epa.gov/aml/tech/kennecott.pdf.

———. "Superfund." Accessed February 10, 2023. https://www.epa.gov/superfund.

———. "Toxics Release Inventory." Accessed February 10, 2023. https://www.epa.gov/toxics-release-inventory-tri-program.

————. "Toxics Release Inventory Explorer." 2021 Dataset, p. 102. Accessed July 11, 2023. https://enviro.epa.gov/triexplorer/release_fac_profile?TRI=84006KNNCT12300&TRILIB=TRIQ1&FLD=&FLD=RELLBY&FLD=TSFDSP&OFFDISPD=&OTHDISPD=&ONDISPD=&OTHOFFD=&YEAR=2018.

Estes, Nick. *Our History Is the Future: Standing Rock Versus the Dakota Access Pipeline, and the Long Tradition of Indigenous Resistance.* New York: Verso, 2019.

Evans, Thomas W. "The GE Years: What Made Reagan." History News Network. Accessed February 10, 2023. https://historynewsnetwork.org/article/32681.

Evernden, Neil. *The Social Creation of Nature.* Cambridge, MA: Harvard University Press, 1992.

Foreman, Dave, and Bill Haywood, eds. *Ecodefense: A Field Guide to Monkeywrenching.* Chico, CA: Abbzug Press, 1993.

Foucault, Michel. "Of Other Spaces." In *Foucault: Aesthetics, Method, and Epistemology,* edited by James Faubian, 175–86. New York: New Press, 1998.

————. *The Order of Things.* New York: Vintage, 1994.

Fox, Courtney. "'Death Valley Days': The Classic Western Series Was Ronald Reagan's Final Acting Job." Wide Open Country. April 21, 2021. https://www.wideopencountry.com/death-valley-days/.

Frosch, Dan. "Seen as Nature Lovers' Paradise, Utah Struggles with Air Quality." *New York Times,* February 13, 2013. https://www.nytimes.com/2013/02/24/us/utah-a-nature-lovers-haven-is-plagued-by-dirty-air.html.

Furniss, Elizabeth. "Pioneers, Progress, and the Myth of the Frontier: The Landscape of Public History in Rural British Columbia." *BC Studies: The British Columbian Quarterly* 115, no. 6 (1997): 7–44.

Gaschk, Matt. "RSL's Fans Provide a Home-Field Advantage at Rio Tinto Stadium: Tony Beltran's Perspective on Real Salt Lake's Fans [Embedded Video File]." Real Salt Lake. March 26, 2015. https://www.rsl.com/post/2015/03/26/rsls-fans-provide-home-field-advantage-rio-tinto-stadium.

Gedicks, Al. *The New Resource Wars: Native and Environmental Struggles Against Multinational Corporations.* Montreal: Black Rose Books, 1994.

Gehl, Robert W., and Brian Cozen. "Passé Media: Communication and Transportation on Commuter and Computer Buses." *Communication Theory* 25, no. 3 (2015): 290–309.

GeoEngineer. "Block Caving: A New Mining Method Arises." GeoEngineer, July 25, 2018. https://www.geoengineer.org/news/block-caving-a-new-mining-method-arises.

Gibbons, Michelle G. "Persona 4.0." *Quarterly Journal of Speech* 107, no. 1 (2021): 49–72.

Gibbs, Lois. "Rio Tinto, Kennecott Sulfide Mine in Northern Michigan Like Infamous Love Canal." YouTube. July 10, 2011. https://www.youtube.com/watch?v=iWIrhDv1zZg.

Gibson, Owen. "Protests Groups Target Olympics Sponsors with New Campaign." *The Guardian,* April 15, 2021. https://www.theguardian.com/sport/2012/apr/15/protest-groups-olympics-sponsors-campaign.

Glasson, Ben. "Environmental Myth-Work: The Discursive Greening of the Olympic Games." *Communication and Critical/Cultural Studies* 19, no. 3 (2022): 217–34.

Goldmacher, Shane. "Flake's Past as Lobbyist at Odds with His Image." Yahoo! News, April 18, 2012. https://news.yahoo.com/flake-past-lobbyist-odds-image-181053586.html.

Gómez-Barris, Macarena. *The Extractive Zone.* Durham, NC: Duke University Press, 2017.

Gorman, Steve. "Locked-Out Rio Tinto Borax Miners in US Get Support." *Reuters,* February 24, 2010. https://www.reuters.com/article/us-usa-mine-lockout/locked-out-rio-tinto-borax-miners-in-u-s-get-support-idUSTRE61O0CV20100225.

Gorrell, Mike. "Kennecott Sells Daybreak Community to Värde." *Salt Lake Tribune,* June 17, 2016. https://archive.sltrib.com/article.php?id=4019288&itype=CMSID.

Gourgouris, Stathis. *Lessons in Secular Criticism*. New York: Fordham University Press, 2013.

Graham, David A. "The Bait-and-Switch President." *The Atlantic*, December 14, 2016. https://www.theatlantic.com/politics/archive/2016/12/the-bait-and-switch -presidency/510530/.

Greene, Ronald Walter. "Another Materialist Rhetoric." *Critical Studies in Media Communication* 15, no. 1 (1998): 21–40.

———. "More Materialist Rhetoric." *Communication and Critical/Cultural Studies* 12, no. 4 (2015): 414–17.

———. "Rhetorical Capital: Communicative Labor, Money/Speech, and Neo-Liberal Governance." *Communication and Critical/Cultural Studies* 4, no. 3 (2007): 327–31.

———. "Rhetoric and Capitalism: Rhetorical Agency as Communicative Labor." *Philosophy and Rhetoric* 37, no. 3 (2004): 188–206.

———. "Towards a New Rhetorical Axiology: Communication as Extraction Industry." Paper presented at the 2021 National Communication Association Conference, Seattle, Washington, November 18, 2021.

———. "Y Movies: Film and the Modernization of Pastoral Power." *Communication and Critical/Cultural Studies* 2, no. 1 (2005): 20–36.

Gregg, Richard B. "The Ego-Function of the Rhetoric of Protest." *Philosophy and Rhetoric* 4, no. 2 (1971): 71–91.

Gunn, Joshua, and Thomas Frentz. "The Da Vinci Code as Alchemical Rhetoric." *Western Journal of Communication* 72, no. 3 (2008): 213–23.

Hammond, E. D. *History of the Mining in the Bingham District, Utah. Geology of the Bingham Mining District and Northern Oquirrh Mountains: Guidebook to the Geology of Utah, Number 16*. Utah Geological Association, 1961.

Haraway, Donna. "Situated Knowledges: The Science Question in Feminism and the Privilege of Partial Perspective." *Feminist Studies* 14, no. 3 (1988): 575–99.

———. *Staying with the Trouble: Making Kin in the Chthulucene*. Durham, NC: Duke University Press, 2016.

Hardt, Michael, and Antonio Negri. *Empire*. Cambridge, MA: Harvard University Press, 2020.

Harman, Graham. *Immaterialism: Objects and Social Theory*. Cambridge, UK: Polity, 2016.

Harold, Christine. *OurSpace: Resisting the Corporate Control of Culture*. Minneapolis: University of Minnesota Press, 2007.

———. "Pranking Rhetoric: 'Culture Jamming' as Media Activism." *Critical Studies in Media Communication* 21, no. 3 (2004): 189–211.

———. *Things Worth Keeping*. Minneapolis: University of Minnesota Press, 2021.

Harris, Rachel. "In Utah, a New Home for Natural History." *New York Times*, November 6, 2011. https://archive.nytimes.com/query.nytimes.com/gst/fullpage-9D00E4D71F3 DF935A35752C1A9679D8B63.html.

Hartnett, Stephen John. "Communication, Social Justice, and Joyful Commitment." *Western Journal of Communication* 74, no. 1 (2010): 68–93.

Hasian, Marouf, Jr. "Remembering and Forgetting the 'Final Solution': A Rhetorical Pilgrimage Through the US Holocaust Memorial Museum." *Critical Studies in Media Communication* 21, no. 1 (2004): 64–92.

Hasian, Marouf, Jr. and Megan D. McFarlane. "A Critique of Jim Aune's Rhetoric, Legal Argumentation, and Historical Materialism." *Argumentation and Advocacy* 50, no. 4 (2014): 210–27.

Hawhee, Debra. *Rhetoric in Tooth and Claw*. Chicago: University of Chicago Press, 2016.

Heffernan, Tim. "The New Bronze Age." *Pacific Standard*, June 14, 2017. https://psmag.com /social-justice/the-new-bronze-age-entering-the-era-of-tough-ore-60868.

Heidegger, Martin. "The Origin of the Work of Art." In *Basic Writings*, edited by David Farrell Krell, translated by William Lovitt, 143–212. New York: Harper, 2008.

———. "The Question Concerning Technology." In *Basic Writings*, edited by David Farrell Krell, translated by William Lovitt, 308–46. New York: Harper, 2008.

Hess, Aaron, Samantha Senda-Cook, Danielle Endres, and Michael K. Middleton. "(Participatory) Critical Rhetoric: Critiqued and Reconsidered." *International Journal of Communication* 14 (2020): 870–84.

Hill, Forbes. "Conventional Wisdom—Traditional Form—the Presidents Message of November 3, 1969." *Quarterly Journal of Speech* 58, no. 4 (1972): 373–86.

Hinck, Ashley. *Politics for the Love of Fandom: Fan-Based Citizenship in a Digital World*. Baton Rouge: Louisiana State University Press, 2019.

"History of Superior Region." n.a. Accessed February 10, 2023. http://zybtarizona.com /suhist.htm.

Hudson Institute of Mineralogy." Rio Tinto Borax Mine." Accessed July 11, 2023. https://www .mindat.org/loc-23409.html.

Hunt, Kathleen, and Nicholas Paliewicz. "'Are You Listening?!': Indecorous Voice as Rhetorical Strategy in Environmental Public Participation." In Conference on Communication and the Environment Proceedings, *Communication for the Commons*, 407–14. Turtle Island: The IECA, 2013.

Hunt, Kathleen, Nicholas Paliewicz, and Danielle Endres. "The Radical Potential of Public Participation Processes." In *Breaking Boundaries: Innovative Practices in Environmental Communication and Public Participation*, edited by Kathleen Hunt, Gregg Walker, and Stephen Depoe, 149–74. Albany: State University of New York Press, 2019.

Irvine, Amy. *Desert Cabal: A New Season in the Wilderness*. Salt Lake City, UT: Torrey House, 2018.

Jackson, Brian. "The Prophetic Alchemy of Jim Wallis." *Rhetoric Review* 29, no. 1 (2009): 8–68.

Jaffe, Matt. "What You'll Find on the Fabled Four-Hour Journey from L.A. to Death Valley." *LA Magazine*, May 3, 2019. https://www.lamag.com/citythinkblog/what-youll-find -on-the-fabled-four-hour-journey-from-l-a-to-death-valley/.

Jamasmie, Cecilia. "Rio Tinto, BHP A Step Closer to Open US Largest Copper Mine." Mining.com. November 12, 2013. https://www.mining.com/rio-tinto-bhp-a-step-closer -to-open-us-largest-copper-mine-94236/.

———. "Rio Tinto's Kennecott Wins Lawsuit in the US." Mining.com. June 9, 2016. http:// www.mining.com/rio-tintos-kennecott-wins-clean-air-lawsuit-in-the-us/.

Jeansonne, Glen, and David Luhrssen. "Reagan and the West: How Jeffersonian Ideals Reached the 40th President." *Historically Speaking* 7, no. 5 (2006): 34–36.

Jensen, Robin E. "Improving Upon Nature: The Rhetorical Ecology of Chemical Language, Reproductive Endocrinology, and the Medicalization of Infertility." *Quarterly Journal of Speech* 101, no. 2 (2015): 329–53.

———. *Infertility: Tracing the History of a Transformative Term*. University Park: Pennsylvania State University Press, 2016.

———. "Theorizing Chemical Rhetoric: Toward an Articulation of Chemistry as a Public Vocabulary." *Journal of Communication* 71, no. 3 (2021), 431–53.

Johnson, Kevin. "Kenneth Burke and the Rhetorical Magic of *The Eminem Show*." In *Critical Problems in Argumentation*, edited by Charles Arthur Willard, 268–74. Washington, DC: National Communication Association, 2005.

Johnson, Timothy. *Rhetoric, Inc.: Ford's Filmmaking and the Rise of Corporatism*. University Park: Pennsylvania State University Press, 2020.

Jung, Carl. *Psychology and Alchemy*. New York: Routledge, 2014.

Kelety, Josh. "Biden Administration Says Oak Flat Land Swap Should Proceed Despite Lawsuit." *Phoenix New Times*, June 2, 2021. https://www.phoenixnewtimes.com /news/biden-administration-says-oak-flat-land-swap-should-proceed-11558259.

Kelly, David. "Borax Miners Locked out In Labor Dispute." *Los Angeles Times*, February 1, 2010. https://www.latimes.com/archives/la-xpm-2010-feb-01-la-me-boron1-2010feb01 -story.html.

———. "A Labor Dispute Threatens to Tear a Kern County Mining Town Apart." *Los Angeles Times*, January 31, 2010. https://www.latimes.com/archives/la-xpm-2010-jan-31 -la-me-boron31-2010jan31-story.html.

Kemp, Deanna, Eleonore Lebre, John Owen, and Richard Valenta. "Clean Energy? The World's Demand for Copper Could be Catastrophic for Communities and Environments." The Conversation, April 12, 2021. https://theconversation.com/clean-energy -the-worlds-demand-for-copper-could-be-catastrophic-for-communities-and-envi ronments-157872.

Kennedy, George A. "A Hoot in the Dark: The Evolution of General Rhetoric." *Philosophy and Rhetoric* 25, no. 1 (1992): 1–21.

King, Claire Sisco. "It Cuts Both Ways: Fight Club, Masculinity, and Abject Hegemony." *Communication and Critical/Cultural Studies* 6, no. 4 (2009): 366–85.

Kirsch, Stuart. *Mining Capitalism*. Berkeley: University of California Press, 2014.

Klaus, Marion, and Dan Mayhew. "Kennecott Causes One-Third of Air Pollution." *Salt Lake Tribune*, February 29, 2012. http://archive.sltrib.com/article.php?id=53600999&itype =CMSID.

Klein, Naomi. *No Logo*. New York: Vintage Books Canada, 2009.

Kolbert, Elizabeth. *The Sixth Extinction: An Unnatural History*. New York: Bloomsbury, 2014.

LaDuke, Winona. *Recovering the Sacred: The Power of Naming and Claiming*. Boston, MA: South End Press, 2005.

Lake, Randall A. "Enacting Red Power: The Consummatory Function in Native American Protest Rhetoric." *Quarterly Journal of Speech* 69, no. 2 (1983): 127–42.

Lamberti, Andre. "Resolution Copper Completes US $75M Mine Reclamation." *Mining Magazine*, January 12, 2021. https://www.miningmagazine.com/life-cycle-end-of-life -management/news/1402411/resolution-copper-completes-ususd75m-mine -reclamation.

Larry H. Miller Group of Companies. "Larry H. Miller Real Estate Acquires Daybreak from Värde Partners." *PRNewswire*, April 12, 2021. https://www.prnewswire.com/news -releases/larry-h-miller-real-estate-acquires-daybreak-from-varde-partners-301266 430.html.

Lasslett, Kristian. *State Crime on the Margins of Empire: Rio Tinto, the War on Bougainville and Resistance to Mining*. London: Pluto Press, 2019.

Latour, Bruno. "From Realpolitik to Dingpolitik." In *Making Things Public: Atmospheres of Democracy*, edited by Peter Weibel and Bruno Latour, 4–31. Cambridge, MA: MIT Press, 2005.

Law, John. "Actor Network Theory and Material Semiotics." In *The New Blackwell Companion to Social Theory*, edited by John Law, 141–58. Oxford: Blackwell, 1996.

LeCain, Timothy J. *Mass Destruction: The Men and Giant Mines That Wired America and Scarred the Planet*. New Brunswick, NJ: Rutgers University Press, 2009.

Lee, Jasen. "Environmentalists Sue Kennecott over Dirty Air." *KSL*, December 19, 2011. https://www.ksl.com/article/18563833/environmentalists-sue-kennecott-over -dirty-air.

———. "Utah Among the Most Toxic States, Report Says." *Deseret News*, November 9, 2007. https://www.deseret.com/2017/11/9/20635999/utah-among-the-most-toxic-states -report-says.

Leighter, James L., and Laura Black. "'I'm Just Raising the Question': Terms for Talk and Practical Metadiscursive Argument in Public Meetings." *Western Journal of Communication* 74, no. 5 (2010): 547–69.

Leopold, Aldo. *A Sand County Almanac, and Sketches Here and There*. New York: Oxford University Press, 1989.

Light, Elinor. "Visualizing Homeland: Remembering 9/11 and the Production of the Surveilling Flâneur." *Cultural Studies↔Critical Methodologies* 16, no. 6 (2016): 536–47.

London Mining Network. "Doctors, Moms, Environmental Groups Sue Rio Tinto's Subsidiary Kennecott." September 24, 2013. https://londonminingnetwork.org/2013/09 /doctors-moms-environmental-groups-sue-rio-tintos-us-subsidiary-kennecott/.

———. "Rio Tinto: A Shameful History of Human and Labour Rights Abuses and Environmental Degradation Around the Globe." April 20, 2010. https://londonmining network.org/2010/04/rio-tinto-a-shameful-history-of-human-and-labour-rights -abuses-and-environmental-degradation-around-the-globe/v.

Lowe, Donald. *History of the Bourgeois Perception*. Chicago: University of Chicago Press, 1983.

Macfarlane, Robert. "Rereading: Robert Macfarlane on *The Monkey Wrench Gang*." *The Guardian*, September 25, 2009. https://www.theguardian.com/books/2009/sep/26 /robert-macfarlane-monkey-wrench-gang.

———. *Underland: A Deep Time Journey*. New York: W. W. Norton, 2019).

Mack, Ashley Noel, and Tiara R. Na'Puti. "'Our Bodies Are Not Terra Nullius'": Building a Decolonial Feminist Resistance to Gendered Violence." *Women's Studies in Communication* 42, no. 3 (2019): 347–70.

Maffly, Brian. "Museum Galleries Explore Utah's Cultural, Natural Landscapes." *Salt Lake Tribune*, November 12, 2012. https://archive.sltrib.com/article.php?id=52879256& itype=cmsid3.

Main, Douglas. "Sacred Native American Land to Be Traded to a Foreign Mining Giant." *National Geographic*, January 15, 2021. https://www.nationalgeographic.com/environ ment/article/oak-flat-exchange-arizona-sacred-site-mining-company.

Malouf, Mary. "Behind the Beehive." *Salt Lake Magazine*, May 2, 2016. https://www.saltlake magazine.com/behind-the-beehive/.

Marx, Karl. *Capital*. Vol. 1. New York: Penguin, [1867] 1976.

Massumi, Brian. *Politics of Affect*. New York: Polity, 2015.

———. "Translator's Foreword." In *Thousand Plateaus: Capitalism and Schizophrenia*, by Gilles Deleuze and Felix Guattari, translated by Brian Massumi. Minneapolis: University of Minnesota Press, 1987.

———. *A User's Guide to Capitalism and Schizophrenia: Deviations from Deleuze and Guattari*. Cambridge, MA: MIT Press, 1992.

Mattera, Philip. "Rio Tinto." Corporate Research Project. Accessed February 10, 2023. https:// www.corp-research.org/rio-tinto.

Maxfield, Susan. "Creation and Erasure: Art of the Bingham Canyon Mine." *Utah Stories*, August 28, 2014. https://utahstories.com/2014/08/creation-and-erasure-art-of-the -bingham-canyon-mine/.

McCright, Aaron M., and Riley E. Dunlap. "Anti-Reflexivity." *Theory, Culture and Society* 27, nos. 2–3 (2010): 100–133.

———. "Challenging Global Warming as a Social Problem: An Analysis of the Conservative Movement's Counter-Claims." *Social Problems* 47, no. 4 (2000): 499–522.

McGee, Michael C. "In Search of 'The People': A Rhetorical Alternative." *Quarterly Journal of Speech* 61, no. 3 (1975): 235–49.

McGreavy, Bridie, Justine Wells, George F. McHendry Jr., and Samantha Senda-Cook, eds. *Tracing Rhetoric and Material Life: Ecological Approaches.* New York: Palgrave Springer, 2017.

McHendry, George F., Jr. "Whale Wars and the Axiomatization of Image Events on the Public Screen." *Environmental Communication: A Journal of Nature and Culture* 6, no. 2 (2012): 139–55.

McHendry, George F., Jr., Michael K. Middleton, Danielle Endres, Samantha Senda-Cook, and Megan O'Byrne. "Rhetorical Critic(ism)'s Body: Affect and Fieldwork on a Plane of Immanence." *Southern Communication Journal* 79, no. 4 (2014): 293–310.

McKerrow, Raymie E. "Critical Rhetoric: Theory and Praxis." *Communications Monographs* 56, no. 2 (1989): 91–111.

McKibben, Bill. *The End of Nature.* New York: Random House, 2006.

———. "Global Warming's Terrifying New Math." *Rolling Stone,* July 19, 2012. https://www.rollingstone.com/politics/politics-news/global-warmings-terrifying-new-math-188550/.

McLemee, Scott. "Towards Helhaven." *Chronicle of Higher Education,* July 9, 2008. https://www.insidehighered.com/views/2008/07/09/towards-helhaven.

McMillan, Jill J. "In Search of the Organizational Persona: A Rationale for Studying Organizations Rhetorically." In *Organization↔Communication: Emerging Perspectives II,* edited by Lee O. Thayer and George A. Barnett, 21–25. New York: Praeger, 1987.

Middleton, Michael, Aaron Hess, Danielle Endres, and Samantha Senda-Cook. *Participatory Critical Rhetoric: Theoretical and Methodological Foundations for Studying Rhetoric in Situ.* New York: Lexington Books, 2015.

Middleton, Michael K., Samantha Senda-Cook, and Danielle Endres. "Articulating Rhetorical Field Methods: Challenges and Tensions." *Western Journal of Communication* 75, no. 4 (2011): 386–406.

Mignolo Walter D., and Catherine E. Walsh. *On Decoloniality.* Durham, NC: Duke University Press, 2018.

Milstein, Tema. "Nature Identification: The Power of Pointing and Naming." *Environmental Communication: A Journal of Nature and Culture* 5, no. 1 (2011): 3–24.

Milstein, Tema, and José Castro-Sotomayor, eds. *Routledge Handbook of Ecocultural Identity.* New York: Routledge, 2020.

Mines and Communities. "Victory for Locked Out." May 16, 2010. http://www.minesandcommunities.org/article.php?a=10122.

Mirzoeff, Nicholas. *The Right to Look.* Durham, NC: Duke University Press, 2011.

Mitchell, Andrew J. *The Fourfold: Reading the Late Heidegger.* Chicago: Northwestern University Press, 2015.

Mitchell, Gordon R. *Strategic Deception: Rhetoric, Science, and Politics in Missile Defense Advocacy.* East Lansing: Michigan State University Press, 2000.

Moody, Roger. *Plunder!* London: Partizans Press, 1991.

Morris, Charles E., III. "Pink Herring and the Fourth Persona: J. Edgar Hoover's Sex Crime Panic." *Quarterly Journal of Speech* 88, no. 2 (2002): 228–44.

Morris, Richard. "Educating Savages." *Quarterly Journal of Speech* 83, no. 2 (1997): 152–71.

Morton, Timothy. "Ecology Without the Present." *Oxford Literary Review* 34, no. 2 (2012): 229–38.

Muir, John. *Steep Trails.* Berkeley: University of California Press, 1994.

Muller, Marek S. "Monkey Business in a Kangaroo Court: Reimagining *Naruto v. Slater* as a Litigious Event." *Rhetoric and Public Affairs* 25, no. 1 (2022): 31–59.

Murray, James. "Profiling the Top Five Mining Companies in the World." NS Energy. April 9, 2021. https://www.nsenergybusiness.com/features/largest-mining-companies/.

Musgrave, Kevin. *Persons of the Market: Conservatism, Corporate Personhood and Economic Theology*. East Lansing: Michigan State University Press, 2022.

Myfootage.com. "Ronald Reagan Boraxo Commercial." YouTube. December 3, 2010. https://youtu.be/hRqRmjbseqk.

Napier-Pearce, Jennifer. "Utah Clean Air Rally Draws Thousands to Capitol." *Salt Lake Tribune*, January 26, 2014. https://archive.sltrib.com/article.php?id=57447995&itype=CMSID.

Nash, William Giles. *The Rio Tinto Mine; Its History and Romance*. London: Simpkin Marshall Hamilton Kent, 1904.

National Institute of Health. "Copper." Accessed February 10, 2023. https://ods.od.nih.gov/factsheets/Copper-HealthProfessional.

National Park Service. "Death Valley: Historic Resource Study: A History of Mining." Accessed February 10, 2023. http://www.npshistory.com/publications/deva/hrs/section3e.htm.

———. "Zabriskie Point: Death Valley National Park." Accessed February 10, 2023. https://www.nps.gov/places/zabriskie-point-scenic-viewpoint.htm.

Natural History Museum of Utah. "Our Building," Last modified 2020. https://nhmu.utah.edu/museum/our-new-home.

"New Frontiers: Extractivism and Activism at Sea." *Salty Geographies*. Accessed February 10, 2023. https://saltygeographies.net/portfolio/new-frontiers-extractivism-activism-at-sea-new-museum-ny-2018/.

Nogrady, Bianca. "There's Gold, Platinum and Other Valuable Materials in Every Phone—The Hard Part Is Getting It Out." BBC, October 18, 2016. https://www.bbc.com/future/article/20161017-your-old-phone-is-full-of-precious-metals.

NoiseCat, Julian Brave. "Apaches Rally at Capitol, Vowing to Continue Fighting for Sacred Oak Flat." *HuffPost*, July 22, 2015. https://www.huffpost.com/entry/apaches-and-allies-rally-at-capitol-to-save-sacred-oak-flat-from-massive-mine_n_55aff2f9e4b08f57d5d3747d.

Nosie, Vanessa. "Apache Wendsler Nosi Going Home to Oak Flat." *Censored News: Indigenous Peoples and Human Rights*, November 29, 2019. http://apache-stronghold.com/going-home.html.

Nye, David E. *American Technological Sublime*. Cambridge, MA: MIT Press, 1996.

Ockey, Natalie. "20 Things to Do on Pioneer Day in Utah." *Utah's Adventure Family*, October 8, 2021. https://www.utahsadventurefamily.com/things-to-do-on-pioneer-day-in-utah/.

O'Donoghue, Amy Joi. "It's Rarer Than Gold and Critical for Green Energy—And It's About to be Mined in Utah." *Deseret News*, March 27, 2021. https://www.deseret.com/utah/2021/3/26/22344673/utah-green-energy-rare-element-for-solar-panels-mined-in-salt-lake-tellurium-rio-tinto.

Olney, Peter. "Battle in the Mojave: Lessons from the Rio Tinto Lockout." *New Labor Forum*, March 2011. https://newlaborforum.cuny.edu/2011/03/04/battle-in-the-mojave-lessons-from-the-rio-tinto-lockout/.

Ong, Walter. *Orality and Literacy*. New York: Routledge, 2013.

Ono, Kent A., and John M. Sloop. "Commitment to Telos—A Sustained Critical Rhetoric." *Communications Monographs* 59, no. 1 (1992): 48–60.

Oravec, Christine. "Conservationism vs. Preservationism: The 'Public Interest' in the Hetch Hetchy Controversy." *Quarterly Journal of Speech* 70, no. 4 (1984): 444–58.

Oravec, Christine, and Tracylee Clark. "Naming, Interpretation, Policy, and Poetry." In *Environmental Communication Yearbook*, vol. 1, edited by Susan Senecah, 1–14. New York: Lawrence Erlbaum, 2004.

Orr, Patti. "History of Boron California." *Mojave Desert News*, July 14, 2021. http://www.desertnews.com/article_796a2a8e-e34c-11eb-b72a-83943450a555.html.

———. "History of Muroc and North Muroc, Calif." *Mojave Desert News*, September 5, 2021. http://www.desertnews.com/news/article_5a3aa2e4-0ff0-11ec-8936-ff255d930907.html.

Ott, Brian L., Eric Aoki, and Greg Dickinson. "Ways of (Not) Seeing Guns: Presence and Absence at the Cody Firearms Museum." *Communication and Critical/Cultural Studies* 8, no. 3 (2011): 215–39.

Paliewicz, Nicholas S. "Arguments of Green Colonialism: A Post-Dialectical Reading of Extractivism in the Americas." *Argumentation and Advocacy* 58, nos. 3–4 (2022): 1–17.

———. "The Country, the City, and the Corporation: Rio Tinto Kennecott and the Materiality of Corporate Rhetoric." *Environmental Communication* 12, no. 6 (2018): 744–62.

———. "Industrial Pioneerism in the Beehive State: Rio Tinto and the Corporate Persona." *Western Journal of Communication* 86, no. 1 (2022): 60–82.

———. "Taking It to the Streets: The Rhetorical Mobility of Expert Arguments in Public Settings." *Argumentation and Advocacy* 51, no. 1 (2014): 42–57.

———. "Thinking Like a Copper Mine: An Ecological Approach to Corporate Ethos and Prosōpon." *Rhetoric Society Quarterly* 53, no. 2 (2023): 231–46.

Paliewicz, Nicholas, and George F. McHendry Jr. "Post-dialectics and Fascistic Argumentation in the Global Climate Change Debate." *Argumentation and Advocacy* 56, no. 3 (2020): 137–54.

———. "When Good Arguments Do Not Work: Post-Dialectics, Argument Assemblages, and the Networks of Climate Skepticism." *Argumentation and Advocacy* 53, no. 4 (2017): 287–309.

Peeples, Jennifer. "Aggressive Mimicry: The Rhetoric of Wise Use and the Environmental Movement." *Environmental Communication Yearbook* 2, no. 1 (2005): 1–18.

———. "Toxic Sublime: Imaging Contaminated Landscapes." *Environmental Communication: A Journal of Nature and Culture* 5, no. 4 (2011): 373–92.

Peters, John Durham. *Speaking into the Air: A History of the Idea of Communication*. Chicago: University of Chicago Press, 2012.

The Petri Dish. "How Much Gold Can be Found in the Human Body?" February 15, 2021. https://thepetridish.my/2021/02/15/how-much-gold-can-be-found-in-human-body/.

Pezzullo, Phaedra C. "Resisting 'National Breast Cancer Awareness Month': The Rhetoric of Counterpublics and Their Cultural Performances." *Quarterly Journal of Speech* 89, no. 4 (2003): 345–65.

———. *Toxic Tourism: Rhetorics of Pollution, Travel, and Environmental Justice*. Tuscaloosa: University of Alabama Press, 2009.

Pezzullo, Phaedra C., and Catalina M. de Onís. "Rethinking Rhetorical Field Methods on a Precarious Planet." *Communication Monographs* 85, no. 1 (2018): 103–22.

Phillips, Aaron T. "Eliding Extraction, Embracing Novelty: The Spatio-Temporal Configuration of Natural History." *Environmental Communication: A Journal of Nature and Culture* 8, no. 4 (2014): 452–67.

Plec, Emily, and Mary Pettenger. "Greenwashing Consumption: The Didactic Framing of ExxonMobil's Energy Solutions." *Environmental Communication: A Journal of Nature and Culture* 6, no. 4 (2012): 459–76.

Powell, Dana E. *Landscapes of Power.* Durham, NC: Duke University Press, 2018.

Racinez, Sheila. "Twenty Mule Team Museum." Behind Every Day (blog). Accessed February 10, 2023. https://behindeveryday.com/twenty-mule-team-museum/.

Rancière, Jacques. *Dissensus: On Politics and Aesthetics.* New York: Bloomsbury Publishing, 2010.

Real Salt Lake Communications. "Rio Tinto Stadium Announces South End Video Board Installation Details." September 18, 2014. https://www.rsl.com/post/2014/09/18/rio -tinto-stadium-announces-south-end-video-board-installation-details.

Redniss, Lauren. *Oak Flat: A Fight for Sacred Land in the American West.* New York: Random House, 2020.

Renzhofer, Martin. "Real Salt Lake's Fan Base Keeps Growing." *Salt Lake Tribune,* August 30, 2012. https://archive.sltrib.com/article.php?id=54788982&itype=CMSID.

Resolution Copper. "Building the Copper Triangle's Economy." https://resolutioncopper.com /sharing-success/building-copper-triangles-economy/.

———. "Magma Copper Smelter Chimney Stack Safely Dismantled," November 10, 2018. https://www.resolutioncopper.com/press-releases/2018/11/10/magma-copper-smelter -chimney-stack-safely-demolished/.

———. "On Site with Mike 'Reclamation.'" YouTube. September 4, 2015. https://www .youtube.com/watch?time_continue=35&v=XTDXF4nlnPw&feature=emb_logo.

———. "Protecting Cultural Resources." YouTube. July 30, 2018. https://www.youtube.com /watch?time_continue=1&v=_rJ6OPST9uA&feature=emb_logo.

———. "Resolution Copper Completes $75 Million Restoration of Historic Mining Land, Arizona." February 18, 2021. https://resolutioncopper.com/resolution-copper -completes-75-million-restoration-of-historic-mining-land/.

———. "Water: Responsible Use of a Vital Resource." Accessed February 10, 2023. https:// resolutioncopper.com/protecting-the-desert/water/.

Rickert, Thomas. *Ambient Rhetoric: The Attunements of Rhetorical Being.* Pittsburgh, PA: University of Pittsburgh Press, 2013.

———. "Toward the Chōra: Kristeva, Derrida, and Ulmer on Emplaced Invention." *Philosophy and Rhetoric* 40, no. 3 (2007): 251–73.

Rio Tinto. "About." Accessed February 10, 2023. https://www.riotinto.com/about.

———. "Borates." Accessed February 10, 2023. https://www.riotinto.com/products/borates.

———. "Rio Tinto Achieves Battery Grade Lithium Production at Boron Plant." April 7, 2021. https://www.riotinto.com/news/releases/2021/Rio-Tinto-achieves-battery-grade -lithium-production-at-Boron-plant.

———. "Rio Tinto Public Comment—Proposed 2021 Critical Minerals List." December 9, 2021. https:// downloads.regulations.gov/DOI-2021-0013-1039/attachment_1.pdf.

Rio Tinto Kennecott, "Operation." Rio Tinto, 2023, https://www.riotinto.com/en/operations /us/kennecott.

———. "Rio Tinto: Daybreak's Environmental History." Accessed on February 10, 2023. http://www.kennecott.com/sites/kennecott.com/files/environment2/environment _landmanagement_historyofdaybreak.pdf.

———. "Rio Tinto to Build New Tellurium Plant at Kennecott Mine." Accessed January 31, 2023. https://riotintokennecott.com/coppercurrents/rio-tinto-to-build-new-tellurium -plant-at-kennecott-mine/.

Robichaud, Denis J.-J. *Plato's Persona: Marsilio Ficino, Renaissance Humanism, and Platonic Traditions.* Philadelphia: University of Pennsylvania Press, 2018.

Rojecki, Andrew. "Rhetorical Alchemy: American Exceptionalism and the War on Terror." *Political Communication* 25, no. 1 (2008): 67–88.

Rookhuzen, David. "Throwback Thursday: Claypool Tunnel." ADOT, July 18, 2019. https://azdot.gov/adot-blog/throwback-thursday-claypool-tunnel.

Rowland, Robert. "On Mythic Criticism." *Communication Studies* 41, no. 2 (1990): 101–16.

Rushing, Janice Hocker. "Mythic Evolution of 'The New Frontier' in Mass Mediated Rhetoric." *Critical Studies in Media Communication* 3, no. 3 (1986): 265–96.

Said, Edward W. *The World, the Text, and the Critic.* Cambridge, MA: Harvard University Press, 1983.

Saindon, Brent Allen. "A Doubled Heterotopia: Shifting Spatial and Visual Symbolism in the Jewish Museum Berlin's Development." *Quarterly Journal of Speech* 98, no. 1 (2012): 24–48.

Sanchez, James Chase. "Trump, the KKK, and the Versatility of White Supremacy Rhetoric." *Journal of Contemporary Rhetoric* 8, no. 1/2 (2018): 44–56.

Schneider, Jen, Steve Schwarze, Peter K. Bsumek, and Jennifer Peeples. *Under Pressure: Coal Industry Rhetoric and Neoliberalism.* New York: Springer, 2016.

Sclafani, Jennifer. *Talking Donald Trump: A Sociolinguistic Study of Style, Metadiscourse, and Political Identity.* New York: Routledge, 2017.

Seegert, Natasha. "Play of Sniffication: Coyotes Sing in the Margins." *Philosophy and Rhetoric* 47, no. 2 (2014): 158–78.

Sekler, Joan, dir. *Locked Out.* Boron, CA: Alternavision Films, 2010.

Semerad, Tony. "Daybreak's Mission vs. Kennecott's Emissions." *Salt Lake Tribune,* March 10, 2014. https://archive.sltrib.com/article.php?id=57641837&itype=CMSID.

Senda-Cook, Samantha. "Long Memories: Material Rhetoric as Evidence of Memory and a Potential Future." *Western Journal of Communication* 84, no. 4 (2020): 419–38.

———. "Rugged Practices: Embodying Authenticity in Outdoor Recreation." *Quarterly Journal of Speech* 98, no. 2 (2012): 129–52.

Shatz, Sallie Dean. "Tall Tailings." *Catalyst Magazine,* August 1, 2011. https://www.catalyst magazine.net/tall-tailings/.

Shaviro, Steven. *Without Criteria: Kant, Whitehead, Deleuze, and Aesthetics.* Cambridge, MA: MIT Press, 2012.

Siegfried, Kate. "Making Settler Colonialism Concrete: Agentive Materialism and Habitational Violence in Palestine." *Communication and Critical/Cultural Studies* 17, no. 3 (2020): 267–84.

Smerecnik, Karl R. and Valerie R. Renegar. "Capitalistic Agency: The Rhetoric of BP's Helios Power Campaign." *Environmental Communication: A Journal of Nature and Culture* 4, no. 2 (2010): 152–71.

Smith, Andrea. *Conquest: Sexual Violence and American Indian Genocide.* Durham, NC: Duke University Press, 2015.

Solis, Holly. "Sparky's Quill: Apache Leap." *The State Press,* February 19, 2013. https://www.statepress.com/article/2013/02/sparkys-quill-the-apache-leap.

Statista. "Revenue of Rio Tinto from 2010 to 2022." Statista. Last modified June 28, 2021. https://www.statista.com/statistics/272615/rio-tinto-revenue-since-2001/.

Stern, Philip J. *The Company-State: Corporate Sovereignty and the Early Modern Foundations of the British Empire in India.* Oxford, UK: Oxford University Press, 2011.

Strong, Kathy. "Ghost Towns of the California Desert." Visit Greater Palm Springs, October 12, 2018. https://www.visitgreaterpalmsprings.com/blog/post/ghost-towns-of-the-california-desert/.

Stuckey, Mary E. "The Donner Party and the Rhetoric of Westward Expansion." *Rhetoric and Public Affairs* 14, no. 2 (2011): 229–60.

Stuckey, Mary E., and John M. Murphy. "By Any Other Name: Rhetorical Colonialism in North America." *American Indian Culture and Research Journal* 25, no. 4 (2001): 73–98.

Sturken, Marita. *Terrorism in American Memory: Memorials, Museums, and Architecture in the Post-9/11 Era.* New York: New York University Press, 2022.

———. *Tourists of History.* Durham, NC: Duke University Press, 2007.

Superior. "Our Story." Accessed February 10, 2023. https://www.superiorarizona.com/our -story.

Sweney, Mark. "Global Shortage in Computer Chips 'Reaches Crisis Point.'" *The Guardian*, March 21, 2021. https://www.theguardian.com/business/2021/mar/21/global-shortage -in-computer-chips-reaches-crisis-point.

Taylor, Chloe. "'Welcome to the Age of Copper': Why the Coronavirus Pandemic Could Spark a Red Metal Rally." CNBC, June 24, 2020. https://www.cnbc.com/2020/06/24 /coronavirus-why-the-pandemic-could-spark-a-copper-rally.html.

This Is the Place Heritage Park. "About Us." Accessed February 10, 2023 https://www.thisis theplace.org/general-info/about-us.

Thoreau, Henry David. "Walking." *The Atlantic*, June 1862. Accessed February 10, 2023. https://www.theatlantic.com/magazine/archive/1862/06/walking/304674/.

Udell, Cherise. "Rio Tinto Should Be Responsible for Damage." *Salt Lake Tribune*, April 16, 2011. https://archive.sltrib.com/article.php?id=51614839&itype=CMSID.

United Nations Sustainable Development Goals. "Goal 12: Ensure Sustainable Consumption and Production Patterns." Accessed February 10, 2023. https://www.un.org/sustain abledevelopment/sustainable-consumption-production/.

United States Department of Agriculture. "EIS Public Hearing." Queen Valley (10/8/19).

———. "EIS Public Hearing." San Tan Valley, AZ (9/12/19).

———. "EIS Public Hearing." Superior, AZ (9/10/19).

———. "EIS Public Hearing." Tempe, AZ (10/10/2019).

United States House of Representatives, House Committee of Natural Resources. "The Irreparable Environmental and Cultural Impacts of the Proposed Resolution Copper Mining Operation." 116th Congress, March 12, 2020. https://www.congress.gov/event /116th-congress/house-event/LC65246/text?s=1&r=1.

United States Securities and Exchange Commission. "List of Subsidiaries of BHP Billiton Limited and BHP Billiton PLC." H.R. 1884: Save Oak Flat Act. 117th Congress (2021–22). https://www.congress.gov/bill/117th-congress/house-bill/1884.

Urry, John. *Mobilities: New Perspectives on Transport and Society.* New York: Routledge, 2016.

"U.S. Borax Salary." SalaryList. Accessed February 10, 2023. https://www.salarylist.com /company/Us-Borax-Salary.htm.

Utah Department of Environmental Quality (UDEQ). Summary—Public Hearing Comments. Available on CD-ROM. February 22, 2011, Salt Lake City.

Vaifanua, Tamara. "Daybreak Homeowners File Lawsuit Accusing Builders of Cutting Corners on Construction." Fox 13, April 12, 2017. https://www.fox13now.com/2017/04/12 /daybreak-homeowners-file-lawsuit-accusing-builders-of-cutting-corners-on -construction/.

Waalkes, Scott. "Does Soccer Explain the World or Does the World Explain Soccer? Soccer and Globalization." *Soccer and Society* 18, nos. 2–3 (2017): 166–80.

Wachowski, Lana, and Lilly Wachowski, dirs. *The Matrix.* Burbank, CA: Warner Home Video, 1999.

Wahlquist, Calla. "Rio Tinto Blasts 46,000-year-old Aboriginal Site to Expand Iron Ore Mine." *The Guardian*, May 26, 2020. https://www.theguardian.com/australia-news /2020/may/26/rio-tinto-blasts-46000-year-old-aboriginal-site-to-expand-iron -ore-mine.

Walker, Gladys, and T. G. Chilton. "The History of Mining at Superior." In *History of Mining in Arizona*, vol. 2, edited by J. Michael Canty and Michael N. Greeley, 231–60. Tucson, AZ: Club of the Southwest Foundation, 1991.

Wallerstein, Immanuel. *The Modern World-System*. Oakland: University of California Press, 2011.

Walton, Douglas. "Ignoratio Elenchi: The Red Herring Fallacy." *Informal Logic* 2, no. 3 (1979): 3–7.

Wander, Philip. "The Third Persona: An Ideological Turn in Rhetorical Theory." *Communication Studies* 35, no. 4 (1984): 197–216.

Wanzer, Darrel Allan. "Delinking Rhetoric, or Revisiting McGee's Fragmentation Thesis Through Decoloniality." *Rhetoric and Public Affairs* 15, no. 4 (2012): 647–57.

Wanzer-Serrano, Darrel. *The New York Young Lords and the Struggle for Liberation*. Philadelphia, PA: Temple University Press, 2015.

Weber, Max. *The Protestant Ethic and the "Spirit" of Capitalism, and Other Writings*. New York: Penguin, 2002.

Welch, John R. "Earth, Wind, and Fire: Pinal Apaches, Miners, and Genocide in Central Arizona, 1859–1874." *Sage Open* 7, no. 4 (2017): 1–19.

Wentling, Michelle. "Ute Brave: Copper's Cradle." Accessed February 10, 2023. https://www .torreyhouse.org/single-post/2019/10/14/ute-brave-copper-s-cradle.

West, Richard. *River of Tears: The Rise of the Rio Tinto-Zinc Mining Corporation*. London: Earth Island Limited, 1972.

Westland Resources. "Remembering the Smelter: The Magma Copper Company Smelter at Superior, Arizona." *Resolution Copper*. Last modified October 2, 2019. https:// storymaps.arcgis.com/stories/09d303bb6bfe4d12814e67661aa559dd.

Whitehead, Alfred North. *Process and Reality*. Free Press, 1979.

Wilsdon, John. R. "A Brief History of Southern Arizona Silver Mining." HubPages, November 3, 2020. https://discover.hubpages.com/education/A-Brief-History-of-Arizona -Silver-Mining.

Wise, J. Macgregor. "Assemblage." In *Gilles Deleuze: Key Concepts*, edited by Charles J. Stivale, 77–87. Montreal: McGill-Queen's University Press, 2005.

Wolff, Kristina. "Strategic Essentialism." In *The Blackwell Encyclopedia of Sociology*, edited by G. Ritzer, 4797–99. Hoboken, NJ: John Wiley & Sons, 2007.

World Socialist Web Site. "Boron, California Mine Workers Denounce Company Lock-Out." YouTube. February 19, 2010. https://www.youtube.com/watch?v=-2azVh6yVis.

———. "Locked-Out Rio Tinto Workers Oppose Concessions." YouTube. February 27, 2010. https://www.youtube.com/watch?v=MmN48mNC-2U.

Yale University. "Energy History." Accessed February 10, 2023. https://energyhistory.yale .edu/video-the-cracking-of-glen-canyon-dam-with-edward-abbey-and-earth-first -1982/.

Young James. *The Texture of Memory: Holocaust Memorials and Meaning*. New Haven, CT: Yale University Press, 1994.

Žižek, Slavoj. *Interrogating the Real*. New York: Bloomsbury Press, 2006.

Index

9 780271 097060